COURAGE
FOR TODAY

365 Daily Devotions for Women

Ann White

BroadStreet
PUBLISHING

BroadStreet Publishing® Group, LLC
Savage, Minnesota, USA
BroadStreetPublishing.com

Courage for Today: 365 Daily Devotions for Women
Copyright © 2024 Ann White

9781424566839 (faux leather)
9781424566846 (ebook)

Cover and interior by Garborg Design Works | garborgdesign.com

Printed in China

24 25 26 27 28 5 4 3 2 1

THE COURAGE TO
Acknowledge God

In the beginning God created the heavens and the earth.
The earth was formless and empty, and darkness covered the deep waters.
And the Spirit of God was hovering over the surface of the waters.

GENESIS 1:1–2

Father, I am surrounded by the evidence of your power, creativity, and intentionality. Remind me to stop and take notice of your creation and help me to honor you by sharing your greatness with others.

Are you in awe of God's greatness? Do his magnificent works inspire you to be courageous? In Genesis chapter 1, we read the account of God's creation. Each verse is detailed, specific, and validated by modern science. This chapter establishes God's sovereignty and reveals his power and creativity. God's intentionality can be seen throughout the complexity of earth's design. The lights he created and perfectly placed permit life on earth to exist. If the sun were farther away, we would freeze; if it were closer, we would burn.

The precise placement, gravitational pull, and orbit of the moon are accredited with primary control over our oceans' tides, which, in turn, significantly impact our weather. The sun, moon, and stars also identify our seasons—exactly as God's Word proclaims!

COURAGE FOR TODAY

Consider the verse below and describe how your surroundings reveal God's power, creativity, and intentionality. Then explain how God's greatness inspires you to courageously honor him today.

They know the truth about God because he has made it obvious to them. For ever since the world was created, people have seen the earth and sky. Through everything God made, they can clearly see his invisible qualities—his eternal power and divine nature. So they have no excuse for not knowing God.

ROMANS 1:19–20

THE COURAGE TO
Be God's Witness

God sent a man, John the Baptist, to tell about the light
so that everyone might believe because of his testimony.

JOHN 1:6–7

Father, because I am a believer in Jesus Christ, your light resides within me. Give me the desire and the courage to be a faithful witness as I share your light and love with others.

Are you negatively influenced by the news and information you see daily? We live in a world that often deems opinions to be fact and regularly considers fact to be subjective. Reflect on John chapter 1, where God beautifully identifies and describes Jesus, his beloved Son and the Savior of the world. God had been silent for four hundred years when he sent Jesus to earth. Some believed Jesus was the Messiah, but others did not.

In John chapter 1 we learn that God sent John the Baptist to give witness to Jesus and to reveal his divine power and glory. When the priests and temple assistants asked John about his own identity, he humbled himself and stated that he was not the Messiah. "I am a voice shouting in the wilderness…not even worthy to be his slave and untie the straps of his sandal" (vv. 23–27). John sought no glory for himself. Instead, as God's witness, he stated all he observed and faithfully testified of the "Chosen One of God" (v. 34).

COURAGE FOR TODAY

Like John the Baptist, how often do you share God's good news with others? Meditate on the verse below and list at least two ways you will courageously share Christ with others today.

I am not ashamed of this Good News about Christ. It is the power of God at work, saving everyone who believes—the Jew first and also the Gentile.

ROMANS 1:16

THE COURAGE TO
Pray Faithfully

Solomon stood before the altar of the Lord in front of the entire community of Israel. He lifted his hands toward heaven, and he prayed "O Lord, God of Israel, there is no God like you in all of heaven above or on the earth below. You keep your covenant and show unfailing love to all who walk before you in wholehearted devotion."

1 KINGS 8:22–23

Father, thank you for allowing me to have a personal relationship with you. As I come before you in prayer, help me remember to lift up the many needs of others too.

How often do you pray? Communication with God is like talking to a loved one, a confidant, a provider, and a protector—all in one. Consider King Solomon's prayer in 1 Kings chapter 8. When the people of Israel had completed God's temple, King Solomon assembled the leaders to celebrate and dedicate their house of worship to almighty God.

We read in these verses about how the leaders of Israel brought the ark of the covenant into the temple. When they had placed it in the inner sanctuary, God's glory filled the temple. Then Solomon offered a prayer of praise and dedication. Notice how he honored God and made specific requests for God to hear the people's prayers, including those of foreigners.

COURAGE FOR TODAY

How much time do you spend in prayer? Read the passage below and write a courageous prayer that honors God, confesses your needs, and lifts up the needs of others.

Are any of you suffering hardships? You should pray. Are any of you happy? You should sing praises. Are any of you sick? You should call for the elders of the church to come and pray over you, anointing you with oil in the name of the Lord.

JAMES 5:13–14

THE COURAGE TO
Take Courage

Jesus spoke to them at once. "
Don't be afraid," he said.
"Take courage. I am here!"
MATTHEW 14:27

Father, at times, I courageously step out in faith only to fall prey to my own negativity and doubt. Remind me that, with you, I can accomplish anything you call me to do.

Are you able to keep your eyes on Jesus when discouragement and fear arise? Let the story of Peter's encounter with Jesus in Matthew chapter 14 encourage you to let God's power and presence see you through. After feeding five thousand followers, Jesus sent his disciples ahead in a boat to the opposite side of the Sea of Galilee. In the middle of the night, while crossing the sea, a strong wind arose and threatened to sink their boat. So Jesus walked across the water to encourage his friends, yet seeing him frightened them even more.

In response, Jesus urged them to "take courage," for he was with them. But Peter wanted proof. So he asked his Savior to call him to walk on water, too, and Jesus did. When Peter first stepped out of the boat, he walked in great faith, but when he gave in to doubt and negativity, he immediately began to sink.

COURAGE FOR TODAY

Like Peter, do you sometimes struggle with doubt and discouragement? Let King David's encouraging words below inspire you to lean into the Lord today and "take courage," no matter what situation or circumstances you find yourself in.

Wait patiently for the LORD.
Be brave and courageous.
Yes, wait patiently for the LORD.
PSALM 27:14

THE COURAGE TO
Embrace Security

Those who live in the shelter of the Most High will find rest in the shadow of the Almighty. This I declare about the Lord: He alone is my refuge, my place of safety; he is my God, and I trust him.

PSALM 91:1–2

Father, you are my place of comfort, care, and refuge. Help me to rely on you daily and find courage in your promise of security.

Do you feel emotionally and physically secure? Our feelings of security directly affect our stress levels, which, in turn, can affect our attitudes, abilities, and peace of mind. Draw encouragement from Psalm 91, one of the most beautiful hymns about security in life. Throughout this prayer, the psalmist vacillates between inviting readers to embrace God's protection and describing the types of protection God provides.

In Psalm 91, verses 1–2 and 9–10, the psalmist invites us to trust in God as a safe place to take refuge. In verses 3–8 and 11–16, he describes the types of security God provides. God can rescue us from attacks by the wicked and threats of deadly diseases. And he places his angels around us to keep us from stumbling or going the wrong way. When we love God and courageously embrace his security, he responds, rescues, satisfies, and saves us.

COURAGE FOR TODAY

Describe areas in your life that tempt you to feel insecure. Then read the following words of wisdom from the book of Job and vow to draw courage today from the hope you find in embracing God's security.

Having hope will give you courage.
You will be protected and will rest in safety.
You will lie down unafraid, and many will look to you for help.

JOB 11:18–19

THE COURAGE TO
Seize Opportunities

*"I know all the things you do, and I have opened a door for you that no one can
close. You have little strength, yet you obeyed my word and did not deny me."*

REVELATION 3:8

Father, you provide countless opportunities in life for me to serve you,
accomplish your will, care for others, and share my faith. Give me the
wisdom to recognize when you've opened or closed certain doors so I can
avoid many pitfalls and instead pursue your perfect plans.

Are you truly seizing your God-given opportunities? Let Jesus' message in
Revelation chapter 3 inspire you to look for and embrace the assignments
God places before you. While he didn't have any constructive criticism for the
church of Philadelphia, Jesus took the opportunity to praise the congregation
for their obedience and perseverance.

Because the Christians at Philadelphia stood firm in their faith when
they were tested, the Lord promised he would protect them from the greater
oppression that was to come. Jesus explained that the doors he opens can
never be shut, and the ones he closes can never be opened. If believers hold on
to their commitment and faithfulness to the Lord, they will be victorious, and
no one will ever take away their heavenly crown.

COURAGE FOR TODAY

How courageous are you when it comes to walking through doors of
opportunity that the Lord has opened? Meditate on the inspiring verse
below and describe the steps you will take today to courageously seize
your God-given opportunities.

*"I am about to do something new. See, I have already begun!
Do you not see it? I will make a pathway through the wilderness.
I will create rivers in the dry wasteland."*

ISAIAH 43:19

THE COURAGE TO
Recognize God's Voice

He said to Samuel, "Go and lie down again, and if someone calls again, say, 'Speak, LORD, your servant is listening.'" So Samuel went back to bed. And the LORD came and called as before, "Samuel! Samuel!" And Samuel replied, "Speak, your servant is listening."

1 SAMUEL 3:9–10

Father, I am grateful for your presence in my life. Give me wisdom to recognize your voice and courage to obey your calling.

How often do you sit quietly and listen for God's voice? Consider the young prophet's encounter with God in 1 Samuel chapter 3. For years, Hannah longed for a child, and in time, God answered her prayers. Because God gave her a son, Hannah vowed to give the child back to the Lord. Once Samuel was weaned, his mother gave him to Eli, the priest.

Samuel grew in God's favor and served the Lord faithfully. One night, when Samuel was sleeping, God called to him three times, but Samuel did not recognize God's voice. Then Eli realized it was the Lord calling Samuel, and he instructed Samuel to listen carefully, recognize God's voice, and answer him appropriately.

COURAGE FOR TODAY

Do you recognize God speaking to you through his Word and his Spirit? Let Samuel's experience and the encouraging verse below motivate you to listen carefully to God's calling and courageously take action today.

"Look! I stand at the door and knock. If you hear my voice and open the door, I will come in, and we will share a meal together as friends."

REVELATION 3:20

THE COURAGE TO
Walk in Love

Live a life filled with love, following the example of Christ.
He loved us and offered himself as a sacrifice for us,
a pleasing aroma to God.

EPHESIANS 5:2

Father, you have taught me that love never gives up, never loses faith, is always hopeful, and endures through every circumstance. Help me walk in great love for you, others, and myself.

Do you sometimes find it hard to love certain people? Let the apostle Paul's words in Ephesians chapter 5 challenge you to embrace a greater love for God, yourself, and others. Paul urged believers in Ephesus to be imitators of Jesus in everything. Since God's greatest attribute is sacrificial love (see John 3:16), exhibiting that type of love is honorable and pleasing to the Lord.

Paul described three ways believers can display this great love: by being morally pure, generous, and verbally respectful. To love sacrificially requires putting other's needs first. Therefore, Paul asked the Ephesians to "submit to one another" (Ephesians 5:21). By lovingly looking out for each other, they would be modeling the love of Christ.

COURAGE FOR TODAY

Do you love others well? Do you consider their needs as more important than yours? Name two people you are struggling to love. Then meditate on the verse below and describe how you will embrace a more courageous and caring love for them today.

Above all, clothe yourselves with love,
which binds us all together in perfect harmony.

COLOSSIANS 3:14

THE COURAGE TO
Treasure God's Knowledge

Hear the word of the LORD, O people of Israel! The LORD has brought charges against you, saying: "There is no faithfulness, no kindness, no knowledge of God in your land…My people are being destroyed because they don't know me. Since you priests refuse to know me, I refuse to recognize you as my priests. Since you have forgotten the laws of your God, I will forget to bless your children."

HOSEA 4:1, 6

Father, you have given us the Bible as our guide for life. Put within me an impenetrable passion to know both you and your Word.

How important is the knowledge of God and his Word to you? Do you rely on God's wisdom and guidance for everyday dilemmas and decisions? Allow God's words in Hosea chapter 4 to challenge you regarding your passion for God's knowledge. Through the prophet Hosea, God indicted the people of Israel for their unfaithfulness, their unkindness, and their lack of knowledge of God.

Because of their willful disregard of God, they were self-destructing. People were lying, murdering, stealing, and committing adultery. And, as a result, everyone and everything wasted away. Israel's leaders refused responsibility, so God aimed his complaint directly at them. Since the priests refused to know God, the people followed suit, and they all suffered the consequences.

COURAGE FOR TODAY

Do you treasure God's knowledge? Meditate on King Solomon's wise proverb below and vow today to courageously rely on the knowledge of God and his Word for wisdom, discipline, and guidance.

*The wise are mightier than the strong,
and those with knowledge grow stronger and stronger.*

PROVERBS 24:5

THE COURAGE TO
Change Your Mind

Don't copy the behavior and customs of this world, but let God transform you into a new person by changing the way you think. Then you will learn to know God's will for you, which is good and pleasing and perfect.

ROMANS 12:2

Father, you created my mind and gave me the ability to control it. Give me the desire and courage to reject the lies, deceptions, distractions, and enticements of this world so I can devote myself faithfully to your perfect will and ways.

Are you currently battling any negative, destructive, or discouraging thoughts? Let the apostle Paul's counsel in Romans chapter 12 inspire you to renew your mind and change your ways. In Paul's letter to the Roman church, he urged members to reject the conduct and customs of this world so they can focus on pleasing the Lord.

In response to God's love and great sacrifice, Paul encouraged believers to dedicate their bodies to their Creator. He further advised Christ followers to openly and honestly evaluate themselves and change their bad behaviors by letting God change their thoughts. For when believers devote their bodies and lives to the Lord, it is truly the greatest way to worship and honor almighty God.

COURAGE FOR TODAY

Evaluate yourself and describe any distractive, discouraging, or detrimental thoughts you are currently experiencing. Then read the familiar verse below and decide today to courageously put aside your current way of thinking so you can focus on all that is good, godly, and productive.

Dear brothers and sisters, one final thing. Fix your thoughts on what is true, and honorable, and right, and pure, and lovely, and admirable. Think about things that are excellent and worthy of praise.

PHILIPPIANS 4:8

THE COURAGE TO
Take Necessary Risks

The Lord turned to him and said, "Go with the strength you have, and rescue Israel from the Midianites. I am sending you!" "But Lord," Gideon replied, "how can I rescue Israel? My clan is the weakest in the whole tribe of Manasseh, and I am the least in my entire family!"

JUDGES 6:14–15

Father, with you working in and through me, I can accomplish more than I could ever dream of achieving. Help me set aside self-doubt and hesitation and take necessary risks as I courageously pursue your calling on my life.

Do you fear you may be underqualified for the task God has assigned you? Consider Gideon's calling in Judges chapter 6. Just as the people of Israel consistently returned to their pattern of evil without godly leadership, God consistently raised up faithful judges to save them when they cried out in regret.

When an angel appeared to Gideon, he felt inadequate to accomplish God's calling. Yet God assured Gideon that he was not only sending Gideon but that God would also be with him. "Mighty hero, the Lord is with you!" (v. 12). God's presence brought Gideon courage and confidence. God often calls us to accomplish tasks that are outside our comfort zone and ability. This way, we learn to rely more on the Lord as we experience his power at work in and through us.

COURAGE FOR TODAY

Read the verse below and describe the courageous assignment you sense God is calling you to. Proclaim your willingness to trust God as you step out in courageous faith today.

All glory to God, who is able, through his mighty power at work within us, to accomplish infinitely more than we might ask or think.

EPHESIANS 3:20

THE COURAGE TO
Be a Faithful Friend

Timothy, please come as soon as you can. Demas has deserted me because he loves the things of this life and has gone to Thessalonica. Crescens has gone to Galatia, and Titus has gone to Dalmatia.

2 TIMOTHY 4:9–10

Father, you command me to be loving at all times. Give me the courage, desire, and ability to be a loyal and loving friend.

How many trustworthy friends do you have? How loyal of a friend are you to others? Consider the apostle Paul's situation in 2 Timothy chapter 4. Paul, who at one time had many friends and followers, found himself mostly alone near the end of his life. While his faith in the Lord remained strong, he still needed human companionship and help. In his darkest hours, Paul experienced emotions of loneliness and betrayal. He considered Timothy his "son in the Lord," and he needed his encouragement (1:2).

Some of Paul's friends and ministry partners had walked away from their faith, and some had even done harm to him. But he refused to hold a grudge. Instead, he drew strength from his relationship with the Lord. In humility and transparency, Paul asked Timothy to please come as the end of his time drew near.

COURAGE FOR TODAY

Do you desire to be a faithful friend and a person who loves unconditionally and wholeheartedly? Meditate on the proverb below and describe how you will exercise your courage muscles today and be a more loyal and loving friend.

A friend is always loyal, and a brother is born to help in time of need.

PROVERBS 17:17

THE COURAGE TO
Cherish God's Wisdom

Choose my instruction rather than silver, and knowledge rather than pure gold. For wisdom is far more valuable than rubies. Nothing you desire can compare with it.

PROVERBS 8:10–11

Father, your wisdom leads me toward a healthier and happier life. Help me avoid the pitfalls of worldly advice by seeking only your understanding and guidance.

Do you rely more on your own judgment and worldly knowledge, or do you truly cherish the wisdom of God and his Word? Be challenged by King Solomon's words in Proverbs chapter 8. For believers, the role of God's Holy Spirit is to give us knowledge and remind us of God's wisdom and words.

In Proverbs chapter 8, Solomon reminds us that, no matter where we go or what we do, God's wisdom is available, offering advice, uncovering truth, and giving clear directions to those who will listen. Therefore, we should cherish God's wisdom above all other advice. When we rely on God for guidance and understanding, we will possess sound judgment, common sense, insight, and strength. Otherwise we can fall prey to what the world promotes: pride, arrogance, corruption, and perverse speech.

COURAGE FOR TODAY

Do you hunger for God to give you knowledge, counsel, and understanding? Meditate on the description of God's wisdom below and describe how following his guidance can help you live a more courageous life today.

The wisdom from above is first of all pure. It is also peace loving, gentle at all times, and willing to yield to others. It is full of mercy and the fruit of good deeds. It shows no favoritism and is always sincere.

JAMES 3:17

THE COURAGE TO
Show Kindness

I appeal to you to show kindness to my child, Onesimus.
I became his father in the faith while here in prison.

PHILEMON 1:10

Father, being kind to someone who has hurt me is difficult. Give me the courage to forgive and be kindhearted even when I don't want to.

How easy is it for you to put the past behind you in order to restore a lost friend or adversary? Consider the apostle Paul's plea in the book of Philemon. Paul wrote a letter to his friend, Philemon, a wealthy man who housed the Colossian church in his home. Onesimus, Philemon's slave, had run away to Rome, where he met Paul and became a believer.

Paul had grown fond of Onesimus and wanted to keep him near, but he knew the right thing to do was to send him back to Philemon. So Paul's letter included a plea for his friend to "show kindness to my child, Onesimus" (v. 10) and to restore him as a repentant brother. In addition, Paul offered to pay any debt Onesimus owed, asking Onesimus to "give me this encouragement in Christ" (v. 20). Paul wrote in confidence, believing Philemon would demonstrate both kindness and favor to his former servant.

COURAGE FOR TODAY

Are you withholding forgiveness and compassion toward someone who has mistreated you? Read the verse below and describe how you will courageously show kindness today to people in your life whom you feel don't deserve it.

Since God chose you to be the holy people he loves, you must clothe yourselves with tenderhearted mercy, kindness, humility, gentleness, and patience. Make allowance for each other's faults, and forgive anyone who offends you. Remember, the Lord forgave you, so you must forgive others.

COLOSSIANS 3:12–13

THE COURAGE TO
Seek God

The Spirit of God came upon Azariah son of Oded, and he went out to meet King Asa as he was returning from the battle. "Listen to me, Asa!" he shouted. "Listen, all you people of Judah and Benjamin! The LORD will stay with you as long as you stay with him! Whenever you seek him, you will find him. But if you abandon him, he will abandon you."

2 CHRONICLES 15:1–2

Father, thank you for your presence in my life. Help me to courageously seek your comfort, care, and guidance daily in both good times and in bad.

How often do you seek God? Consider God's message to King Asa, recorded in 2 Chronicles chapter 15. Throughout Scripture, God repeatedly affirms, "If you seek me, you will find me." King Asa honored God and commanded his people to faithfully seek God. In 2 Chronicles 15:1–4, God's prophet reassured King Asa and the Israelites of God's presence and promises. God reminded them to "be strong and courageous" (v. 7). In response to God's words, Asa and his people vowed to seek God "with all their heart and soul" (v. 12). As a result of their faithfulness, God gave them rest and protection.

Today, God's Spirit resides in all believers, providing comfort, care, and guidance to all who rely on him.

COURAGE FOR TODAY

Do you seek God's presence daily? Or do you mostly call on him when you are in need? Memorize the following verse and make a commitment today to courageously seek God in both good and bad times.

Search for the LORD and for his strength;
continually seek him.

1 CHRONICLES 16:11

THE COURAGE TO
Celebrate Your Value

"The very hairs on your head are all numbered. So don't be afraid;
you are more valuable to God than a whole flock of sparrows."

LUKE 12:7

Father, I can sometimes be my own worst enemy, beating myself up for the mistakes I've made. Help me remember that my value is not a result of what I do or don't do but that only you define my value.

Do you ever stop to think about how valuable you are to God? Let Jesus' words in Luke chapter 12 comfort and encourage you today. Jesus regularly confronted religious leaders about their hypocrisy and fixation on adherence to religious laws. In this chapter of Luke, Jesus warned his followers to beware of the Pharisees' hypocrisy because it could spread throughout and infect many people. He encouraged them not to worry about what people think of them but to be concerned about what God thinks. After all, eternal judgment is forever.

Then Jesus went on to explain that God knows everything about his creation and that "the very hairs on your head are all numbered" (v. 7), for God values every human being and never forgets a single one.

COURAGE FOR TODAY

Are you more concerned about how the world sees you? Or do you rely on God's view to determine your value? Read the familiar passage below and draw courage and confidence today from God's unconditional, sacrificial, and loving view of you.

You saw me before I was born. Every day of my life was recorded in your book. Every moment was laid out before a single day had passed. How precious are your thoughts about me, O God. They cannot be numbered!

PSALM 139:16–17

THE COURAGE TO
Trust God's Power

Don't be afraid, for I am with you. Don't be discouraged, for I am your God.
I will strengthen you and help you.
I will hold you up with my victorious right hand.

ISAIAH 41:10

Father, life on earth is filled with foolishness and temptation. Help me deny the idols in my life and trust only in your power and presence.

Do you respect God's supremacy and rely on his power? Allow God's words in Isaiah chapter 41 to confront the areas of your life that need to be reformed. The prophet Isaiah heard from God and faithfully delivered his messages to the people of Israel. In chapter 41, God presented his case against his people. He scolded those who were captivated by their idols and encouraged those who were faithful. He recounted his sovereignty that establishes kings, overthrows armies, strengthens his people, and physically protects the faithful.

Twice in this chapter, God tells believers, "Don't be afraid," because he is with them, to strengthen them and to help them. God's power is revealed and is real while worthless, manmade idols can do nothing.

COURAGE FOR TODAY

Do worldly preoccupations hinder your relationship with God? Read the passage below and courageously set aside any enticements and trust only in the Lord today.

Yours, O LORD, is the greatness, the power, the glory, the victory, and the majesty.
Everything in the heavens and on earth is yours, O LORD, and this is your kingdom.
We adore you as the one who is over all things. Wealth and honor come from you
alone, for you rule over everything. Power and might are in your hand, and at your
discretion people are made great and given strength.

1 CHRONICLES 29:11–12

THE COURAGE TO
Be Unmistakable

In everything we do, we show that we are true ministers of God. We patiently endure troubles and hardships and calamities of every kind...We prove ourselves by our purity, our understanding, our patience, our kindness, by the Holy Spirit within us, and by our sincere love.

2 CORINTHIANS 6:4, 6

Father, although it is uncomfortable to stand out in a crowd, I want it to be known that you are living in and through me. Help me consistently reveal my dedication to you by the way I act and respond, no matter what hardship or difficulty I may be going through.

Do others see your behavior and conclude that you're a believer? Let the apostle Paul's confession in 2 Corinthians chapter 6 compel your walk and relationship with God to be unmistakable.

Paul had endured hardship, abuse, imprisonment, rejection, exhaustion, and hunger, yet these struggles never kept him from being patient, kind, honorable, and loving toward believers and unbelievers alike. Paul made a deliberate effort to live in a way that displayed God's presence and encouraged others to do the same. He honored God no matter how others treated him, and he maintained his character no matter how difficult life became.

COURAGE FOR TODAY

How often do you consider your reputation and legacy when making important choices and decisions? Do you sometimes let your problems determine your responses? Consider the verse below and describe how you will courageously strive to let your walk with God be unmistakable today.

We are God's masterpiece. He has created us anew in Christ Jesus, so we can do the good things he planned for us long ago.

EPHESIANS 2:10

THE COURAGE TO
Be a Good Shepherd

You drink the milk, wear the wool, and butcher the best animals, but you let your flocks starve. You have not taken care of the weak. You have not tended the sick or bound up the injured. You have not gone looking for those who have wandered away and are lost. Instead, you have ruled them with harshness and cruelty.

EZEKIEL 34:3–4

Father, you sent Jesus to be our perfect Savior and Shepherd. Let his life inspire me and his calling drive me to be a godly mentor to others.

Are you a faithful disciple maker and a good shepherd to others? Be challenged by God's reprimand in Ezekiel chapter 34. In this passage, God commanded his prophet Ezekiel to scold Israel's leaders, who were only looking out for themselves. Because of their leaders' negligence, God's people were suffering and vulnerable.

God concluded his rebuke by vowing to rescue and shepherd his people. "I myself will search and find my sheep" (v. 11). He promised to recover, provide for, tend to, strengthen, and make a covenant of peace with his followers. And today, every Christ follower is called to shepherd others by caring for their spiritual well-being and investing in their spiritual growth.

COURAGE FOR TODAY

Who are you spiritually mentoring? Would you say you are doing a good job as their shepherd? Read the passage below and explain how you can be a more courageous and reliable influence on others today.

Care for the flock that God has entrusted to you. Watch over it willingly, not grudgingly—not for what you will get out of it, but because you are eager to serve God. Don't lord it over the people assigned to your care, but lead them by your own good example.

1 PETER 5:2–3

THE COURAGE TO
Embrace Ancestry

Salmon was the father of Boaz (whose mother was Rahab). Boaz was the father of Obed (whose mother was Ruth). Obed was the father of Jesse. Jesse was the father of King David. David was the father of Solomon (whose mother was Bathsheba, the widow of Uriah).

MATTHEW 1:5–6

Father, on the day I was saved, I became your child. Help me honor your great love and sacrifice as I embrace my life as a member of your family.

Have you ever felt unworthy of God's forgiveness and salvation because of your past behavior or that of your family of origin? Consider Jesus' ancestry in Matthew chapter 1 that includes men and women from all walks of life. Genealogies are an important part of Jewish history because they confirm a person's identity and their relationship to Abraham and his blessing.

The presence of both Abraham and David in Jesus' lineage establishes his legal right to fulfill God's promises to both of these great patriarchs. The fact that imperfect men and women, including women who were not Jewish, are in Christ's ancestry shows that God's covenant promises are for all people, from every nationality and background, who accept his Son, Jesus.

COURAGE FOR TODAY

Do you consider yourself a genuine child of God, regardless of your past or family background? Meditate on the verse below and describe how accepting that you are a genuine child of God gives you more courage for life today.

To all who believed him and accepted him, he gave the right to become children of God. They are reborn—not with a physical birth resulting from human passion or plan, but a birth that comes from God.

JOHN 1:12–13

THE COURAGE TO

Say Yes to God

When the LORD saw Moses coming to take a closer look,
God called to him from the middle of the bush, "Moses! Moses!"
"Here I am!" Moses replied.

EXODUS 3:4

Father, you always prepare me for your calling even when I don't feel adequately equipped. Give me the courage to say "yes" to you no matter what you ask me to do.

Have you told God "maybe" regarding a particular assignment or opportunity he has put before you? Allow the account of Moses in Exodus chapter 3 to inspire you to say "yes" to God. After being raised by Pharaoh's daughter and later killing a man while defending a Hebrew slave, Moses fled to Midian, got married, and began raising a family. One day, while Moses was tending to his father-in-law's flock, God appeared to him in the form of a burning bush. God explained how he had seen the oppression of his people and had heard their cries.

So God called Moses to lead the Israelites out of Egypt. Five times Moses protested, and each time God reassured him. God promised to be with him, displayed his power, and even gave Moses a spokesman. Finally, Moses agreed, and with God's help, he accomplished everything the Lord asked him to do.

COURAGE FOR TODAY

Are you ready to put your excuses aside and say "yes" to God? Read the prophet Isaiah's response below and take courageous and intentional steps today to accomplish God's calling on your life.

I heard the Lord asking, "Whom should I send as a messenger to this people?
Who will go for us?" I said, "Here I am. Send me."

ISAIAH 6:8

THE COURAGE TO
Hold On to Joy

You received the message with joy from the Holy Spirit in spite of the severe suffering it brought you. In this way, you imitated both us and the Lord.

1 THESSALONIANS 1:6

Father, sometimes others reject or exclude me because of my faith. Help me hold on to the joy I receive from my relationship with you, especially when I face hardship or suffering.

Do you try to find joy in the midst of painful circumstances? Or are you more prone to letting hardships keep you down? Consider the apostle Paul's compliments in 1 Thessalonians chapter 1. In Paul's first letter to the church in Thessalonica, he recalled his first visit, when enemies of the gospel had tormented him, forced him to leave town, and persecuted new believers.

But rather than giving into self-pity or giving up on God, Thessalonian believers held on to their faith and embraced joy in anticipating Christ's return. The perseverance and enthusiasm this church had for Jesus made a profound impression on believers in Greece. Instead of returning to their idols, the Thessalonians endured persecution and continued to serve God. Nothing deterred them from their faith and joy. In fact, it only multiplied.

COURAGE FOR TODAY

Do you struggle to hold on to your faith and joy in challenging times? Let the verse below inspire you to lean into your relationship with God and courageously embrace joy in the Lord, no matter what today may bring.

I pray that God, the source of hope, will fill you completely with joy and peace because you trust in him. Then you will overflow with confident hope through the power of the Holy Spirit.

ROMANS 15:13

THE COURAGE TO
Start Over

The Lord spoke to Jonah a second time: "Get up and go to the great city of Nineveh, and deliver the message I have given you."

JONAH 3:1–2

Father, thank you for allowing me to begin again. Though at times I've failed you and others, you have given me the courage to start over. Help me be a vessel of truth wherever I go.

Have you ever failed to obey God and desired a second chance? Observe the life of God's rebellious prophet in Jonah chapter 3. Jonah was a man who disobeyed God and almost lost his life. After a miraculous rescue from the belly of a fish, God allowed Jonah to try again.

When Jonah finally delivered God's warning of judgment and destruction to the Ninevites, the people and their king abandoned their evil ways and turned their hearts toward the Lord. They, too, received a fresh start with God. Jonah's do-over changed the direction of his life and profoundly impacted the lives of countless others too.

COURAGE FOR TODAY

Do you need a second chance to embrace God's calling? Doing so can have an eternal impact on your life and on the lives of others around you. Read the verse below and make the decision to courageously follow God's lead, speak his truth, and pursue his will today.

The faithful love of the Lord never ends! His mercies never cease. Great is his faithfulness; his mercies begin afresh each morning.

LAMENTATIONS 3:22–23

THE COURAGE TO
Love Wholeheartedly

"'You must love the Lord your God with all your heart, all your soul, all your mind, and all your strength.' The second is equally important: 'Love your neighbor as yourself.' No other commandment is greater than these."

MARK 12:30–31

Father, you command that everything I do should be done in love. Help me to love you and others wholeheartedly, in both practical and meaningful ways.

Do you truly love God with all your heart, soul, mind, and strength? And do you genuinely love others as well? Be motivated by Jesus' discussion with religious leaders in Mark chapter 12. After Jesus taught the parable about the evil farmers, the Sadducees questioned him about taxes and marriage in heaven. In response, Jesus challenged their misunderstanding of Scripture and clarified that believers are to pay what is owed and that all people will be like the angels when they enter heaven, meaning that they will neither marry nor be given in marriage.

After Jesus' reply, the religious teachers asked, "Of all the commandments, which is the most important?" (v. 28). And Jesus said to love the Lord with all your heart, soul, mind, and strength. Then he went on to say, "The second is equally important: 'Love your neighbor as yourself'" (v. 31).

COURAGE FOR TODAY

What does it mean to genuinely love God and others? Read the following verse and describe how you will courageously display your love for the Lord and people in your life today.

If I had the gift of prophecy, and if I understood all of God's secret plans and possessed all knowledge, and if I had such faith that I could move mountains, but didn't love others, I would be nothing.

1 CORINTHIANS 13:2

THE COURAGE TO

Embrace Faith over Fear

Then the whole community began weeping aloud, and they cried all night.
Their voices rose in a great chorus of protest against Moses and Aaron.
"If only we had died in Egypt, or even here in the wilderness!" they complained.
NUMBERS 14:1–2

Father, you call me to be courageous and to trust you completely. Help me determine if my concerns are valid or if I need to proceed in faith, knowing that with you, all things are possible.

Does fear keep you from experiencing new adventures or taking on new challenges? Fear should serve as a warning, but adopting a spirit of fear will keep you from the abundant life God created you for. Consider Numbers chapter 14 and discover how the Israelites rebelled against God out of fear.

In Numbers chapter 13, Moses sent twelve men to explore God's promised land. When they returned, ten scouts spread their fears among the people while two scouts, Joshua and Caleb, encouraged the people to take the land. "Don't be afraid of the people of the land…They have no protection, but the Lord is with us!" (v. 9). But the people decided to believe the naysayers, choosing fear over faith. Due to their faithless decision, an eleven-day journey turned into forty years of wandering, and an entire generation perished before the people of Israel entered God's promised land.

COURAGE FOR TODAY

Memorize the verse below and identify your fears. Ask God to help you determine if your fears are justified and to guide you to godly counsel if needed. Then decide to courageously embrace your faith over your fears today.

This is why I remind you to fan into flames the spiritual gift God gave you when I laid my hands on you. For God has not given us a spirit of fear and timidity, but of power, love, and self-discipline.
2 TIMOTHY 1:6–7

THE COURAGE TO
Risk Everything

The jailer woke up to see the prison doors wide open. He assumed the prisoners had escaped, so he drew his sword to kill himself. But Paul shouted to him, "Stop! Don't kill yourself! We are all here!"

ACTS 16:27–28

Father, you call me to trust you with everything, including my life. Help me to fully surrender my life and all I have to you.

Do you fear losing your job, health, relationships, or possessions if you faithfully obey God? Consider Paul's response to the Philippian jailer in Acts chapter 16. The jailer's responsibility was to ensure that no prisoners escaped. Yet one night, when a great earthquake occurred, the cell doors flew open, and the chains of every prisoner fell off. Fearing the inmates had escaped and thinking he would face an execution for losing the prisoners, the jailer drew his sword to end his own life.

But Paul shouted to the jailer, "Stop! Don't kill yourself! We are all here!" (v. 28). Instead of escaping and saving his own life, Paul risked everything and stayed. As a result of Paul's courage and compassion, the jailer surrendered his life to Christ, saving his entire household.

COURAGE FOR TODAY

Do you fear losing something you value if you were to obey God and share his truth? Meditate on the verse below and describe ways you will pick up your cross to courageously follow God today.

Jesus said to his disciples, "If any of you wants to be my follower, you must give up your own way, take up your cross, and follow me. If you try to hang on to your life, you will lose it. But if you give up your life for my sake, you will save it. And what do you benefit if you gain the whole world but lose your own soul? Is anything worth more than your soul?"

MATTHEW 16:24–26

THE COURAGE TO
Be Blessed

The LORD is my shepherd; I have all that I need…Surely your goodness and unfailing love will pursue me all the days of my life, and I will live in the house of the LORD forever.

PSALM 23:1, 6

Father, you are faithful, trustworthy, and true. Help me courageously set aside any selfish desires and focus fully on receiving the perfect blessings you have prepared for me.

Are you willing to set aside your personal wants and trust God to give you what you truly need? Reflect on Psalm 23, one of the Bible's most familiar and encouraging hymns. In this psalm, David recalls his confidence in God as his shepherd and provider. Verse 1 celebrates God as the one who oversees, cares for, and protects his children.

His divine peace can restore the soul. His presence and divine guidance can alleviate fear, and his protection can provide comfort. God prepares great blessings and abundantly provides for those who follow him. And his goodness and unfailing love are ever-present for those who choose to live in his presence forever. Therefore, when we need nourishment, restoration, guidance, and protection, we must consistently seek almighty God and willingly receive his blessings.

COURAGE FOR TODAY

Do you trust in God's protection and provisions? Are you confident he will give you all you need? Be encouraged by the passage below and decide to receive the blessings God has prepared for you and, in turn, freely bless others who also are in need today.

God will generously provide all you need. Then you will always have everything you need and plenty left over to share with others.

2 CORINTHIANS 9:8

THE COURAGE TO
Motivate Others

Let us think of ways to motivate one another
to acts of love and good works.

HEBREWS 10:24

Father, in response to all you've done for me, I long to inspire others to also embrace a great love and respect for you. Give me the opportunity to be a good influence and help me know how to motivate others toward acts of love and good works.

Do you regularly offer words of encouragement and inspiration to friends, family members, and acquaintances? Let the author's message in Hebrews chapter 10 inspire you to influence others toward godly behavior and good deeds. Just before writing one of the greatest essays on faith, the author of Hebrews addressed the weakness in the old sacrificial system. Rather than taking away the guilt of a sinner once and for all, animal sacrifices only reminded God's people of their sins year after year.

Through Jesus, God had made a new covenant with humankind, so there is no longer a need for religious rituals. So in response to Jesus' profound sacrifice that took away God's judgment of believers' sins, Christ followers can now confidently enter God's presence. Therefore, in response to all the Lord has done for us, believers should continually look for ways to inspire one another to do good deeds and love others well.

COURAGE FOR TODAY

Describe how you inspire others toward godly behavior and good deeds. Then meditate on King Solomon's wise sayings below and explain how you will courageously motivate those around you today.

Worry weighs a person down; an encouraging word cheers a person up.
The godly give good advice to their friends; the wicked lead them astray.

PROVERBS 12:25–26

THE COURAGE TO
Serve God Faithfully

"Fear the Lord and serve him wholeheartedly. Put away forever the idols your ancestors worshiped when they lived beyond the Euphrates River and in Egypt. Serve the Lord alone."

JOSHUA 24:14

Father, I often allow myself to be pulled in many directions. Help me choose today to courageously serve you no matter how difficult or what trial or temptation comes my way.

Are you committed to serving God faithfully? Consider Joshua's final words to the Israelites in Joshua chapter 24. In the first twelve verses of Joshua, God provided a historical review of his faithfulness that should inspire his people to be faithful in return. In verse 13, God reminded the people of Israel that he was the one who provided the land and all its resources. Therefore, the Israelites, in humility and out of gratitude, should "fear the Lord and serve him wholeheartedly."

So Joshua gave the people of Israel an ultimatum in verse 15: "Choose today whom you will serve." Two times in verses 16–30, the people of Israel proclaimed, "We will serve the Lord," and all those who had experienced God's faithfulness remained committed to him for the rest of their lives. We should do the same.

COURAGE FOR TODAY

Are you fully committed to God out of gratitude for all he has done for you? Or do you prioritize your own wants and needs over God's will? Read the verse below and describe how you will courageously serve God today.

"No one can serve two masters. For you will hate one and love the other; you will be devoted to one and despise the other. You cannot serve God and be enslaved to money."

MATTHEW 6:24

THE COURAGE TO
Engage in the Harvest

These were his instructions to them: "The harvest is great, but the workers are few.
So pray to the Lord who is in charge of the harvest; ask him to send more workers
into his fields."

LUKE 10:2

Father, there's no time better than now for me to lead someone to faith in you. Give me the opportunity and courage to reach, teach, and minister to unbelievers today.

How often do you share God's love and salvation with others? Let Jesus' instructions in Luke chapter 10 inspire you. As Jesus sought to expand his ministry, he enlisted seventy-two disciples and sent them from town to town sharing God's good news. He instructed them to go, pray, and be aware of opposition.

When they entered someone's home, they were to bless the family with peace. If they received a warm reception, they were to stay and minister to the town. But if the town rejected them, the disciples were to let the people be and move on. For anyone who refused their message was rejecting God and Jesus, not the disciples. Therefore, as believers, we, too, must persevere in sharing God's love and salvation, striving to reach everyone who will listen.

COURAGE FOR TODAY

How are you engaging in God's harvest of new believers? Read Jesus' familiar calling below and describe how you will courageously engage unbelievers and lead new people to God today.

"Therefore, go and make disciples of all the nations, baptizing them in the name of the Father and the Son and the Holy Spirit. Teach these new disciples to obey all the commands I have given you. And be sure of this: I am with you always, even to the end of the age."

MATTHEW 28:19–20

THE COURAGE TO
Ask Questions

How long, O LORD, must I call for help? But you do not listen!
"Violence is everywhere!" I cry, but you do not come to save.

HABAKKUK 1:2

Father, I don't always understand your silence or the reason evil prevails.
Help me believe you will right the wrongs in your perfect timing.

Are you sometimes bewildered by God's silence, or do you wonder why he allows the prolonged continuation of evil? You're not alone. Consider the book of Habakkuk, in which the courageous prophet stepped up and asked God some tough questions. While most prophets received God's messages and delivered them to an audience, Habakkuk directly approached God for answers when things didn't make sense.

The prophet abhorred the evil behavior of God's people and wondered why the Almighty only gazed on inactively. In response, God told Habakkuk to watch and be amazed at what he would do. God then told his prophet that he'd be sending in the wicked Chaldeans to overthrow his own people—those who'd turned their backs on him. Though he questioned how and when God would move, Habakkuk waited, listened, and prayed. And in the end, his misunderstanding of the Lord turned into praise for the God of his salvation.

COURAGE FOR TODAY

Does God's inactivity sometimes baffle or frustrate you? Embrace the verse below and ask God to help you understand his ways. Then explain how you will courageously wait on God today and never lose hope.

"Just as the heavens are higher than the earth, so my ways are higher than your ways and my thoughts higher than your thoughts."

ISAIAH 55:9

THE COURAGE TO
Control Your Tongue

We all make many mistakes. For if we could control our tongues,
we would be perfect and could also control ourselves in every other way.

JAMES 3:2

Father, I want to honor you in all my conversations. Give me the desire and courage to control my tongue, speaking words that will build people up, not tear them down.

When you speak, are you careful or careless with your words? Are your conversations hurtful or helpful to others? Be challenged by the words of wisdom in James chapter 3. In his letter, James encouraged believers to be mindful of their speech. He addressed their need to listen carefully, speak slowly, and avoid anger. Now James chose to highlight how harmful words pack a powerful punch.

The tongue allows words to flow. So like a bit that controls a horse or a rudder that turns a ship, believers must learn to control their tongues. For the tongue is a flame of fire that will spread corruption throughout the entire body—if we allow it. While people can tame all kinds of animals, no one can completely subdue their tongue. The same mouth that blesses God can also curse others.

COURAGE FOR TODAY

Do you need to work harder at honoring God and others with your words? Meditate on the verse below and make a commitment to courageously control your tongue today.

Don't use foul or abusive language. Let everything you say be good and helpful,
so that your words will be an encouragement to those who hear them.

EPHESIANS 4:29

THE COURAGE TO
Trust God

*The serpent was the shrewdest of all the wild animals the L*ord *God had made. One day he asked the woman, "Did God really say you must not eat the fruit from any of the trees in the garden?"*

GENESIS 3:1

Father, from the very beginning, you made a way. Help me courageously embrace your salvation that allows me to enjoy a close relationship with you.

Are you aware that God prepared a way for reconciliation immediately after Adam and Eve sinned? In Genesis chapter 3, we read about the fall of humankind and God's plan for restoration. While there are many "firsts" in the book of Genesis, we find the most important one in this chapter, when God first mentioned restoration.

In verses 14–19, God announced consequences for Adam and Eve's sin. But in verse 15, God promised Christ's victory over Satan. Here we learn that Eve's offspring will strike Satan's seed on the head—a lethal blow that will defeat evil once and for all. And Satan's offspring will strike Eve's seed on the heel—an act that was accomplished at Christ's crucifixion when his hands and heels were pierced to pay for our transgressions.

COURAGE FOR TODAY

Read the verses below and consider God's sacrifice. How does knowing that God immediately established a way for you to return to a close relationship with him help you embrace a more courageous faith today?

God called you to do good, even if it means suffering, just as Christ suffered for you. He is your example, and you must follow in his steps…He personally carried our sins in his body on the cross so that we can be dead to sin and live for what is right. By his wounds you are healed.

1 PETER 2:21, 24

THE COURAGE TO
Cling to Faith

The disciples went and woke him up, shouting, "Lord, save us! We're going to drown!" Jesus responded, "Why are you afraid? You have so little faith!" Then he got up and rebuked the wind and waves, and suddenly there was a great calm.

MATTHEW 8:25–26

Father, you did not give me a spirit of fear. Instead, you gave me power, love, and self-discipline. Help me cling to my faith in you when I am tempted to embrace my fears.

When facing a frightening situation, are you comforted by your confidence in God, or do you tremble in fear? Consider the disciples circumstances in Matthew chapter 8 and let Jesus' response inspire you to trust God completely.

After healing many people and applauding a Roman officer's great faith, Jesus boarded a boat with his disciples and headed across the lake. When a storm arose and threatened to destroy their boat, the disciples woke Jesus and begged him to save their lives. But before calming the storm, their Savior addressed the issue that had caused them to fear. In response to their plea for help, Jesus first focused on their lack of confidence in him, saying, "Why are you afraid? You have so little faith!" (v. 26).

COURAGE FOR TODAY

Do you trust more in human ability and wisdom or in the power of God? Meditate on the apostle Paul's explanation below and vow to courageously cling to your faith when responding to anything that concerns you today.

When I first came to you, dear brothers and sisters, I didn't use lofty words and impressive wisdom to tell you God's secret plan…I did this so you would trust not in human wisdom but in the power of God.

1 CORINTHIANS 2:1, 5

THE COURAGE TO

Honor and Protect Love

Promise me, O women of Jerusalem,
by the gazelles and wild deer,
not to awaken love until the time is right.

SONG OF SONGS 2:7

Father, you designed love and relationships for us to cherish and respect. Help me honor and protect your plan and purpose for intimacy.

Do you cherish and safeguard your romantic relationships? Let King Solomon's words in Song of Songs inspire and challenge you. This beautiful poem artistically describes the love relationship between King Solomon and his bride. Throughout the book, the lovers exchange words of attraction, appreciation, and longing for one another. But there are two primary themes that emerge when reading this song: 1) the celebration of intimacy and 2) the importance of keeping physical love both sacred and alive.

Three times in this book, Solomon advises readers that they should not awaken sexual passions until the right time or in advance of the right person (see 2:7; 3:5; 8:4). In the final chapter, Solomon's bride asks him to receive her unbreakable devotion as she explains that the joy of true love is both powerful and everlasting.

COURAGE FOR TODAY

Do you intentionally protect and preserve love and intimacy in your life? Read the passage below and describe how you currently safeguard your sexuality and relationships. Are there any courageous changes you believe God is encouraging you to make today?

Because there is so much sexual immorality, each man should have his own wife, and each woman should have her own husband. The husband should fulfill his wife's sexual needs, and the wife should fulfill her husband's needs.

1 CORINTHIANS 7:2–3

THE COURAGE TO
Never Give Up

Since God in His mercy has given us this new way, we never give up.

2 CORINTHIANS 4:1

Father, I need courage to stay the course and not give up when life gets tough. Give me the desire to do your will and the ability to persevere.

Do you press on in difficult situations? Or are you more apt to give up when the going gets tough? Examine the apostle Paul's words recorded in 2 Corinthians chapter 4. After his conversion to Christianity, Paul faced never-ending challenges throughout his new life and ministry. Saul the persecutor became Paul the persecuted, and he often spoke of the obstacles he faced while carrying out his mission for God.

Paul was consistently crushed, perplexed, and hunted down by those who opposed his message. Yet amid every challenge, Paul drew strength from God's promises. Even though Paul and his companions constantly suffered for their faith, they never gave up. "Though our bodies are dying, our spirits are being renewed every day" (v. 16). Paul refused to focus on his affliction. Instead he considered his troubles small in comparison to the glory that awaited him in heaven.

COURAGE FOR TODAY

Do you need more courage to keep going? Read the verse below and list situations in your life where you are tempted to give up. Then ask God for guidance to courageously persevere today.

Let's not get tired of doing what is good.
At just the right time we will reap a harvest of blessing
if we don't give up.

GALATIANS 6:9

THE COURAGE TO
Commit

Ezra arrived in Jerusalem in August of that year. He had arranged to leave Babylon on April 8, the first day of the new year, and he arrived at Jerusalem on August 4, for the gracious hand of his God was on him. This was because Ezra had determined to study and obey the Law of the LORD and to teach those decrees and regulations to the people of Israel.

EZRA 7:8–10

Father, your will and ways are superior to anything I can think of or hope for. Give me the desire to seek your will and the courage to obey your guidance and calling.

How committed are you to God and his Word? Consider Ezra's passion and dedication to learning, obeying, and teaching God's Word recorded in Ezra chapter 7. Ezra is mentioned by name for the first time in this chapter. It is here that we learn that Ezra was a scribe and a priest. Years after the first group of Israelite exiles returned to their homeland, King Artaxerxes permitted and prepared Ezra to return to Jerusalem to establish leadership over the people and ensure that they learned and obeyed God's Word.

Ezra chapter 7 concludes with him praising God for his sovereignty and faithfulness in allowing him to return to Jerusalem with not only the support of his own people but also the physical and spoken blessings of a pagan king.

COURAGE FOR TODAY

How strong is your commitment to God and his Word? Read the following familiar verse out loud and describe what it means to you to love God with all your heart, soul, and strength. What courageous changes do you need to make today to strengthen your commitment to God.

You must love the LORD your God with all your heart, all your soul, and all your strength.

DEUTERONOMY 6:5

THE COURAGE TO
Remove Obstacles

Let's stop condemning each other. Decide instead to live in such a way that you will not cause another believer to stumble and fall…For the Kingdom of God is not a matter of what we eat or drink, but of living a life of goodness and peace and joy in the Holy Spirit.

ROMANS 14:13, 17

Father, sometimes I disagree with the religious opinions and beliefs of others. Help me remember that I am not their judge and give me the desire and ability to lovingly and peacefully live out my convictions, without causing another believer to stumble.

Are you ever tempted to argue with other believers about their beliefs? Heed the apostle Paul's warning in Romans chapter 14 and remove any obstacles between you and other Christ followers. Paul was a knowledgeable, faithful, and dedicated follower of Christ. He committed his life to strengthening the faith of others and made a point to avoid doing anything that might cause a believer to stumble.

In his letter to the church in Rome, Paul urged members to stop arguing with other members and instead to accept those who may be weaker in their faith. For if someone tries to prove their point or insist that everyone believe like they do, they may cause another Christ follower to stumble. Therefore, one must do all one can to eliminate any roadblocks hindering another person's faith.

COURAGE FOR TODAY

Are you aware of any obstacles you've placed in the way of other believers? Memorize the familiar verse below and list the courageous steps you will take today to build others up, not tear them down.

Encourage each other and build each other up, just as you are already doing.

1 THESSALONIANS 5:11

THE COURAGE TO

Heed God's Correction

"I destroyed some of your cities, as I destroyed Sodom and Gomorrah. Those of you who survived were like charred sticks pulled from a fire. But still you would not return to me," says the Lord. "Therefore, I will bring upon you all the disasters I have announced. Prepare to meet your God in judgment, you people of Israel!"

Amos 4:11–12

Father, you are merciful and forgiving. You allow second chances—and even more. Allow me to recognize my sin and give me the courage and desire to heed your correction and return to you in obedience.

Have you recently jumped headfirst into sin or been led there by a friend? Have you considered the pain it causes you, others, and the heart of God when you run after worldly pleasure? Notice how the Israelites simply ignored God when he sent incentives in the forms of a famine, drought, plagues, and even death to deter them.

In Amos chapter 4, we learn that even though God warned the people and delivered consequences, they still chose evil over good. Notice how God attempted to capture their attention; the phrase "You would not return to me" is repeated five times in this one chapter alone.

COURAGE FOR TODAY

How many times has God prompted you to change your ways? Were you willing then and are you willing now to heed his correction and make courageous modifications to your life? Consider the wise proverb below and take responsibility, turn away from sin, and courageously pursue God's will today.

Trust in the Lord with all your heart; do not depend on your own understanding. Seek his will in all you do, and he will show you which path to take.

Proverbs 3:5–6

THE COURAGE TO
Reach for Jesus

*A woman in the crowd had suffered for twelve years with constant bleeding, and
she could find no cure. Coming up behind Jesus, she touched the fringe of his robe.
Immediately, the bleeding stopped.*

LUKE 8:43–44

Father, I often try to fix my problems myself before turning to you.
Help me remember to immediately reach out to you for comfort, guidance,
and healing when I am in need.

How quickly do you reach for Jesus when you need encouragement or
restoration? Consider the account of the bleeding woman in Luke chapter
8. By the time Jesus encountered this woman, he was well-known as the
Messiah who had the power to heal. While making his way through a crowd of
supporters, a lady who had been suffering for twelve years approached him.

As she reached for Jesus and touched his robe, her bleeding
immediately stopped. Yet when Jesus asked who had brushed up against him,
everyone denied having done it. So the woman fell to her knees in front of her
Savior and confessed what she had done. In response, Jesus commended her.
"Your faith has made you well. Go in peace" (v. 48).

COURAGE FOR TODAY

Where do you turn first when you need comfort, encouragement, or
healing? Meditate on the verse below and reach for Jesus regarding
anything you need help or guidance with today.

*Jesus replied, "I am the bread of life. Whoever comes to me will never be hungry
again. Whoever believes in me will never be thirsty…For it is my Father's will that
all who see his Son and believe in him should have eternal life. I will raise them up
at the last day."*

JOHN 6:35, 40

THE COURAGE TO
Choose Godly Mentors

Elisha picked up Elijah's cloak, which had fallen when he was taken up. Then Elisha returned to the bank of the Jordan River. He struck the water with Elijah's cloak and cried out, "Where is the LORD, the God of Elijah?" Then the river divided, and Elisha went across.

2 KINGS 2:13–14

Father, many inspiring and godly people have traveled life's road before me. Let their courageous journeys inspire me to embrace a more courageous faith and lead me to encourage others to do the same.

Are you inspired by godly leaders? Be encouraged by the relationship of two great and godly prophets recorded in 2 Kings chapter 2. The story of Elijah and Elisha's alliance begins in verse 21. Elijah mentored Elisha, and Elisha ministered to Elijah. In this chapter of 2 Kings, we learn that Elijah had reached the end of his time on earth. He was faithful to God's calling, and he completely trusted God in every situation.

So when it came time for Elijah to die, God took him to heaven in a whirlwind. Even though Elijah was no longer on earth, his spirit and all that he had taught his successor remained with Elisha. His relationship with Elijah profoundly affected Elisha, and he, too, faithfully served God for the remaining days of his life.

COURAGE FOR TODAY

Name the people in your life who motivate you to embrace a more courageous faith. Read the verse below and list ways you can courageously inspire others to draw closer to God today.

Let us think of ways to motivate one another to acts of love and good works.

HEBREWS 10:24

THE COURAGE TO
Let Your Actions Speak

When he found him, he brought him back to Antioch. Both of them stayed there with the church for a full year, teaching large crowds of people. (It was at Antioch that the believers were first called Christians.)

ACTS 11:26

Father, I want to be a positive influence on people, inspiring them to love and serve you faithfully. Strengthen my ability to resist temptation so others will witness my behavior and attribute it to my relationship with you.

Do your actions speak louder than your words? Let the reputation of Christ followers in Acts chapter 11 inspire you to let your good character precede you. When Jesus' disciples began preaching to gentiles in the ancient city of Antioch, many believed and turned to the Lord. One of Jesus' disciples named Barnabas was known to be a good man who was filled with God's Spirit and had a strong faith. As he and Paul were teaching large crowds in Antioch, it was there that believers "were first called Christians" (v. 26).

Rather than bragging about their position as followers of Christ, believers in this Syrian city let their actions speak louder than their words, which led others to begin calling them "Christians."

COURAGE FOR TODAY

Do you have a good reputation, and does it precede you? Memorize King Solomon's wise proverb below and let it inspire you to be courageous and careful in all you say and do today so that others will see your actions and conclude that you are a follower of Christ.

*Choose a good reputation over great riches;
being held in high esteem is better than silver or gold.*

PROVERBS 22:1

THE COURAGE TO
Believe in God's Salvation

"You will not even need to fight. Take your positions; then stand still and watch the Lord's victory. He is with you, O people of Judah and Jerusalem. Do not be afraid or discouraged. Go out against them tomorrow, for the Lord is with you!"

2 CHRONICLES 20:17

Father, you are all knowing, all powerful, and ever present. Give me the courage to trust in your Word and take comfort in your protection.

How strong is your faith in God's salvation? Do you completely trust him both in this life and for your eternity? Consider King Jehoshaphat's confidence in God, recorded in 2 Chronicles chapter 20. Jehoshaphat was a good king. He followed in the faithful ways of King David, he cleansed Judah of idol worship, he promoted the study of God's Word, and he sought God's guidance when facing his enemies.

In 2 Chronicles 20, we read a remarkable story of faith. When Jehoshaphat was faced with the fear of a potential enemy attack, he chose to believe in God and the power of prayer for their salvation. In response, God said, "Do not be afraid! Don't be discouraged...for the battle is not yours, but God's" (v. 15).

COURAGE FOR TODAY

Do you trust God for your deliverance? Read the verse below out loud with conviction. Then describe ways you will courageously demonstrate your confidence in God's salvation today.

I wait quietly before God,
for my victory comes from him.
He alone is my rock and my salvation,
my fortress where I will never be shaken.

PSALM 62:1–2

THE COURAGE TO
Be Reborn

Jesus replied, "I assure you, no one can enter the Kingdom of God
without being born of water and the Spirit."
JOHN 3:5

Father, you designed me on purpose to honor and serve you faithfully. Yet because sin lures me from your will, I had to be reborn and receive your Holy Spirit. Help me recognize your presence in my life and let your Spirit lead me to honor you in everything I do.

Has your life genuinely changed because of your rebirth? Allow Jesus' teaching in John chapter 3 to inspire you to fully embrace your new life in Christ. When a Pharisee named Nicodemus asked Jesus, "How can an old man go back into his mother's womb and be born again?" (v. 4), Jesus explained that humankind's first birth is of flesh, and a believer's rebirth is of the spirit. For unless the Holy Spirit resides within a person, giving them new life, they cannot enter the kingdom of God.

Jesus went on to tell Nicodemus that he, the Son of Man, came down from heaven so that "everyone who believes in him will have eternal life" (v. 15). A believer's rebirth not only removes judgment of their sin, but it also draws them to live life in Christ's light that hates evil and pursues the will of God.

COURAGE FOR TODAY

How has your life changed as a result of believing and receiving Jesus as your Savior? Meditate on the verse below and describe the changes you will make, beginning today, to courageously display your new life in Christ.

He saved us, not because of the righteous things we had done, but because of his
mercy. He washed away our sins, giving us a new birth and new life through the
Holy Spirit.
TITUS 3:5

THE COURAGE TO
Flee

"Flee from Babylon! Leave the land of the Babylonians.
Like male goats at the head of the flock, lead my people home again."

JEREMIAH 50:8

Father, when I am tempted to sin or I am in a compromising situation, you promise to provide a way out. Give me the wisdom to recognize the danger and the courage to flee from what will harm me.

Have you found yourself in a situation that you sensed could lead to disaster? Or have you been tempted by a choice that would likely end in regret? Consider Jeremiah chapter 50 and the plight of God's people who experienced the painful aftermath of their disobedience and rebellion.

While God had allowed the Israelites to be held captive in a foreign land for seventy years, in time he permitted them to return to their homes. So while the prophet Jeremiah encouraged the Israelites to flee their captivity, go back to their beloved home, and serve God faithfully, he also pronounced judgment on their captors who had viciously destroyed the Israelites' great city. God not only promises to forgive sin and restore those who love him, but he also gives wisdom and guidance so we know when to flee a dangerous situation.

COURAGE FOR TODAY

How often do you experience the uneasy feelings of conviction? When you do, do you drop everything and run, or do you question your conscience and take the risk? Find inspiration and courage in the verse below and decide today to courageously flee every compromising situation.

Run from anything that stimulates youthful lusts. Instead, pursue righteous living, faithfulness, love, and peace. Enjoy the companionship of those who call on the Lord with pure hearts.

2 TIMOTHY 2:22

THE COURAGE TO
Eliminate Pride

*Humble yourselves before the Lord,
and he will lift you up in honor.*

JAMES 4:10

Father, I need to rid myself of pride that prevents humility. Help me see myself, others, and this world through your eyes so I can resist temptation and be humble.

Does pride keep you from acknowledging your weaknesses? Be motivated by the insightful teaching recorded in James chapter 4. James was the half brother of Jesus, yet there was a time when he refused to believe his sibling was the Messiah. But after Jesus' resurrection, James humbly confessed and confidently believed.

In his letter to Jewish believers, James introduced himself as "a slave of God and of the Lord Jesus Christ" (1:1). He urged believers to humble themselves and to repent over the disloyal things they had done. If they would draw nearer to God, the Lord would come closer to them. James warned Christ followers against boasting and making plans without seeking God's will first, saying, "It is sin to know what you ought to do and then not do it" (4:17).

COURAGE FOR TODAY

Are you willing to set your pride aside and admit when you've been wrong? Is it easy for you to ask for and give forgiveness when someone has treated you unfairly or when you have mistreated someone else? Meditate on the verse below and describe how you will courageously humble yourself before God and others today.

Because of the privilege and authority God has given me, I give each of you this warning: Don't think you are better than you really are. Be honest in your evaluation of yourselves, measuring yourselves by the faith God has given us.

ROMANS 12:3

THE COURAGE TO
Embrace God's Compassion

The LORD passed in front of Moses, calling out,
"Yahweh! The LORD! The God of compassion and mercy!
I am slow to anger and filled with unfailing love and faithfulness."

EXODUS 34:6

Father, your unconditional love, mercy, and compassion are beyond comprehension. Give me the ability to put all obstacles behind me so I can fully embrace your affection.

Are you in need of God's compassion? Do you know others who need it too? Let his words to his beloved servant Moses in Exodus chapter 34 encourage you to draw closer to the Lord today. From the time Moses was an infant, God protected and prepared him for his calling. Despite Moses' protests, God consistently displayed great compassion and patience for his servant. Even after Moses broke the original stone tablets, God graciously told him to get two new ones for God to again inscribe his Ten Commandments. Moses followed God's instructions and brought the new stones before the Lord on Mount Sinai.

When God came down and stood before Moses, God passed before him, proclaiming his compassion, mercy, unfailing love, and faithfulness. He also affirmed his lavish love that forgives iniquity, sin, and rebellion. In response, Moses threw himself to the ground, worshiped the Lord, and fasted for forty days and nights.

COURAGE FOR TODAY

Have you truly embraced God's unconditional affection for you? Do you accept that he offers the same to everyone? Meditate on the verse below and describe the ways you welcome God's compassion and courageously extend it to others today.

You, O Lord, are a God of compassion and mercy, slow to get angry
and filled with unfailing love and faithfulness.

PSALM 86:15

THE COURAGE TO
Work God's Plan

We are God's masterpiece. He has created us anew in Christ Jesus,
so we can do the good things he planned for us long ago.

EPHESIANS 2:10

Father, I may not know your plans for my life, but I can trust that they are good. Give me the courage to say "yes!" so I can accomplish what you've created me for.

Do you believe God created you "on purpose" and "for a purpose"? What would it take for you to begin following through with God's plan for your life today? Consider the apostle Paul's encouraging words in Ephesians chapter 2. Paul understood from his own history that human beings without Christ are like dead men walking. He used the term "were" repeatedly in this chapter to refer to the status of believers before they came to faith in Jesus.

Because of God's great mercy and love, he gives new life to all who believe in Christ and his sacrifice. Paul made it clear that salvation is God's free gift, not a result of anything people can do. The apostle regarded believers as God's *masterpiece*, and he warned them about boasting, for grace saved them, and they could take no credit. Paul then reminded the church that both Jews and gentiles were part of God's salvation plan. Together they make up God's complete family.

COURAGE FOR TODAY

Do you believe you are God's masterpiece? Read the verse below and describe how you can be more courageous and enthusiastic about God's plan for your life today.

He gave his life to free us from every kind of sin, to cleanse us, and to make us his very own people, totally committed to doing good deeds.

TITUS 2:14

THE COURAGE TO
Receive God's Good News

The Spirit of the Sovereign LORD is upon me, for the LORD has anointed me to bring good news to the poor. He has sent me to comfort the brokenhearted and to proclaim that captives will be released and prisoners will be freed.

ISAIAH 61:1

Father, because of your unconditional love and grace, you never give up on me. Help me regularly embrace and share your good news that fills me with hope.

Have you ever felt as if your sin were so great that God had written you off? Be encouraged by God's prophecy in Isaiah chapter 61. Although the Israelites had blatantly rebelled and willingly distanced themselves from him, God mercifully promised that one day, he would save and restore them.

This prophecy, delivered by Isaiah, must have been an overwhelming relief and a great source of hope for the women and men who likely believed God had given up on them. God, through his appointed Savior, would bring hope and deliverance to the poor, the brokenhearted, the captive, and those in mourning. Israel's cities would once again be rebuilt, prosperity would abound, and nations would recognize and honor their blessings. God's anointed savior would be filled with joy and clothed in righteousness, and he would offer salvation to all who would receive him.

COURAGE FOR TODAY

Are you confident in your relationship with God? Read the familiar passage below and describe how God's good news empowers you to be more courageous today.

The angel reassured them. "Don't be afraid!" he said. "I bring you good news that will bring great joy to all people. The Savior—yes, the Messiah, the Lord—has been born today in Bethlehem, the city of David!"

LUKE 2:10–11

THE COURAGE TO
Avoid Bitterness

Look after each other so that none of you fails to receive the grace of God. Watch out that no poisonous root of bitterness grows up to trouble you, corrupting many.

HEBREWS 12:15

Father, you warn me to avoid jealousy, anger, strife, and other destructive behaviors. Help me heal from hurtful experiences that may have caused me
to become bitter.

Have you ever allowed bitterness to grow? Learn from the author's words in Hebrews chapter 12 and be inspired by the lives of men and women of the Bible. Consider Adam and Eve's son Cain, whose bitterness led him to murder his brother; Esau, who also sought to kill his brother over his birthright; Job whose heartache caused him to speak out in bitterness; Jezebel who tried to kill the Lord's prophets; Jonah who had no compassion for the Ninevites; King David's son Absalom, who murdered his brother and tried to take over his father's throne; Haman who tried to destroy the Jews; and the chief priests, rulers, and people of Israel whose hatred toward Jesus caused them to cry out, "Crucify him!" (Luke 23:21).

The writer of Hebrews reminded believers that Jesus preached forgiveness not vengeance. Living in God's grace and extending it to others is the only way to truly overcome bitterness.

COURAGE FOR TODAY

Do you need to let go of any hurt that has caused you to become bitter? Read the verse below and ask God to give you the desire and courage to overcome animosity and frustration today.

Make allowance for each other's faults, and forgive anyone who offends you. Remember, the Lord forgave you, so you must forgive others.

COLOSSIANS 3:13

THE COURAGE TO
Choose God's Path

Oh, the joys of those who do not follow the advice of the wicked, or stand around with sinners, or join in with mockers. But they delight in the law of the LORD, meditating on it day and night.

PSALM 1:1–2

Father, your Word is a lamp to guide my feet and a light for my path. Give me the courage to always pursue your will and ways even when others around me choose corruption and immorality.

How often do you stop to think about your path in life? Psalm 1 describes the two pathways we can take: God's way or the way of the wicked. While each path is available, and the choice is ours, God has established the consequences, clearly defined in this psalm, for choosing wickedness.

When we listen to and follow people who pursue evil, our lives will ultimately be unstable, unproductive, and unsuccessful. But when God and his Word are our guide, we will be secure, productive, and profitable. Even when it seems like wicked people prosper, we must remember that it is only for a time, for their judgment is inevitable unless they leave their sinful life behind and turn faithfully to the Lord.

COURAGE FOR TODAY

How important is it to you to pursue godly behavior? Are you more apt to follow the crowd or to stand out and be different? Read the familiar verse below and state your commitment to courageously pursue God's plan for your life today over the short-lived pleasure you may gain from chasing the unethical ways of this world.

"I know the plans I have for you," says the LORD.
"They are plans for good and not for disaster,
to give you a future and a hope."

JEREMIAH 29:11

THE COURAGE TO
Fan the Flame

This is why I remind you to fan into flames the spiritual gift God gave you
when I laid my hands on you.

2 TIMOTHY 1:6

Father, I don't want to grow cold in my faith or neglect the abilities and talents you created in me. Give me guidance and a lasting passion to honor and serve you faithfully.

Have you ever felt distant from God? Or become disinterested in serving him? Consider the apostle Paul's words of advice in 2 Timothy chapter 1. Though he had reason to give up, nothing discouraged Paul from sharing the gospel or building up the body of Christ. As he awaited death, Paul sent a letter to Timothy, his ministry partner and son in the faith. In this letter, Paul urged Timothy to keep fanning the flames of his faith and passion for discipleship.

Throughout his two letters to Timothy, Paul encouraged him more than twenty times to be bold, strong, and to not shy away from confrontation. By strengthening his faith and using the gifts within him, Timothy would enlarge the kingdom of God. So Paul listed three God-given attributes that would keep Timothy from being fearful or timid: power, love, and self-discipline.

COURAGE FOR TODAY

Do you need more courage to persevere in your faith and use your talents for God? Be encouraged by the verse below and list the ways you will grow closer to God and courageously use your abilities to serve him today.

My health may fail, and my spirit may grow weak,
but God remains the strength of my heart; he is mine forever.

PSALM 73:26

THE COURAGE TO
Stand for Justice

As for me, I am filled with power—with the Spirit of the LORD.
I am filled with justice and strength to boldly declare Israel's sin and rebellion.

MICAH 3:8

Father, the world appears to be heading for moral destruction. Injustice trumps integrity while everyone sits and watches. Give me the courage to speak up for what is right, honorable, and just in your sight.

Does your heart break for those displaced in war-torn countries? Are you sickened when people turn a blind eye to evil in order to support their own agendas? Perhaps you feel guilty because of your own complacency or silence. Examine Micah's response to the corruption of his day in Micah chapter 3.

Disobedience was rampant, and God held Israel's leaders accountable. So Micah confronted the bribe takers, paid prophets, and foundations built by murder. Micah longed for his people to return to true worship. So he faithfully stood for justice and warned the corrupt nation that God would destroy all they had built in response to their rebellion.

COURAGE FOR TODAY

When you witness an offense, do you act or turn a blind eye? Are you willing to courageously speak out against wrongdoing and meet the needs of victims? Read the verse below and list the ways you will seek justice, help the helpless, and stand up for all that is good and godly today.

O people, the LORD has told you what is good, and this is what he requires of you: to do what is right, to love mercy, and to walk humbly with your God.

MICAH 6:8

THE COURAGE TO
Prioritize God

*We speak as messengers approved by God
to be entrusted with the Good News.
Our purpose is to please God, not people.
He alone examines the motives of our hearts.*

1 THESSALONIANS 2:4

Father, forgive me for wanting to please people instead of you. Give me
the courage to seek your approval over everyone else's.

Do you care more about what people think or what God thinks? Consider the
apostle Paul's experiences that he recorded in 1 Thessalonians chapter 2. Paul
had a reputation as God's ambassador to the Christian world. He established
churches, taught people how to grow in their faith, and promoted unity among
believers. He didn't wait until it was convenient or safe to share the gospel. He
willingly endured suffering from government officials and the religious elite for
preaching God's good news.

While some missionaries took money from their listeners and used
flattering speech for personal gain, Paul never did. Instead, he compared
himself to a nursing mother who cherishes her children and a father who
lovingly looks after them. Paul genuinely loved his people, and he honored
their suffering. Not only did he prioritize God, but he also urged other believers
to do so. For one day, all Christ followers will receive God's reward when they
stand before the Lord.

COURAGE FOR TODAY

Do you sometimes place the opinions of others over God's view? Let the
verse below motivate you to courageously put God first in everything you
do today.

Fearing people is a dangerous trap, but trusting the LORD means safety.

PROVERBS 29:25

THE COURAGE TO

Withstand Your Circumstances

When Daniel learned that the law had been signed, he went home and knelt down as usual in his upstairs room, with its windows open toward Jerusalem. He prayed three times a day, just as he had always done, giving thanks to his God.

DANIEL 6:10

Father, no matter what, I can always trust you with my circumstances. Give me the courage to withstand anything and the wisdom to believe that you will see me through.

When facing hardships or difficulties, how do you endure? Be encouraged by one man's perilous account in Daniel chapter 6. After spending more than eighty years navigating his captivity, servanthood, and eventual prosperity in Babylon, Daniel faced a life-threatening predicament: he could agree to either pray only to Babylon's king or be thrown into a den of lions.

Despite the risk, Daniel refused intimidation and continued to openly worship almighty God. When jealous officials reported him to the king, Daniel was arrested and tossed into the lion's den. But God did not allow Daniel's story to end there. The next morning, when the stone at the opening of the lion's den was rolled away, Daniel did not have a scratch on him, for he had faithfully trusted God to protect him.

COURAGE FOR TODAY

Do you truly believe that "with God" all things are possible? Will you set aside your doubts and trust God with all your concerns? Read the passage below and describe how, with God, you will courageously withstand your circumstances today.

We are always confident, even though we know that as long as we live in these bodies we are not at home with the Lord. For we live by believing and not by seeing.

2 CORINTHIANS 5:6–7

THE COURAGE TO
Do All You Can

Jesus was in Bethany at the home of Simon, a man who had previously had leprosy. While he was eating, a woman came in with a beautiful alabaster jar of expensive perfume made from essence of nard. She broke open the jar and poured the perfume over his head.

MARK 14:3

Father, I desire to serve you and others faithfully. Motivate me to do all I can to honor and serve you devotedly and to comfort and care for people.

When you serve God and others, do you do all you can? Be inspired by the account of Jesus' anointing in Mark chapter 14. Not long before Jesus was arrested, beaten, and crucified, a woman anointed his body by pouring a beautiful jar of expensive perfume over his head. When others saw this, they were appalled and verbally scolded the woman for wasting money that she could have given to the poor.

In response, Jesus told them to "leave her alone" (v. 6). He then made it clear to those listening that the poor would always be with them but that he would not. The woman had done all she could to bless and honor her Lord and Savior, preparing his body ahead of time for the burial that was to come.

COURAGE FOR TODAY

Are you wholeheartedly faithful and generous in serving the Lord? Meditate on the poor widow's generosity below and describe how you will courageously do all you can to give to God and others today.

"I tell you the truth," Jesus said, "this poor widow has given more than all the rest of them. For they have given a tiny part of their surplus, but she, poor as she is, has given everything she has."

LUKE 21:3–4

THE COURAGE TO
Acknowledge God's Sovereignty

I will raise my fist of judgment against you.
I will give you as plunder to many nations.
I will cut you off from being a nation and destroy you completely.
Then you will know that I am the Lord.

EZEKIEL 25:7

Father, you alone are Lord over everyone and everything. Give me wisdom and a desire to faithfully acknowledge and honor your sovereignty.

Do you recognize God's supremacy and respect his authority? Let God's message in Ezekiel chapter 25 inspire you to acknowledge God's supremacy. In this chapter, God asks his great prophet Ezekiel to deliver a message of judgment against nations who had oppressed Israel. Because Ammon cheered when God's temple was defiled and laughed when God's people were taken into exile, God promised to give Ammon's land to the nomads. Since Moab ignored the importance of Israel, God would make of Moab a wasteland. And because Philistia took revenge against the Israelites, God planned to destroy the Philistine territory and people. God would allow judgment to take place to ensure that everyone knew that he alone is the Lord.

COURAGE FOR TODAY

What does it mean to you to acknowledge God's sovereignty? Meditate on the passage below and describe how you can be a more courageous witness for God today.

Yours, O Lord, is the greatness, the power, the glory, the victory, and the majesty. Everything in the heavens and on earth is yours, O Lord, and this is your kingdom. We adore you as the one who is over all things. Wealth and honor come from you alone, for you rule over everything. Power and might are in your hand, and at your discretion people are made great and given strength.

1 CHRONICLES 29:11–12

THE COURAGE TO
Persevere

*Such things were written in the Scriptures long ago to teach us.
And the Scriptures give us hope and encouragement
as we wait patiently for God's promises to be fulfilled.*

ROMANS 15:4

Father, when I encounter hurt, hardship, or loss, I sometimes find it hard to keep going. In times like these, please remind me of your presence and give me great hope and courage so I can press on.

Do you sometimes find it difficult to move forward? Consider the life of the apostle Paul and let his teaching in Roman's chapter 15 encourage you to persevere. Paul was no stranger to suffering. He endured rejection, abandonment, abuse, and imprisonment. Yet he always found a way to stand firm in his faith, find joy in his circumstances, and press on.

In his letter to Roman church members, Paul taught them to care for others and live for the Lord. Through his presence and by his Word, God promises Christ followers constant patience and encouragement. For God never said believers have a right to be happy. In contrast, he makes it clear that, on this earth, many challenges will arise. Yet with God, believers can always prevail.

COURAGE FOR TODAY

Are you currently experiencing any difficult or upsetting challenges? Do you know someone who is? Read the verse below and let it motivate you today to rely on God's presence and guidance as you courageously persevere while encouraging others to do the same.

Dear brothers and sisters, when troubles of any kind come your way, consider it an opportunity for great joy. For you know that when your faith is tested, your endurance has a chance to grow.

JAMES 1:2–3

THE COURAGE TO
Celebrate God's Character

*Let all that I am praise the L*ORD*; with my whole heart, I will praise his holy name.*
*Let all that I am praise the L*ORD*; may I never forget the good things he does for me.*
PSALM 103:1–2

Father, you are all powerful, all knowing, ever present, and in complete control. Help me remain humble in your presence and faithful to your will.

How often do you take time to appreciate the many attributes of God? Reflect on King David's words of praise in Psalms 103 and 104 as he celebrates and describes God's holy character. In the first two verses of Psalm 103, David expresses his adoration for the Lord. In verses 3 through 5, the psalmist lists five benefits we receive when we accept him as our Lord and Savior. These benefits include: 1) he forgives our sins, 2) he heals our diseases, 3) he redeems us from death, 4) he crowns us with love and tender mercies, and 5) he fills our lives with good things.

God is compassionate, gracious, slow to anger, and full of lovingkindness. He is clothed in splendor and majesty and created the earth in his wisdom and by his words. So like David, let us bless the Lord, celebrate his character, and praise his name forever.

COURAGE FOR TODAY

Describe the ways you acknowledge and celebrate God's many attributes. Read the verse below and name several ways God's character can give you courage today.

*Have you never heard? Have you never understood? The L*ORD *is the everlasting God, the Creator of all the earth. He never grows weak or weary. No one can measure the depths of his understanding.*
ISAIAH 40:28

THE COURAGE TO
Grow Spiritually

You have been believers so long now that you ought to be teaching others. Instead, you need someone to teach you again the basic things about God's word. You are like babies who need milk and cannot eat solid food…Solid food is for those who are mature, who through training have the skill to recognize the difference between right and wrong.

HEBREWS 5:12, 14

Father, nothing is more important than my relationship with you. Lead me to consistently grow stronger in my faith so that I can always discern right from wrong and share your truth with others.

Are you persistently growing spiritually stronger? Or are your love for and devotion to God at a standstill? Consider the author's rebuke and advice in Hebrews chapter 5. The author of Hebrews felt discouraged by the lack of maturity among Christ followers in his day. So in his letter to believers, he critiqued their spiritual dullness and their inability to discern right from wrong.

Because Jesus sacrificed so much for all who would believe in him, the writer of this message felt it was vital for Christ followers to continually grow in their faith and dedication to the Lord.

COURAGE FOR TODAY

Describe the ways you strengthen your faith daily. Then meditate on the passage below and decide how you plan to grow courageously stronger in the grace and knowledge of your Savior today.

You already know these things, dear friends. So be on guard; then you will not be carried away by the errors of these wicked people and lose your own secure footing. Rather, you must grow in the grace and knowledge of our Lord and Savior Jesus Christ. All glory to him, both now and forever! Amen.

2 PETER 3:17–18

THE COURAGE TO
Go

The Lord had said to Abram, "Leave your native country, your relatives,
and your father's family, and go to the land that I will show you."

GENESIS 12:1

Father, you prepare, provide for, and protect me as I pursue your will and
ways. Give me courage and confidence to embrace your calling and great
faith as I rely on you to see me through.

Is God calling you to go? To relocate, take a new job, resolve a conflict, or begin
a new relationship? In Genesis chapter 12, we learn about Abram's calling. In
the previous chapter, Genesis 11, we meet Abram (whom God later named
Abraham), through whom the nation of Israel was born. Abram embraced
God's calling and trusted in God's promises.

At the beginning of chapter 12, God spoke to Abram, instructed him to
relocate, and promised him blessings in return for obedience. Abram obeyed
God immediately, and as the man traveled, God reassured Abram of his presence
and promises. In a moment of weakness, Abram gave in to his fear, disregarded
God, and endangered his wife's life. Yet God, in his abundant grace and mercy,
rescued Abram and Sarai so they could resume their God-given journey.

COURAGE FOR TODAY

Read the passage below and underline ways God prepares, provides for,
and protects his followers. How do God's words inspire you to heed his
calling and walk in more courage today?

The Lord is my shepherd; I have all that I need. He lets me rest in green meadows;
he leads me beside peaceful streams. He renews my strength.
He guides me along right paths, bringing honor to his name.
Even when I walk through the darkest valley, I will not be afraid,
for you are close beside me. Your rod and your staff protect and comfort me.

PSALM 23:1–4

THE COURAGE TO
Escape Temptation

*The temptations in your life are no different from what others experience.
And God is faithful. He will not allow the temptation to be more than you can stand.
When you are tempted, he will show you a way out so that you can endure.*

1 CORINTHIANS 10:13

Father, temptation is a part of life. Help me resist worldly enticements by
relying on you to show me the way of escape.

Do you find it difficult to resist temptation? Let the apostle Paul's teaching in
1 Corinthians chapter 10 encourage you to choose God's escape route so you
can overcome enticements.

In his letter to the Corinth church, Paul begged the new Christians to
learn from the past and stop craving sin. He warned them to flee from the
desires of this life because temptation leads believers away from God. He then
encouraged the Corinthians to always look to the Lord for guidance because
God will not allow his followers to be tempted with more than they can stand.
Instead, God will show believers "a way out" (v. 13).

COURAGE FOR TODAY

Are you currently being enticed to sin against God? Or do you know
someone who is? Meditate on the familiar passage below and let the Lord
help you courageously escape temptation today as you inspire others to
do so as well.

*We are not fighting against flesh-and-blood enemies, but against evil rulers and
authorities of the unseen world, against mighty powers in this dark world, and
against evil spirits in the heavenly places. Therefore, put on every piece of God's
armor so you will be able to resist the enemy in the time of evil. Then after the
battle you will still be standing firm.*

EPHESIANS 6:12–13

THE COURAGE TO
Embrace Redemption

O Jacob, listen to the Lord who created you. O Israel, the one who formed you says,
"Do not be afraid, for I have ransomed you. I have called you by name; you are mine."

ISAIAH 43:1

Father, you redeemed my life by your Son's great sacrifice. Help me set
aside any shame to fully embrace my new life in your presence.

Have you fully embraced the fact that your past no longer defines you because
God has purchased your freedom? Consider the great prophecy in Isaiah
chapter 43 that our Savior, Jesus Christ, precisely fulfilled. The prophet Isaiah
delivered God's message of both judgment and hope to the people of Israel.
While God gave them consequences in response to their disobedience, he also
promised salvation to those who would return to him in genuine faith.

Although the Israelites faced oppression and captivity for their rebellion,
God vowed never to desert them or allow them to perish. He would see them
through their suffering and ultimately give a ransom for their freedom. Twice
in this prophecy, God told his people, "Do not be afraid" (vv. 1, 5). For God
promised his followers a new and refreshing life, where they again would
honor him faithfully and God would erase their sins.

COURAGE FOR TODAY

Do your past mistakes hinder your future opportunities? Memorize the
familiar verse below and list the courageous steps you will take today to
fully embrace your new life in Christ.

My old self has been crucified with Christ. It is no longer I who live, but Christ lives
in me. So I live in this earthly body by trusting in the Son of God, who loved me and
gave himself for me.

GALATIANS 2:20

THE COURAGE TO
Love like Jesus

We know what real love is because Jesus gave up his life for us.
So we also ought to give up our lives for our brothers and sisters.

1 JOHN 3:16

Father, you command me to love like you do, without any conditions. Help me let go of any obstacles that keep me from expressing genuine and godly love and give me wisdom and discernment to know if and when I should reconcile with people who have offended or mistreated me.

Do you truly love others like Jesus loves them? Are you willing to offer forgiveness and grace to those who have failed you? Are you open to reconciliation when offenders demonstrate genuine remorse? In his letter, John urged all followers of Jesus to be inspired by the Lord's great love for them.

John reminded believers that God had adopted them as his very own children, and he encouraged them to pursue purity and avoid habitual sin. He then discussed the importance of loving our brothers and sisters in Christ. For Christ demonstrated real love when he gave up his life for those who would receive him. Therefore, when believers see someone in need, they are to demonstrate godly love by helping the person out. For actions always speak louder than words.

COURAGE FOR TODAY

Is it sometimes challenging for you to offer love to certain people? Meditate on Jesus' commandment below and describe how you will courageously and faithfully extend love like Jesus today.

"I am giving you a new commandment: Love each other.
Just as I have loved you, you should love each other."

JOHN 13:34

THE COURAGE TO
Be Brave

"No one will be able to stand against you as long as you live. For I will be with you as I was with Moses. I will not fail you or abandon you. Be strong and courageous, for you are the one who will lead these people to possess all the land I swore to their ancestors I would give them."

JOSHUA 1:5–6

Father, it requires courage to take on many of life's challenges. Thank you for being my unending source of courage and confidence. With you, all things within your will are truly possible.

Do you find it difficult some days to muster up the courage for life? Courage is a choice, and God and his Word are the two essential sources of daily courage and confidence. Take note of how many times God said, "Be strong and courageous" in the first chapter of Joshua. In verses 1 through 9 alone, God told Joshua three times to "be strong and courageous" as Joshua prepared to bring the Israelites into God's promised land.

While fear and unbelief overtook Israel's first generation, the new generation was prepared to take the land. Today, God also often calls us to complete tasks and seize opportunities that are outside our comfort zone or physical ability. We, too, must "be strong and courageous."

COURAGE FOR TODAY

Is God calling you to a task or opportunity that requires great courage? Recite the familiar verse below and make it your battle cry. What steps will you take today to courageously move forward in God's calling regardless of your ability or comfort zone?

I can do everything through Christ, who gives me strength.

PHILIPPIANS 4:13

THE COURAGE TO
Share Responsibility

You know how Timothy has proved himself.
Like a son with his father, he has served with me in preaching the Good News.

PHILIPPIANS 2:22

Father, too often I find myself going it alone. Give me wisdom and the courage to enlist trustworthy people when I need help so I can bring more glory to you and opportunity to others.

Do you enjoy taking credit for a job well done? Or do you share the praise and compliments with those who've helped you succeed? Be motivated by the apostle Paul's words in Philippians chapter 2. Paul was a high achiever, but he never was a one man show. Instead he enlisted help, traveled with companions, and complimented everyone who worked with him. Incarceration and other hindrances often limited Paul's ability to minister directly to churches. But rather than giving up on his calling, Paul chose to enlist great women and men who were loyal to him and were eager to serve.

Paul praised Timothy for proving himself and for caring deeply for the Philippians. And he also mentioned Epaphroditus, a brother, coworker, fellow soldier, and one who kept Paul and the church connected. When Epaphroditus' service to the church had left him seriously ill, Paul thanked God for sparing Epaphroditus' life. Like Paul, his helpers risked their lives to support their mentor and to share in Christ's mission and ministry.

COURAGE FOR TODAY

How good are you at sharing your workload and responsibilities? Memorize the verse below and describe how you plan to courageously enlist others to help you accomplish your tasks and goals today.

Two people are better off than one, for they can help each other succeed.

ECCLESIASTES 4:9

THE COURAGE TO
Seek God's Help

Some time later Samson fell in love with a woman named Delilah, who lived in the valley of Sorek. The rulers of the Philistines went to her and said, "Entice Samson to tell you what makes him so strong and how he can be overpowered and tied up securely. Then each of us will give you 1,100 pieces of silver."

JUDGES 16:4–5

Father, this world is full of distractions and temptations. Give me discernment and protect me from being deceived.

Do your emotions or others' desires tempt you to compromise your faith, morals, or calling? Consider Judges chapter 16 and recall how Delilah relentlessly deceived Samson. After the Philistines suppressed the Israelites for forty years, God chose a barren couple to conceive a son who would become Israel's deliverer. As Samson grew, God's Spirit empowered him with great strength.

In Judges chapter 16, we learn of Samson's love for Delilah and Delilah's heartless betrayal. Samson's passion for Delilah caused him to reveal the secret of his strength, and in turn, Delilah sold his secret to Samson's enemies for financial gain. The Philistines captured and imprisoned Samson, blinding him and humiliating him for their entertainment. In his despair, Samson cried out to God for one final dose of supernatural strength. God granted Samson's request and allowed him to sacrifice himself and destroy the Philistines as he physically collapsed their temple.

COURAGE FOR TODAY

How often do you seek God's guidance when making important decisions? Memorize the verse below and explain how you will seek God's help today.

Don't copy the behavior and customs of this world, but let God transform you into a new person by changing the way you think. Then you will learn to know God's will for you, which is good and pleasing and perfect.

ROMANS 12:2

THE COURAGE TO
Get Moving

Jesus told him, "Stand up, pick up your mat, and walk!"
JOHN 5:8

Father, hardships sometimes overwhelm me. Give me the courage to get up when I'm down and to persevere when I'm discouraged.

Have you ever struggled with depression? Is it sometimes hard to believe there are brighter days ahead? Take into consideration John chapter 5 and the account of a man in Jerusalem who'd been paralyzed for thirty-eight years. Daily he'd been carried to a pool in Bethesda for healing, yet the paralyzed man had never been able to enter its healing waters.

Though many sick people lay by the pool seeking help, Jesus singled out the paralytic man and asked, "Would you like to get well?" (v. 6). Instead of eagerly replying, "Yes," the man clung to his hardship. Jesus dismissed his hesitation and instead commanded him to get up and walk. No rehab, no help, just "pick up your mat, and walk" (v. 8). Instantaneously, the man was healed and walked away. Later when Jesus encountered him once again, he reminded the man of his healing and that he needed to stop sinning. God knew the secret areas of the man's life and longed to see those wounds healed as well.

COURAGE FOR TODAY

Has the weight of your circumstances left you depressed or unable to enjoy life? Memorize the popular verse below and embrace your God-given courage today to take on your challenges with hope and help from God.

Since we are surrounded by such a huge crowd of witnesses to the life of faith, let us strip off every weight that slows us down, especially the sin that so easily trips us up. And let us run with endurance the race God has set before us.

HEBREWS 12:1

THE COURAGE TO
Seek God and Live

*This is what the L*ORD *says to the family of Israel:*
"Come back to me and live!"

AMOS 5:4

Father, you remind me that there are good or bad consequences for every decision I make. Help me heed your warnings and seek your guidance as I aim to accomplish your will.

Does your life illustrate your faith in God? Let God's plea in Amos chapter 5 challenge you. God commissioned Amos to warn the Southern Kingdom of Israel during a time of peace and prosperity, around 760 BC. Even knowing that most would ignore his warning, Amos faithfully urged the people of Judah to return to God before it was too late.

In his message, God said: "Come back to me and live!" And to broaden his plea, God urged the Israelites to "do what is good and run from evil" (v. 14). That way, the Lord could once again display his mercy and help his people prosper. For if they continued to ignore his warnings, they were doomed to experience great destruction and inescapable sorrow.

COURAGE FOR TODAY

How close is your relationship with God? Meditate on the verses below and describe how you will courageously seek God today and live.

*Seek the L*ORD *while you can find him. Call on him now while he is near. Let the wicked change their ways and banish the very thought of doing wrong. Let them turn to the L*ORD *that he may have mercy on them. Yes, turn to our God, for he will forgive generously.*

ISAIAH 55:6–7

THE COURAGE TO
Defend Your Faith

"I admit that I follow the Way, which they call a cult. I worship the God of our ancestors, and I firmly believe the Jewish law and everything written in the prophets."

ACTS 24:14

Father, in a society that is obsessed with pleasures and possessions, it can be challenging, at times, to defend my faith. Give me courage and confidence to stand firm and stand up for my love and dedication to you and your Word.

How prepared are you to defend your faith? Be inspired by the apostle Paul's experiences and perseverance recorded in Acts chapters 21–24.

When Jewish leaders disputed Paul's teaching and tried to persecute him, Paul courageously defended himself, his testimony, and his faith in Jesus. When more than forty unbelievers came together and conspired to kill Paul, God personally encouraged him, and he was moved to Caesarea. When Paul appeared before the governor, the high priest, and the religious elders, he presented his defense and confidently confessed his faith in Jesus.

COURAGE FOR TODAY

How prepared are you to explain your faith? Read the familiar verse below, describe your current spiritual growth routine, and list the changes you will make beginning today to be more properly equipped to courageously defend your love for God and his Word.

Preach the word of God. Be prepared, whether the time is favorable or not. Patiently correct, rebuke, and encourage your people with good teaching.

2 TIMOTHY 4:2

THE COURAGE TO
Use Your Influence

"If you keep quiet at a time like this, deliverance and relief for the Jews will arise from some other place, but you and your relatives will die. Who knows if perhaps you were made queen for just such a time as this?"

ESTHER 4:14

Father, you assure me in your Word that you work all things together for the good of those who love and serve you. Give me wisdom, guidance, and courage to use my position and clout to accomplish your will and for the benefit of your kingdom work.

God places each of us in strategic positions of influence. Are you willing to use your position or influence for the benefit of God's people and kingdom? Consider Queen Esther's bravery in Esther chapters 4–5. Shortly after being crowned Queen of Persia, Esther, who was born Jewish, found herself in a precarious situation when her husband, King Ahasuerus, issued an order for all Jews to be destroyed. Esther chapters 4–7 describe her cautious and courageous response.

When her cousin Mordecai informed her of the king's plans, Esther fasted and prayed for three days and encouraged Mordecai and the Jewish people to do the same. After seeking God's blessing and guidance, Esther presented herself before the king, won his favor, and secured mercy for her people.

COURAGE FOR TODAY

Does fear or uncertainty hinder you from using your influence or circumstances to benefit the body of Christ or the kingdom of God? Memorize the familiar verse below and list the courageous steps you will take today to begin pursuing the will of God.

"This is my command—be strong and courageous! Do not be afraid or discouraged. For the Lord your God is with you wherever you go."

JOSHUA 1:9

THE COURAGE TO
Avoid Insincerity

Jesus replied, "You hypocrites! Isaiah was right when he prophesied about you, for he wrote, 'These people honor me with their lips, but their hearts are far from me.'"

MARK 7:6

Father, you deserve genuine honor, obedience, and praise. Help me refrain from insincere traditions and inspire me to worship and serve you with sincerity instead.

Are you sincere in your worship of God, or are you going through the motions? Be challenged by Jesus' reprimand in Mark chapter 7. When the Pharisees and scribes confronted him with their concerns over his disciples' behavior, Jesus responded by calling them hypocrites. The religious leaders were upset that Jesus' disciples were eating before going through a religious hand-washing ceremony. Yet they were insincere regarding their own faithfulness to religious laws. Instead of following God's law, they substituted it for their own traditions.

Jesus further explained that his disciples and others were not being defiled by what they ate but that it is what comes from the heart that defiles a person. For "out of a person's heart, come evil thoughts, sexual immorality, theft, murder, adultery, greed, wickedness, deceit, lustful desires, envy, slander, pride, and foolishness" (vv. 21–22).

COURAGE FOR TODAY

Do you worship God with sincerity, or do you participate in religious practices out of habit or obligation? Consider the verses below and describe how you will courageously and sincerely honor and worship God today.

If you claim to be religious but don't control your tongue, you are fooling yourself, and your religion is worthless. Pure and genuine religion in the sight of God the Father means caring for orphans and widows in their distress and refusing to let the world corrupt you.

JAMES 1:26–27

THE COURAGE TO
Be Grateful

"These are the commands, decrees, and regulations that the Lord your God commanded me to teach you. You must obey them in the land you are about to enter and occupy, and you and your children and grandchildren must fear the Lord your God as long as you live. If you obey all his decrees and commands, you will enjoy a long life."

DEUTERONOMY 6:1–2

Father, thank you for loving me and establishing limits that help me avoid hardships and heartaches. In light of all you have done for me, remind me to remain grateful and help me to be faithful.

Do God's presence and promises inspire you to obey his commands? After forty years of wandering in the desert, Moses prepared the Israelites to finally enter God's promised land. He restated God's Ten Commandments, going into greater detail as to how Israel should live out these commands.

Consider Moses' instructions to the people in Deuteronomy chapter 6. God's guidelines in this chapter are not meant to simply restrict behavior but also to prevent God's people from falling into hardship and harm. In the New Testament, Jesus described Deuteronomy 6:5 as God's greatest commandment, of which God's entire law is based (Matthew 22:34–39; Mark 12:28–31; Luke 10:25–28). Out of gratitude for God's great sacrifice and faithfulness, we should make every effort to obey his commandments and teach them to the next generation.

COURAGE FOR TODAY

Are you grateful for God's mercy, forgiveness, and presence in your life? Consider the verse below and describe ways you demonstrate your gratitude to the Lord. Name specific ways your appreciation compels you to courageously obey God today.

Since we are receiving a Kingdom that is unshakable, let us be thankful and please God by worshiping him with holy fear and awe.

HEBREWS 12:28

THE COURAGE TO

Help Restore Others

Dear brothers and sisters, if another believer is overcome by some sin,
you who are godly should gently and humbly help that person back onto the right
path. And be careful not to fall into the same temptation yourself.

GALATIANS 6:1

Father, give me the desire to help those who have fallen into sin. Help me refrain from either judging or looking the other way and instill within me the wisdom and passion to encourage those who have strayed from you.

Do you know someone who is entangled in sin? Are you willing to help, or are you tempted to look away? Be inspired by the apostle Paul's passionate plea in Galatians chapter 6. Paul's heart went out to believers who were struggling. So he encouraged the members in Galatia to look out for one another.

Realizing that everyone is susceptible to temptation and sin, Paul urged believers to "gently and humbly help that person back onto the right path" (v. 1). We are not to ignore, excuse, or destroy sinners. Instead, they need compassion and restoration. So Paul encouraged the Galatians to never grow weary or miss an opportunity to care for others. Realizing that God's grace would lead them into a proper relationship with one another, Paul closed his letter by praying that the grace of God would be upon them all.

COURAGE FOR TODAY

Have you developed a critical spirit, judging others rather than helping? Read the verse below and describe how you can be more courageous and give encouragement to someone today.

Do not withhold good from those who deserve it
when it's in your power to help them.

PROVERBS 3:27

THE COURAGE TO
Embrace God's Boundaries

"Do not make idols or set up carved images, or sacred pillars, or sculptured stones in your land so you may worship them. I am the LORD your God."

LEVITICUS 26:1

Father, for years I believed that obedience to your law would keep me from enjoying my everyday life. Now I realize that following your commands provides boundaries that protect me from sin and its devastating aftereffects.

Do you love God's law? Countless readers avoid the book of Leviticus when studying the Bible because its focus is on the laws of God. But located within its pages, we can discover great hope, encouragement, and wisdom. While the main purpose of this book is to teach and inspire holiness, God's heart behind his law is to provide boundaries that protect us from making harmful mistakes.

For every action there is a reaction, and for every act there is a consequence—good or bad. Consider Leviticus chapter 26. Verses 1 through 13 describe God's promise to bless believers for obedience. Verses 14 through 40 outline consequences for disobedience. And verses 40 through 46 communicate God's grace and faithfulness to restore those who humble themselves and repent. God's law makes us aware of our sin, and following his law sets us free to experience his abundant blessings.

COURAGE FOR TODAY

Is God prompting you to change a particular attitude, behavior, relationship, or situation? Read the following verse and decide today to courageously heed God's warning and embrace the freedom and blessings found within his boundaries.

If you look carefully into the perfect law that sets you free, and if you do what it says and don't forget what you heard, then God will bless you for doing it.

JAMES 1:25

THE COURAGE TO
Release Worry

Don't worry about anything; instead, pray about everything.
Tell God what you need, and thank him for all he has done.

PHILIPPIANS 4:6

Father, I need to let go of worry so I can confidently embrace
your promises. Help me keep my thoughts fixed on you and
not on my problems.

Do you consider yourself a warrior or a worrier? If you are a worrier, let the apostle Paul's words in Philippians chapter 4 motivate you to change the way you think. Paul wrote from a prison cell, not knowing what his future held. Yet his letter to the Philippians was full of joy and encouragement. He wanted the church to also maintain a proper attitude. So he instructed them to set their concerns aside so they could trust God, pray without reservation, and be grateful.

He then urged believers to focus on the things in life that are true, honorable, right, pure, lovely, and admirable—things that are excellent and worthy of praise. For by doing so, their anxiety and disunity would decrease. Paul modeled a joyful life, which was a result of his intentional and positive thinking, not his circumstances. He longed for other believers to adopt this same point of view too.

COURAGE FOR TODAY

Are you willing to replace any negative thoughts with a confident and positive point of view? Meditate on the familiar verse below and describe how you plan to courageously take your eyes off your problems and focus on the things in your life that are worthy of praise today.

"That is why I tell you not to worry about everyday life—
whether you have enough food and drink, or enough clothes to wear…
Can all your worries add a single moment to your life?"

MATTHEW 6:25, 27

THE COURAGE TO
Act

Noah did everything exactly as God had commanded him.
GENESIS 6:22

Father, you place opportunities before me that I feel unqualified to achieve. Give me the enthusiasm, wisdom, and courage to accept your assignment and motivate me to act right away.

Do you need more courage to say yes to God's calling on your life? Consider Noah's response in Genesis chapters 6 and 7. Noah lived at a time when all people on earth were corrupt and violent, yet he maintained his integrity and a close fellowship with God. So God, after observing the condition of his creation, decided to destroy all living creatures and start over.

God planned to flood the earth and preserve only Noah, his family, and a pair of every kind of animal. When God told Noah to build a large boat and prepare for a flood, "Noah did everything exactly as God had commanded him" (v. 22). When the boat was ready, God instructed Noah to take himself, his family, and the animals on board. And again, "Noah did everything as the LORD commanded him" (7:5).

COURAGE FOR TODAY

Has God placed an opportunity before you? Are you ready to take action? Consider Jesus' words in the passage below and let them inspire you to courageously heed God's calling today.

"Why do you keep calling me 'Lord, Lord!' when you don't do what I say? I will show you what it's like when someone comes to me, listens to my teaching, and then follows it. It is like a person building a house who digs deep and lays the foundation on solid rock. When the floodwaters rise and break against that house, it stands firm because it is well built."
LUKE 6:46–48

THE COURAGE TO
Fight Satan

A final word: Be strong in the Lord and in his mighty power. Put on all of God's armor so that you will be able to stand firm against all strategies of the devil.

EPHESIANS 6:10–11

Father, I need more courage to defend myself against Satan's attacks. Remind me to put on your armor every day so I can be prepared to withstand any temptation or opposition to my faith.

Do you sometimes feel powerless against temptation? Be encouraged by the words of the apostle Paul in Ephesians chapter 6. Paul concluded his letter to the church in Ephesus by reminding them to embrace God's strength. Paul knew that the only way for a believer to be truly protected was to be spiritually clothed in God's armor.

To "put on" is a deliberate action that implies a willingness to wear God's protective gear. So Paul listed each item in God's armor: the belt of truth, the shoes of peace, the shield of faith, the helmet of salvation, and the sword of God's Word. He then urged believers to be alert and pray at all times. If a soldier went into battle only partially armed, he'd risk being wounded. So Paul strongly advised the Ephesians to "put on all of God's armor" (v. 11), for that is the only way to fight Satan and win.

COURAGE FOR TODAY

Do you need more courage to withstand the devil's tactics? Memorize the verse below and let it challenge you to put on all of God's armor today so you can courageously fight Satan's deception and temptations.

Stay alert! Watch out for your great enemy, the devil.
He prowls around like a roaring lion, looking for someone to devour.

1 PETER 5:8

THE COURAGE TO
Invest in the Church

*A proclamation was sent throughout Judah and Jerusalem, telling the people
to bring to the LORD the tax that Moses, the servant of God, had required of the
Israelites in the wilderness. This pleased all the leaders and the people, and they
gladly brought their money and filled the chest with it.*

2 CHRONICLES 24:9–10

Father, thank you for my local church. Reveal to me ways that
I can courageously support, strengthen, and protect our fellowship,
teaching, and worship.

Do you regularly and generously invest in your local church? Consider
King Joash's commitment to repair the temple in Jerusalem, recorded in 2
Chronicles chapter 24. Joash became king at a very young age, but despite his
youth, he was committed to honoring God and investing in Jerusalem's house
of worship.

The temple needed repair following the destruction caused by Athaliah's
sons. So Joash instructed the priests and Levites to use the people's offerings
specifically to restore the temple. Although King Joash was ultimately led
astray, betrayed God, and was murdered by his own servants, history still
remembers him for having preserved Jerusalem's house of worship.

COURAGE FOR TODAY

Are you an active member of a local church or fellowship? Read the verses
below and list ways you will courageously support, strengthen, and protect
believers' ability to gather, learn, and worship the Lord today.

*They worshiped together at the Temple each day, met in homes for the Lord's
Supper, and shared their meals with great joy and generosity—all the while
praising God and enjoying the goodwill of all the people. And each day the Lord
added to their fellowship those who were being saved.*

ACTS 2:46–47

THE COURAGE TO
Consider the Times

Look! He comes with the clouds of heaven.
And everyone will see him—even those who pierced him.
And all the nations of the world will mourn for him. Yes! Amen!

REVELATION 1:7

Father, life on earth is filled with challenges, responsibilities, and distractions. Help me remember that this is not my eternal home so I can live a balanced life while keeping all my concerns in perspective.

Do you let the enticements of this life distract you from taking eternity into consideration? Let the apostle John's vision in Revelation chapter 1 inspire you to fix your eyes on Jesus.

While John was exiled on the island of Patmos, he experienced a visitation from the Lord. In his vision, John saw a man standing among seven gold lampstands. The heavenly figure's hair was white as snow, his eyes were like fire, his feet were like shining bronze, and his voice was like the thunder of mighty ocean waves. As he recorded his experience, John proclaimed that Jesus was worthy of all glory and power and that he is "the one who is, who always was, and who is still to come" (v. 8).

COURAGE FOR TODAY

Are you more concerned about your time here on earth, or is your eternity also a priority in your life? Meditate on the passage from James below and describe how you will consider the times and courageously make your relationship with God a priority in your life today.

How do you know what your life will be like tomorrow? Your life is like the morning fog—it's here a little while, then it's gone. What you ought to say is, "If the Lord wants us to, we will live and do this or that."

JAMES 4:14–15

THE COURAGE TO
Trust That God Knows Best

"What?" his servant exclaimed. "Feed a hundred people with only this?" But Elisha repeated, "Give it to the people so they can eat, for this is what the LORD says: Everyone will eat, and there will even be some left over!"

2 KINGS 4:43

Father, I sometimes struggle to wait for your perfect plan and timing. Help me to refrain from choosing my own way and give me the courage to trust and follow your guidance.

Do you truly trust God to provide for your needs? Consider the three accounts in 2 Kings chapter 4 that record God caring for those who faithfully trusted him to do so. In 2 Kings 4:1–7, God helped a poor widow survive by sending the prophet Elisha to instruct her. In 4:8–37, God not only arranged for Elisha's care, but he also blessed and answered the prayers of a woman who generously gave Elisha a place to stay. In the third account, verses 38–44, God provided an abundance of food during a famine.

God can and will give us everything we need, but we must trust in him to do so.

COURAGE FOR TODAY

How often do you run ahead of God? Read the passage below and list your current prayer requests. Go to God, ask for his help, and make a commitment today to courageously trust him to do what is best.

The LORD must wait for you to come to him so he can show you his love and compassion. For the LORD is a faithful God. Blessed are those who wait for his help… Your own ears will hear him. Right behind you a voice will say, "This is the way you should go," whether to the right or to the left.

ISAIAH 30:18, 21

THE COURAGE TO
Show Mercy

"You will be treated as you treat others. The standard you use in judging is the standard by which you will be judged. And why worry about a speck in your friend's eye when you have a log in your own?"

MATTHEW 7:2–3

Father, thank you for forgiving me when I fail you. Help me also to forgive others when they mistreat or fail me.

How often do you judge others even if you don't acknowledge it out loud? Take to heart Jesus' words in Matthew chapter 7. As he concluded his Sermon on the Mount, Jesus addressed an important topic every human struggles with: judgment. In the first few verses of chapter 7, he compared the judgment of others with the judgment believers will receive from God in return. He then challenged his audience by reminding them how easy it is for us to concern ourselves with the mistakes of others while at the same time ignoring the seriousness of our own wrongdoings.

In his remaining remarks, Jesus spoke on the importance of prayer, sincerity, treating others well, bearing good fruit, and building your life on a firm foundation as well as the challenges of living an honest, faithful, and righteous life. And he reminded his listeners—and us—that to concern themselves with self-reflection, self-control, genuineness, and goodwill is far better than focusing on other people's issues.

COURAGE FOR TODAY

Are you quick to criticize others, or are you willing to give them grace? Let the verse below challenge you to avoid judgment and courageously and consistently show mercy to others today.

There will be no mercy for those who have not shown mercy to others. But if you have been merciful, God will be merciful when he judges you.

JAMES 2:13

THE COURAGE TO
Trust God's Word

In the first year of King Cyrus of Persia, the Lord fulfilled the prophecy he had given through Jeremiah. He stirred the heart of Cyrus to put this proclamation in writing and to send it throughout his kingdom.

EZRA 1:1

Father, your Word is trustworthy and true. Give me a passion for reading your Word, wisdom to recognize its life-changing lessons, and courage to apply it to my life in practical ways.

Do you believe God's Word is true and trust that its prophecies and promises are reliable? Consider God's fulfilled prophecy in Ezra chapter 1. Beginning in 739 BC, God commissioned several prophets to inform his people about their coming exile and future restoration. While God would allow his people to be exiled for seventy years, he also prepared ahead of time for their release.

Through the prophets Isaiah and Jeremiah, God explained the reason for Israel's displacement, disclosed how long their relocation would last, and revealed exactly how and by whom they would be allowed to return home. Just as God had promised, the Southern Kingdom of Israel was conquered in 605 BC, and many of the Israelites were exiled to Babylon. And in 539 BC, God raised up a king named Cyrus who conquered Babylon and set God's people free so they could return home and rebuild their great city.

COURAGE FOR TODAY

Do you truly trust God's Word? Meditate on the verse below and let your faith in Scripture give you courage and confidence for your challenges today.

"It is the same with my word. I send it out, and it always produces fruit. It will accomplish all I want it to, and it will prosper everywhere I send it."

ISAIAH 55:11

THE COURAGE TO
Encourage Others

"Take courage! For I believe God.
It will be just as he said."
ACTS 27:25

Father, you tell me that I am to speak words that lift people up and not tear them down. Give me the longing and ability to encourage any family, friends, coworkers, and acquaintances who need support today.

Are you consistent in your faith and in your desire to encourage others regardless of your circumstances? Let the apostle Paul's persistence in Acts chapter 27 inspire you to reassure anyone who is experiencing doubt or discouragement. After having been imprisoned for several years and then defending himself and his faith before the king and a crowd in Caesarea, Paul was placed on a ship with other prisoners to set sail for Rome.

When major storms threatened their travel, Paul approached the ship's officers and recommended that they seek shelter in a safe harbor. But the officers refused to listen, so they battled the storm head-on. When all hope was lost and everyone was starving, Paul approached the crew again to offer his help and wise counsel. Although no one had listened to his earlier advice, Paul refused to feel discouraged and continued encouraging the sailors to set aside their fears and "take courage!" (v. 22). For Paul had great confidence in God's protection and promises, and he chose to share his faith with others.

COURAGE FOR TODAY

How often do you make a conscious effort to reassure others? Let the verse below inspire you to courageously comfort family, friends, coworkers, or acquaintances who need encouragement today.

Let us not neglect our meeting together, as some people do, but encourage one another, especially now that the day of his return is drawing near.
HEBREWS 10:25

THE COURAGE TO
Make Friends

Baruch did as Jeremiah told him and read these messages from the Lord to the people at the Temple.

JEREMIAH 36:8

Father, you urge me to have healthy and loving relationships with others. Lead me to people whom I can encourage and who will inspire and support me as well.

Do you tend to be a loner? Or are you outgoing, inviting lots of people to share your life? Reflect on Jeremiah chapter 36 and the life of the great prophet who needed a partner to help him achieve God's calling. God called Jeremiah to encourage the Israelites to turn away from wickedness and receive God's forgiveness. But at one point, he had been imprisoned and was unable to visit the temple to declare God's message. So he entrusted his assignment to Baruch, his assistant and secretary.

After seventeen years of companionship, Jeremiah new he could trust Baruch, so he gave his God-given task to his friend. Baruch took no glory for himself. Instead he gave Jeremiah all the credit for dictating God's words. Together Jeremiah and Baruch risked their lives to fulfill God's calling, and in return, they received God's guidance and protection.

COURAGE FOR TODAY

Do you have a friend like Baruch, someone you can rely on in any situation? Read the verse below and name the friends you can count on. If you are not sure whom you can trust, ask God to reveal your faithful friends and make a point to courageously nurture your relationship with them today.

There are "friends" who destroy each other,
but a real friend sticks closer than a brother.

PROVERBS 18:24

THE COURAGE TO
Serve with Devotion

I am saying this for your benefit, not to place restrictions on you. I want you to do whatever will help you serve the Lord best, with as few distractions as possible.

1 CORINTHIANS 7:35

Father, you call me to put my relationship with you above all others. Help me know how to honor you while being kind, respectful, and loving to my family, friends, and neighbors.

Are there people, places, or things that hinder your relationship with God? Consider the apostle Paul's teaching in 1 Corinthians chapter 7. Paul knew that believers lived in a sexually saturated world, so he wrote to the church in Corinth to encourage them in their relationships.

While he highlighted the benefits of remaining single, Paul also emphasized the importance of being faithful and devoted to loved ones. He urged husbands and wives to remain physically and emotionally close so that Satan could not lure them away toward sexual sin. But, for those who were alone, Paul encouraged them to, if possible, remain single so they could have an undistracted relationship with God. And for those who were married to unbelievers, Paul instructed them to maintain their faith and try to remain married, for possibly, their devotion to God would lead their spouses to salvation.

COURAGE FOR TODAY

Describe how you currently honor God and nurture your relationships. Then meditate on King Solomon's wisdom below and decide how you will avoid distractions and courageously care for your relationships with God and others today.

Look straight ahead, and fix your eyes on what lies before you.
Mark out a straight path for your feet; stay on the safe path.
Don't get sidetracked; keep your feet from following evil.

PROVERBS 4:25–27

THE COURAGE TO
Forgive and Set Boundaries

*Joseph could stand it no longer. There were many people in the room,
and he said to his attendants, "Out, all of you!" So he was alone with
his brothers when he told them who he was.*

GENESIS 45:1

Father, I sometimes find it hard to forgive. Help me let go of my need for
retaliation and give me the courage to establish healthy boundaries with
people who are toxic.

Do you struggle with unforgiveness? Do you find it hard to set boundaries with
toxic people? In the later chapters of Genesis (Chapters 37–50), we read the
story of Joseph and his complicated relationship with his family. After suffering
abuse at the hands of his jealous brothers, Joseph found himself in an unlikely
position of leadership in Egypt during a time of worldwide famine. When his
brothers traveled to Egypt to buy grain, they did not know Joseph oversaw the
stockpiles, so Joseph seized the opportunity to test their integrity and humility.
In response to their brokenness, Joseph revealed his identity as their brother,
forgave his brothers for their abuse, and provided for them and their families.

Joseph pardoned his brothers and reconciled with them because of their
genuine remorse. Joseph's courage came from knowing that God had allowed
his suffering to ultimately prepare for his family's salvation.

COURAGE FOR TODAY

Read the passage below on forgiveness and boundaries. Name people who
have mistreated you and courageously commit to forgive them today. Then
ask God to give you wisdom regarding reconciliation and boundaries.

*Get rid of all bitterness, rage, anger, harsh words, and slander, as well as all types of
evil behavior. Instead, be kind to each other, tenderhearted, forgiving one another,
just as God through Christ has forgiven you.*

EPHESIANS 4:31–32

THE COURAGE TO

Approach God

Let us come boldly to the throne of our gracious God. There we will receive his mercy, and we will find grace to help us when we need it most.

HEBREWS 4:16

Father, I am eternally grateful for your unconditional love, grace, and presence. Give me the courage to come boldly before you even when I've sinned and feel ashamed.

Have there been times when you were ashamed to approach the Lord? Be inspired by the writer's wise words in Hebrews chapter 4. The author of this letter to the Hebrews reminded believers that they had access to the throne of God. Though their sin likely made the Hebrews feel unclean and unfit, Jesus, their High Priest, had paid their sin-debt in full, making them worthy to be in God's presence.

Under Old Testament law, the forgiveness of sins required a sacrifice. Yet under the new covenant of grace, believers are cleansed by the blood of Jesus, making them appear clean and holy before the Lord. Not only do Christ followers have access to God's throne, but they can also come boldly before him at all times.

COURAGE FOR TODAY

Does your past or present life cause you to feel unworthy before God? Meditate on the passage below and courageously approach the Lord today, confessing your sins and boldly sharing your requests.

By his death, Jesus opened a new and life-giving way through the curtain into the Most Holy place. And since we have a great High Priest who rules over God's house, let us go right into the presence of God with sincere hearts fully trusting him. For our guilty consciences have been sprinkled with Christ's blood to make us clean, and our bodies have been washed with pure water.

HEBREWS 10:20–22

THE COURAGE TO
Endure

"I came naked from my mother's womb, and I will be naked when I leave.
The Lord gave me what I had, and the Lord has taken it away.
Praise the name of the Lord!" In all of this, Job did not sin by blaming God.

JOB 1:21–22

Father, loss is part of life. Give me courage and hope when I am grieving and help me remember that all I have, including my loved ones, comes from you. For as I draw closer to you, I will be comforted, cared for, and restored.

When you lose something or someone you treasure, how do you respond? Consider Job's initial response in Job chapter 1. In the first two chapters of Job, God allows us to see Satan's disdain for God and his creation.

The beginning of the book introduces us to Job, a good and godly man with a large family and an abundance of possessions. Then we see that Satan challenged God to prove that Job's loyalty was unshakable. When God agreed to the test, he allowed the Enemy to destroy all of Job's livestock, his servants, and his ten children. Yet even after receiving the devastating news that he had lost everything, Job courageously chose to continue worshiping and honoring the Lord.

COURAGE FOR TODAY

How do you handle loss? Do you worship God amid your grief, or do you blame him? Read the following verses and decide today to draw closer to God, allowing him to comfort and care for you as you courageously endure any difficulty or hardship.

"God blesses those who are poor and realize their need for him, for the Kingdom of Heaven is theirs. God blesses those who mourn, for they will be comforted."

MATTHEW 5:3–4

THE COURAGE TO
Recognize God

*They know the truth about God because he has made it obvious to them.
For ever since the world was created, people have seen the earth and sky.
Through everything God made, they can clearly see his invisible qualities—his
eternal power and divine nature. So they have no excuse for not knowing God.*

ROMANS 1:19–20

Father, I can clearly see the truth of your existence, power, creativity, and complexity in every visible and invisible feature of earth. Remind me to take time each day to appreciate all aspects of your creation.

How often do you truly delight in the Lord? Let the apostle Paul's words in Romans chapter 1 motivate you to appreciate God and the world around you today. Prior to his conversion, Paul focused on religious rules and persecuting Christians. But after surrendering his life to Jesus, Paul dedicated his remaining years to preaching salvation through belief in Christ alone.

As he began his letter to the church in Rome, Paul described his enthusiasm and boldness in sharing his faith with others. He then explained God's anger toward people who oppose the Lord's grace-filled gift of salvation. For, since the beginning of time, God has made his existence, invisible attributes, eternal power, and divine nature obvious through the existence of everything he created. Therefore, no one has any excuse for not believing in or knowing almighty God.

COURAGE FOR TODAY

Do you regularly acknowledge and appreciate the Lord? Memorize the familiar verse below and vow to courageously share your gratitude and praise for God today.

*The heavens proclaim the glory of God. The skies display his craftsmanship.
Day after day they continue to speak; night after night they make him known.*

PSALM 19:1–2

THE COURAGE TO
Lead Reform

Seek the LORD, all who are humble, and follow his commands. Seek to do what is right and to live humbly. Perhaps even yet the LORD will protect you—protect you from his anger on that day of destruction.

ZEPHANIAH 2:3

Father, please don't let me become complacent with the downfall of our nation. Give me the courage to be a reformer and to not sit idly by as a conformer.

Do you wish to see changes in the morals, values, or direction in which your family, community, or country is heading? Consider the book of Zephaniah and the courage it took for the great prophet to preach reform. The prophet Zephaniah, whose name means "hidden of Jehovah," spoke up before the nation of Judah when idol worship, social injustice, and moral corruption were rampant.

Zephaniah described both the severity of God's judgment as well as his loving nature as he issued a cry for repentance. Seven times Zephaniah mentioned the day of the Lord's judgment, but the people ignored God's warning. Eventually the enemy nation of Babylon carried Judah into exile. Even so, Zephaniah concluded his prophecy with a message of encouragement and hope, declaring a day when God would delight in his people and rejoice over them again.

COURAGE FOR TODAY

Would you like to see your family, community, or nation improve their behavior? Draw strength from the verse below and vow to courageously make a difference in your spheres of influence today.

Josiah removed all detestable idols from the entire land of Israel and required everyone to worship the LORD their God. And throughout the rest of his lifetime, they did not turn away from the LORD, the God of their ancestors.

2 CHRONICLES 34:33

THE COURAGE TO
Receive Freedom

*"You will know the truth,
and the truth will set you free."*
JOHN 8:32

Father, you have cleansed me and given me your Holy Spirit,
so I am no longer a slave to sin. Give me the desire and courage to
resist the pressures and enticements of this world so I can
fully embrace your freedom.

Are you a prisoner of peer pressure, stress, success, or worldly expectations? Be encouraged by Jesus' message in John chapter 8. After defending a woman caught in adultery and encouraging her to "sin no more" (v. 11), Jesus told his followers that he is "the light of the world," and therefore, they no longer have to walk in darkness (v. 12).

To further encourage those who believe in him, Jesus went on to explain that those who are faithful to his teachings "will know the truth, and the truth will set [them] free" (v. 32). When followers asked him to clarify his statement, Jesus stated that everyone who sins is a slave to sin, yet he has the power to truly set them free. Therefore, believers must resist the temptation to engage in sinful behaviors and release themselves from the pressures of man-made expectations. That way, they can focus on their true purpose and pursue God's will.

COURAGE FOR TODAY

Do your behaviors and actions reveal God's presence in your life? Meditate on the prophetic verse below and describe how you will courageously engage your freedom in Christ today.

The Spirit of the Sovereign LORD is upon me, for the LORD has anointed me to bring good news to the poor. He has sent me to comfort the brokenhearted and to proclaim that captives will be released and prisoners will be freed.

ISAIAH 61:1

THE COURAGE TO
Embrace Humility

When Jezebel, the queen mother, heard that Jehu had come to Jezreel, she painted her eyelids and fixed her hair and sat at a window. When Jehu entered the gate of the palace, she shouted at him, "Have you come in peace, you murderer? You're just like Zimri, who murdered his master!"

2 Kings 9:30–31

Father, pride can sneak up on me when I least expect it,
and I often don't even realize it. Help me remain thoughtful, humble,
and grateful in every situation.

Does pride tempt you to ignore God's voice? Discover how pride led to the downfall of Queen Jezebel and her family in 2 Kings chapter 9. When the king of Israel married Jezebel, a pagan princess, Ahab turned his back on God to worship Jezebel's false deities and worldly pleasures instead.

When Jezebel executed a vicious scheme to have Naboth killed and seize his vineyard, God promised to destroy her entire family and put an end to their arrogant and wicked reign. Several years later, when the queen's son Joram ruled over Israel, God appointed Jehu, the commander of Israel's army, to demolish Jezebel's entire family and become king of Israel. Jehu carried out God's assignment and eliminated the wicked kings of both Israel and Judah, leaving their bodies to wither away on the very land Jezebel had stolen from Naboth. Shortly after, Jehu had Jezebel killed and then destroyed the remaining descendants of the corrupt king and queen.

COURAGE FOR TODAY

How often does pride arise in your life? Read the following verses and describe the courageous changes you will make today to avoid ungodly and prideful behavior.

Pride goes before destruction, and haughtiness before a fall.

Proverbs 16:18

THE COURAGE TO
Please God

Obviously, I'm not trying to win the approval of people, but of God.
If pleasing people were my goal, I would not be Christ's servant.
GALATIANS 1:10

Father, you put me first when you sacrificed your one and only Son to save me from my sins. Give me the desire and courage to always place pleasing you above satisfying friends, acquaintances, or loved ones.

Are you a people pleaser? Or do you consistently put God's view and truth before everything else? Consider the apostle Paul's message in Galatians chapter 1 and let it motivate you to focus more on pleasing God than satisfying the expectations of other people. Paul began his letter to the church in Galatia by reminding them that he had been called into ministry directly by Jesus and the Lord, not by a person or group of people. He did this to highlight the fact that believers must always put God first.

The Galatians had fallen prey to a message that deliberately twisted God's truth. So Paul immediately addressed their offense and reminded them that the gospel he preached and that they had received came directly from his personal encounter with Jesus. This message was not based on human reasoning, and he did not preach it to win human approval.

COURAGE FOR TODAY

Is it more important to you to please God or to make your friends, acquaintances, or loved ones happy? Meditate on the verse below and let it challenge you to determine specific ways you can courageously put God first today.

We speak as messengers approved by God to be entrusted with the Good News. Our purpose is to please God, not people. He alone examines the motives of our hearts.
1 THESSALONIANS 2:4

THE COURAGE TO
Fear Not

"See, God has come to save me. I will trust in him and not be afraid.
The Lord God is my strength and my song; he has given me victory."

ISAIAH 12:2

Father, you are my strength and salvation. Help me rely on your presence
and promises throughout every situation and give me great gratitude,
courage, and motivation to share your majesty and truth with others.

When you are anxious, concerned, or afraid, where do you go? Whom do
you turn to? Be emboldened by the Song of Praise for Salvation recorded in
Isaiah chapter 12. The prophet Isaiah, whose name means "God is salvation,"
delivered messages of both judgment and hope to the people of Israel. But in
this chapter, Isaiah addressed another important feature of God's relationship
with his people: their gratitude. For one day, God would save them from their
enemies and end their suffering.

In response, the Israelites were to praise the Lord and give him thanks.
Because God is their strength and salvation, the people of Israel were also to
set aside their fears and totally trust in him. God's followers were to call upon
his name, give thanks for his presence and promises, praise his holiness, and
tell the whole world about him.

COURAGE FOR TODAY

Do you truly recognize God's presence and power in your life? Are you
willing to set your fears aside and trust solely in the Lord? Memorize the
familiar verse below and describe the courageous steps you will take today
to subdue your fears to fully trust your Savior.

"Don't be afraid, for I am with you. Don't be discouraged, for I am your God. I will
strengthen you and help you. I will hold you up with my victorious right hand."

ISAIAH 41:10

THE COURAGE TO
Excel in Giving

Since you excel in so many ways—in your faith, your gifted speakers, your
knowledge, your enthusiasm, and your love from us—I want you to excel also in
this gracious act of giving.

2 CORINTHIANS 8:7

Father, you have given me so much and you call me to pay it forward.
Place within me a desire to give generously out of my love for you
and others.

Do you still give even when your finances and circumstances are challenging?
Be inspired by the apostle Paul's words recorded in 2 Corinthians chapter 8. The
churches in Macedonia were located in an impoverished area. Yet despite their
difficult living conditions, they gave joyfully, generously, willingly, and freely,
even beyond their own ability to afford.

In speaking to the Corinthians, Paul praised them for excelling in many
areas of Christian living, but he wanted them to be more like the Macedonians
in the spiritual discipline of giving. So he urged them to give eagerly out of
the overflow of their blessings, for the Lord had set the example. Though Jesus
possessed everything, he surrendered all he had to become poor for the sake
of those who followed him. For it is good to care for others in need because
who knows, one day the recipient may be in a position to help the giver in a
time of hardship.

COURAGE FOR TODAY

Are you willing to give generously? Meditate on the proverbs below and
list the people you know who need help. What courageous steps will you
take today to generously meet their needs?

Give freely and become more wealthy; be stingy and lose everything.
The generous will prosper;
those who refresh others will themselves be refreshed.

PROVERBS 11:24–25

THE COURAGE TO

Pray for Your Country

*They said to me, "Things are not going well for those who returned to the province
of Judah. They are in great trouble and disgrace. The wall of Jerusalem has been
torn down, and the gates have been destroyed by fire." When I heard this, I sat down
and wept. In fact, for days I mourned, fasted, and prayed to the God of heaven.*

NEHEMIAH 1:3–4

Father, you are sovereign and holy. Thank you for your unconditional love
and forgiveness. Inspire me to pray faithfully for my country and give me
courage to be a source of inspiration for others to do the same.

Do you regularly pray for your country? When you do, are you genuinely
broken over its condition? Consider Nehemiah's sorrow and passionate plea
recorded in Nehemiah chapter 1. When Nehemiah heard about Jerusalem's
condition of trouble and disgrace, he was heartbroken. He immediately
humbled himself and began fasting and praying. In his prayer, Nehemiah
praised God's greatness and recognized God's loving-kindness. In his heartfelt
confession, Nehemiah pleaded with God to remember his promise to intervene
for the sake of Judah's future.

COURAGE FOR TODAY

Do you consistently intercede on behalf of your leaders and country? Read
the passage below and write a prayer to the Lord today courageously
confessing the sins of the nation and begging God to intervene.

*I urge you, first of all, to pray for all people. Ask God to help them; intercede on
their behalf, and give thanks for them. Pray this way for kings and all who are in
authority so that we can live peaceful and quiet lives marked by godliness and
dignity. This is good and pleases God our Savior, who wants everyone to be saved
and to understand the truth.*

1 TIMOTHY 2:1–4

THE COURAGE TO

Be Content

True godliness with contentment is itself great wealth.

1 TIMOTHY 6:6

Father, you warn me to avoid greed and discontent. Remind me to be grateful for the resources you have given me and to be satisfied in my current circumstances.

Are you content with your wealth, health, or status in life? Do your current circumstances cause you to be envious, jealous, or resentful of others? If so, let the apostle Paul's words in 1 Timothy chapter 6 challenge you. Paul understood that godly contentment was more valuable than worldly treasures. He had personally learned that he couldn't achieve satisfaction by being rich, smart, popular, or living in beautiful surroundings. For Paul wrote many of his letters from a prison cell and house arrest. Many hated him and would not allow him to enter certain areas.

Yet Paul proclaimed, "Not that I was ever in need, for I have learned how to be content with whatever I have" (Philippians 4:11). By focusing on heaven and eternal treasures, Paul's eyes were drawn away from the deception of his surroundings. So he shared his experiences with Timothy and taught him that chasing riches leads only to temptation, destruction, and sorrow.

COURAGE FOR TODAY

Are you enticed by the things you see? Meditate on Paul's declaration below and describe how you will courageously embrace or address your current circumstances and choose to be content today.

Not that I was ever in need, for I have learned how to be content with whatever I have. I know how to live on almost nothing or with everything. I have learned the secret of living in every situation, whether it is with a full stomach or empty, with plenty or little.

PHILIPPIANS 4:11–12

THE COURAGE TO
Dismiss Negativity

"The LORD came from Mount Sinai and dawned upon us from Mount Seir; he shone forth from Mount Paran and came from Meribah-kadesh with flaming fire at his right hand. Indeed, he loves his people; all his holy ones are in his hands. They follow in his steps and accept his teaching."

DEUTERONOMY 33:2-3

Father, you tell me repeatedly to "be strong and courageous." Thank you for loving me unconditionally and encouraging me continually. Allow your great love to give me courage and to remind me that with you, I can face anything.

No matter what, God's love never fails. Consider Moses' blessing in Deuteronomy chapter 33. Before publicly reciting an entire song to remind the people of God's covenant and their responsibilities, Moses told the people of Israel and Joshua, his predecessor, the Lord's admonition to "be strong and courageous!" (Deuteronomy 31:6, 7, 23). After reciting his song of encouragement and warning, Moses reminded the Israelites of God's unfailing love, and he blessed each tribe individually.

Despite any struggles (such as those prophesied in Moses' song), we can be sure that the Lord has and always will choose to love his people unconditionally. Nothing we ever do will separate us from the grace-filled love of God. This fact alone should instill comfort, courage, and confidence in us each day.

COURAGE FOR TODAY

What negativity plagues you today? Commit the verse below to memory and let it remind you of God's love and give you courage and confidence when your inner voice seeks to discourage you. Explain how you will courageously move forward in faith today.

What shall we say about such wonderful things as these?
If God is for us, who can ever be against us?

ROMANS 8:31

THE COURAGE TO
Stand before Crowds

Peter saw his opportunity and addressed the crowd. "People of Israel," he said, "what is so surprising about this? And why stare at us as though we had made this man walk by our own power or godliness?"

ACTS 3:12

Father, help me courageously use the influence you've given me to share my faith in you with others no matter how large the crowd.

Are you comfortable speaking in front of groups? Or do crowds cause you to shy away? Be inspired by Peter's courage recorded in Acts chapters 2 through 4. Though he once cowered before a servant girl and denied knowing Jesus, Peter later eagerly embraced his God-given courage to stand before an audience to defend his faith, preach the gospel, and profess the gift of the Holy Spirit.

After healing a man who was lame, Peter then used the miracle of Christ's power to denounce sin and share God's good news. Then even after being arrested with his fellow disciple John, he continued to courageously share his faith, leading thousands to the Lord.

COURAGE FOR TODAY

Do you find it difficult to share your faith in a crowd? Be challenged by the apostle Paul's words below and let them inspire you to courageously stand before others and share Jesus with them today.

We are Christ's ambassadors; God is making his appeal through us. We speak for Christ when we plead, "Come back to God!"

2 CORINTHIANS 5:20

THE COURAGE TO
Trust God's Favor

Esther had not told anyone of her nationality and family background, because Mordecai had directed her not to do so. Every day Mordecai would take a walk near the courtyard of the harem to find out about Esther and what was happening to her.

ESTHER 2:10–11

Father, you often call me to step out of my comfort zone to pursue your will. Help me take courage in knowing that I can always count on you to give me favor, no matter whom or what I encounter.

When you find yourself in an uncertain or delicate situation, do you trust God to give you favor? Consider Esther's unsettling circumstances recorded in Esther chapter 2. King Ahasuerus, king of Persia, had removed his queen due to her disobedience. In the second chapter of Esther, we read that the king's attendants were searching for a replacement.

A young Jewish girl, being raised by her cousin Mordecai, was among those whom the king's attendants chose to be part of the king's harem. Having been taken into the custody of King Ahasuerus' servant, Esther quickly became well-liked and was placed in a promising position among the king's wives (Esther 2:9). Three times in chapter 2, God states that Esther found favor. As a result, Esther was crowned queen of Persia, a position that later permitted her to help save the Jewish people from extermination.

COURAGE FOR TODAY

Do you regularly rely on God's help? Receive God's words of blessing in the passage below and decide today to courageously trust God to give you favor in your current circumstances.

"May the Lord bless you and protect you. May the Lord smile on you and be gracious to you. May the Lord show you his favor and give you his peace."

NUMBERS 6:24–26

THE COURAGE TO
Be Watchful

The day of the Lord will come as unexpectedly as a thief. Then the heavens will pass away with a terrible noise, and the very elements themselves will disappear in fire, and the earth and everything on it will be found to deserve judgment.

2 PETER 3:10

Father, you tell me that your return will come unexpectedly. Give me the desire to live as if each day may be the day that you come back.

Do you believe today might be the day that Jesus returns? Let the apostle's words in 2 Peter chapter 3 inspire you to be watchful. The apostle Peter boldly instructed believers to live in light of Jesus' second coming. Jesus promised he would be back. However, when he didn't return soon after ascending into heaven, some people began to doubt he ever would.

God's timetable dramatically differs from ours, and his patience allows time for more people to be saved. When Jesus does come again, everyone will face judgment, and there will be a new heaven and earth. Therefore, Peter instructed believers to look forward to Christ's return. And in the meantime, they were to live "holy and godly lives" (v. 11), striving to be peaceful, pure, and blameless in God's sight.

COURAGE FOR TODAY

Do you live as if today may be your last? Read the verses below and vow to be watchful and make courageous changes as if Jesus were coming back today.

"You, too, must keep watch! For you don't know what day your Lord is coming… You also must be ready all the time, for the Son of Man will come when least expected."

MATTHEW 24:42, 44

THE COURAGE TO

Consider Your Ways

"It was the LORD who appointed Moses and Aaron," Samuel continued. "He brought your ancestors out of the land of Egypt. Now stand here quietly before the LORD as I remind you of all the great things the LORD has done for you and your ancestors."

1 SAMUEL 12:6–7

Father, you are loving, patient, and kind to me even when I fail you. Give me the courage to examine my ways, the wisdom to recognize my faults, and a longing to honor you in everything I do.

Does your life show evidence of a close relationship with God? Heed the warning by God's prophet in 1 Samuel chapter 12. God called Samuel to be a priest, prophet, judge, and the one who anointed Israel's first two kings. This important chapter records Samuel's speech that concluded his position as a leader and judge over Israel.

In his address, Samuel challenged God's people to consider their ways and reminded them how God had rescued them from Egypt, given them victory over their enemies, and answered their request for an earthly king. Samuel urged the Israelites to honor God in response to all he had done for them. If they listened and followed God's commands, they would prosper. But if they refused and rebelled, God would remove his favor from them.

COURAGE FOR TODAY

Are you compelled to obey God in response to all he has done for you? Or are you more focused on building your own kingdom? Meditate on the verse below and describe any courageous changes you will begin making today.

The LORD sent this message through the prophet Haggai:
"Why are you living in luxurious houses while my house lies in ruins?"

HAGGAI 1:3–4

THE COURAGE TO
Plant Seeds

"The seed that fell on good soil represents those who truly hear and understand God's word and produce a harvest of thirty, sixty, or even a hundred times as much as had been planted!"

MATTHEW 13:23

Father, you call me to share my testimony with as many people as possible. Inspire me to talk about my faith regularly so others will have the opportunity to experience salvation and pass on their faith to others too.

Are you preparing yourself and others for God's harvest? Let Jesus' teaching in Matthew chapter 13 inspire you to plant seeds of faith more often. After expressing that his followers were his family, Jesus taught several parables about God's harvest. In his parable about the farmer scattering seeds, Jesus clarified that the ground receiving the seeds referred to people learning about God.

As he explained the parable further, Jesus revealed that the seed that altogether missed the soil represented individuals who hear the Word of God but don't understand. The seed that fell on rocky soil symbolized those who receive God's good news but wither away because they are spiritually weak. The seed that settled in the thorns illustrated believers who fall away when worldly worries dominate their lives. But the seed that landed on good soil described people who hear and understand God's truth, receive it, and in turn, share it with countless others.

COURAGE FOR TODAY

How often do you share your love of God and his Word with friends, loved ones, and acquaintances? Read the following verse and describe your plan to courageously plant seeds of faith in the lives of others today.

"Pray to the Lord who is in charge of the harvest; ask him to send more workers into his fields."

MATTHEW 9:38

THE COURAGE TO
Acknowledge the Obvious

They saw the fingers of a human hand writing on the plaster wall of the king's palace, near the lampstand. The king himself saw the hand as it wrote.

DANIEL 5:5

Father, morality in our culture is deteriorating. Give me the wisdom to not ignore the obvious and the courage to take any necessary steps to protect my faith and my relationship with you.

Are you consumed by the fast pace, instant gratification, pleasure-seeking world we live in? Are worldly distractions causing a spiritual decline in your life? Consider God's message to an unbelieving king in Daniel chapter 5. Daniel was a young man when he was taken to Babylon in 605 BC. Because of his faithfulness and God's favor, Daniel rose to power in the pagan kingdom.

In 539 BC, while King Belshazzar was hosting a party for a thousand friends and toasting false gods with the gold and silver cups that they had stolen from God's temple in Jerusalem, a mysterious hand appeared and wrote a message on the wall. None of the king's men could understand the words, so Belshazzar called on Daniel to interpret the declaration. When Daniel was brought before the king, he confronted Belshazzar regarding his corrupt character and arrogance, and then revealed God's message that announced the termination of Belshazzar's reign.

COURAGE FOR TODAY

Do you acknowledge the people, places, and things that interfere with your faithfulness to God? Meditate on the verse below, identify any obstacles in your relationship with God, and list the courageous changes you will make today to allow the Holy Spirit to unconditionally guide your life.

Let the Holy Spirit guide your lives.
Then you won't be doing what your sinful nature craves.

GALATIANS 5:16

THE COURAGE TO
Walk with Christ

Jesus turned to the Twelve and asked,
"Are you also going to leave?"
JOHN 6:67

Father, when I am discouraged and believe you've forsaken me, reassure
me and give me the courage to continue walking faithfully with you.

Are you a fair-weather friend or one who goes the distance in both good
times and bad? Be motivated by Jesus' response in John chapter 6. While his
miracles attracted some who had long awaited his arrival, others followed him
only for the benefits he could bestow. When Jewish leaders and those with
hardened hearts raised doubts about his true identity, Jesus' skeptical followers
walked away. When he declared himself to be the bread of life and said that his
followers would eat from him, many others also abandoned him.

God has never been concerned about the number of followers his Son
would attract. His plan all along was to give life to all who would receive him,
no matter what it cost. When Jesus asked his twelve disciples if they desired
to leave him, too, Peter's response was filled with courage and humility. "Lord,
to whom would we go? You have the words that give eternal life" (v. 68). Peter
knew it was worth the risk to walk faithfully with Jesus, for only Jesus can grant
eternal life.

COURAGE FOR TODAY

Do you need courage to walk with God in difficult times? Draw strength
from the verses below and describe how you will courageously pursue
God's will and ways today no matter what it costs.

"Those who love their life in this world will lose it. Those who care nothing for their
life in this world will keep it for eternity. Anyone who wants to serve me must follow
me, because my servants must be where I am. And the Father will honor anyone
who serves me."
JOHN 12:25–26

THE COURAGE TO
Praise God's Character

Give thanks to the LORD and proclaim his greatness.
Let the whole world know what he has done.

1 CHRONICLES 16:8

Father, you are worthy of persistent praise. Help me see past myself and my circumstances and always praise your mighty name.

How often do you publicly praise God? Consider 1 Chronicles chapter 16 that records King David's public praise of God once the ark of the covenant was brought into the city. While 1 Chronicles chapters 1 through 9 record Israel's ancestry and announce the Southern Kingdom's captivity and return, chapters 10 through 29 describe the death of King Saul, the reigns of both King David and King Solomon, and the preparation for building God's holy temple.

First Chronicles chapter 16 specifically acknowledges, celebrates, and praises God's presence among his people and prepares the way for God's covenant promise to David in chapter 17. Whether in fortunate circumstances or even dire distress, King David consistently acknowledged and praised almighty God.

COURAGE FOR TODAY

Do you praise God even when you are struggling? Read the following verses and underline God's attributes. Explain how God's character gives you courage today and inspires you to publicly praise him.

The LORD is compassionate and merciful, slow to get angry and filled with unfailing love. He will not constantly accuse us, nor remain angry forever. He does not punish us for all our sins; he does not deal harshly with us, as we deserve. For his unfailing love toward those who fear him is as great as the height of the heavens above the earth. He has removed our sins as far from us as the east is from the west. The LORD is like a father to his children, tender and compassionate to those who fear him.

PSALM 103:8–13

THE COURAGE TO
Admit Sin

If we claim we have no sin, we are only fooling ourselves and not living in the truth.

1 JOHN 1:8

Father, I am grateful that you love me unconditionally and forgive me when I fail you. Remind me that I will always be a sinner in need of your salvation. And help me admit and turn away from my sins and lovingly encourage others to do the same.

Do you quickly admit when you've fallen into sin, treated someone poorly, or put power, possessions, or pleasure above your relationship with the Lord? Let the apostle's warning in 1 John chapter 1 inspire you to admit your sins. John wrote this letter to oppose false teachings that had corrupted the faith of many believers. In his introduction, he reminded readers that he had personally witnessed, touched, and learned directly from Jesus. He explained that God gives believers the ability to live in his light and that because of Christ's sacrifice, the sins of believers have been washed away.

But John also clarified that those who claim they have no sin are only fooling themselves. Therefore, God's people must always be humble in their assessment of themselves and willingly admit that they will always be a sinner in need of God's saving grace.

COURAGE FOR TODAY

Do you quickly confess your wrongdoings and make necessary changes to avoid making the same mistakes again? Meditate on King David's confession below then admit your sins and courageously seek God's forgiveness and restoration today.

I confessed all my sins to you and stopped trying to hide my guilt. I said to myself, "I will confess my rebellion to the LORD." And you forgave me! All my guilt is gone.

PSALM 32:5

THE COURAGE TO
Be Unafraid

The Lord is my light and my salvation—so why should I be afraid?
The Lord is my fortress, protecting me from danger, so why should I tremble?

PSALM 27:1

Father, fear is a natural emotion, but being controlled by fear inhibits my ability to accomplish your will. Help me choose courage over caution and faith over fear.

Do you struggle with any fear, such as the fear of failure, rejection, loss, or mistreatment? There is a great difference between fears that cause us to reevaluate our situation and fears that prevent us from experiencing the abundant life God has planned for us. When fear is present, are you willing to put it aside and trust God to guide and protect you through your circumstances?

Consider Psalm 27, in which David expressed his complete confidence in God despite his stressful situation. David confessed that because of God's presence, there was no need to be afraid. He sought God's nearness and relied on his protection. Even when his enemies threatened him with violence, David chose courage over fear, patience over anxiety, and confidence in God's goodness over doubt.

COURAGE FOR TODAY

Are you hindered by fear? Confidently recite the passage below and vow today to courageously give God your concerns, trust him with your outcomes, and praise him for his promised presence and provisions.

When I am afraid, I will put my trust in you. I praise God for what he has promised.
I trust in God, so why should I be afraid? What can mere mortals do to me?

PSALM 56:3–4

THE COURAGE TO

Renew Your Love

*"Look how far you have fallen! Turn back to me and do the works you did at first.
If you don't repent, I will come and remove your lampstand from its place
among the churches."*

REVELATION 2:5

Father, when I received you as my Lord and Savior, I was thrilled about my
new life with you. As time has gone by, my dedication has wavered some
because of life's many challenges and distractions. Help me renew my
passion for you and give me a longing to share my love for you
with others.

Do you still have the same love and enthusiasm for God that you had when you
were first saved? Be challenged by Jesus' assessment of the church in Ephesus
in Revelation chapter 2. Although the Ephesians worked hard, endured
suffering and persecution, and had no tolerance for evil, their love for God had
faded. So Jesus told them to remember how they first loved God.

He then encouraged them to confess their lack of enthusiasm, show
genuine remorse for having let their love decline, and regain the passion
for the Lord they had when they were first saved. For if they didn't do as he
instructed, Jesus would remove their reputation from among fellow believers.

COURAGE FOR TODAY

Take an inventory of your love and dedication to the Lord. Then meditate
on Jesus' words below and decide how you will courageously renew your
love for God today.

*"No one can serve two masters.
For you will hate one and love the other;
you will be devoted to one and despise the other.
You cannot serve God and be enslaved to money."*

MATTHEW 6:24

THE COURAGE TO

Reflect on God's Faithfulness

The faithful love of the LORD never ends! His mercies never cease.
Great is his faithfulness; his mercies begin afresh each morning. I say to myself,
"The LORD is my inheritance; therefore, I will hope in him!"

LAMENTATIONS 3:22–24

Father, when I search for you, you are there, and when I return to you, you receive me. Help me honor your great faithfulness by allowing it to have a lasting impact on the way I live.

Have you ever doubted God's faithfulness in a season of suffering? Consider the book of Lamentations that records Jeremiah's grief over his homeland's sin and suffering. Lamentations chapters 1 to 2 and 4 through 5 describe the condition of Israel due to the consequences of their disobedience. In contrast, chapter 3 unveils Jeremiah's heart and heartache over his people's condition, hope in almighty God, and prayer for salvation.

In his season of suffering, Jeremiah remembered that God's faithful love never ends. Therefore, those who examine their ways, confess their sin, and turn back to the Lord will receive his salvation and experience his goodness. For great is God's faithfulness; his mercies are new every morning.

COURAGE FOR TODAY

Does God's trustworthiness and love give you courage and confidence?
Memorize the familiar verse below and describe how reflecting on God's
great faithfulness gives you hope and inspiration today.

He will cover you with his feathers. He will shelter you with his wings.
His faithful promises are your armor and protection.

PSALM 91:4

THE COURAGE TO
Be at Peace

Do all that you can to live in peace with everyone.
ROMANS 12:18

Father, because of your sacrifice, presence, and promises, I have everything
I need to experience joy and peace. Help me to apply your Word and
your guidance each day so that my life will be filled with hope, harmony,
serenity, and contentment.

Are you at peace? Let the apostle Paul's encouraging words in Romans chapter
12 inspire you to pursue a calm, composed, and balanced life. In spite of the
challenges and suffering he faced as a believer, Paul urged all Christ followers
to work toward a content and peaceful life.

In his letter to the Roman church, Paul advised members to genuinely
love others, not simply to pretend to care. He promoted patience, hard work,
hospitality, enthusiastic service, and helping others. Believers were to "bless"
and "pray" for those who persecuted them, strive to live in harmony with all
people, set aside their pride, and admit they didn't have all the answers. For if
Christ followers repaid evil by doing good, lived honorable lives, and aimed to
be a peace with everyone, others would be influenced, God would be honored,
and they would be blessed.

COURAGE FOR TODAY

Do you strive to be at peace with all people? List the people, places, and
things that bring calmness and contentment to your life. Meditate on the
verse below and describe how you will make a courageous effort to
be at peace today.

*God blesses those who work for peace,
for they will be called the children of God.*
MATTHEW 5:9

THE COURAGE TO
Choose Carefully

Young people, it's wonderful to be young! Enjoy every minute of it.
Do everything you want to do; take it all in.
But remember that you must give an account to God for everything you do.

ECCLESIASTES 11:9

Father, every day I face a multitude of choices. Help me choose carefully and courageously as I seek to honor you in everything I do.

Do you contemplate all important decisions or sometimes proceed without consideration? Be challenged by King Solomon's teaching in Ecclesiastes chapter 11. In this chapter, Solomon addressed how we should consider potential outcomes before choosing certain directions. His words remind us that it's impossible to predict the future or to know all things, for only God has that ability. Therefore, we should make the best decisions possible, diversify, work hard, and never give up.

But we must also keep in mind that while God wants us to live our lives to the fullest and find joy in all our circumstances, there are consequences affiliated with every choice we make. So let us set aside our worries, pursue good health, and choose very carefully.

COURAGE FOR TODAY

What steps do you take when making decisions? Is God part of the process? Read the familiar passage below and commit to be courageous and careful as you seek to please God in all your choices today.

Those who live only to satisfy their own sinful nature will harvest decay and death from that sinful nature. But those who live to please the Spirit will harvest everlasting life from the Spirit. So let's not get tired of doing what is good. At just the right time we will reap a harvest of blessing if we don't give up.

GALATIANS 6:8–9

THE COURAGE TO
Stand Up

Peter stepped forward with the eleven other apostles and shouted to the crowd, "Listen carefully, all of you, fellow Jews and residents of Jerusalem! Make no mistake about this. These people are not drunk, as some of you are assuming."

ACTS 2:14–15

Father, I pray for the courage to stand up and speak out against wrong accusations when you prompt me to do so.

Do you shy away from confrontation? Or are you bold and willing to use your words for the greater good? Be inspired by the apostle Peter's words in Acts chapter 2. Before becoming well known for speaking up, Peter, out of fear, denied even knowing Jesus three times. But he learned from his mistakes, and after Jesus' death, Peter never missed an opportunity to further Christ's mission and ministry.

After Judas' betrayal and demise, Peter stood boldly before one hundred twenty believers, addressing the need to appoint someone else to take the deceased disciple's position. When Jesus ascended into heaven and the apostles were gathered in one place, the Holy Spirit descended on them, empowering them to speak other languages as they shared all that God had done. Those who heard the truth in their native tongue were amazed. However, others accused the apostles of being drunk. In response, Peter boldly stood and testified that Jesus was the fulfillment of the prophecies of old. And as a result, over three thousand souls were saved.

COURAGE FOR TODAY

Are you in need of more courage to stand up and speak boldly about your faith? Memorize the verse below and vow to let nothing hinder you from courageously declaring God's truth today.

God has not given us a spirit of fear and timidity, but of power, love, and self-discipline.

2 TIMOTHY 1:7

THE COURAGE TO
Turn Back to God

*Return, O Israel, to the Lord your God, for your sins have brought you down.
Bring your confessions, and return to the Lord. Say to him, "Forgive all our sins
and graciously receive us, so that we may offer you our praises."*

HOSEA 14:1–2

Father, no one can save me other than you. Give me the ability to see my sins, the courage to confess unfaithfulness, and the wisdom to turn back to you so I can fully embrace your great love, forgiveness, and restoration.

Is there anything in your life that pulls you away from the Lord? Let the prophet's words in Hosea chapter 14 encourage you to turn back to God. The book of Hosea portrays God's love for the people of Israel despite their unfaithfulness. In order to demonstrate God's endless and unconditional love, God told Hosea to marry a prostitute. While chapters 1 and 3 describe Hosea's marriage and family, chapters 2 and 4 through 13 outline God's messages of judgment and restoration.

In this final chapter, God made one more appeal to the people of Israel to repent and return to him. For if they would confess their sins and turn back to God, he would put away his anger forever, heal their unfaithfulness, and once again take great care of them.

COURAGE FOR TODAY

Is there distance between you and God? Meditate on his grace-filled offer below and decide to courageously confess any unfaithfulness and return whole-heartedly to the Lord today.

This is how the Lord responds: "If you return to me, I will restore you so you can continue to serve me. If you speak good words rather than worthless ones, you will be my spokesman. You must influence them; do not let them influence you!"

JEREMIAH 15:19

THE COURAGE TO
Leave the Past Behind

Put on your new nature, created to be like God—
truly righteous and holy.
EPHESIANS 4:24

Father, give me the courage to start each day renewed by your spirit and help me stay far away from my old habits and sinful ways.

Have you ever been told you look like or act like another person? On occasion, some might mean the comparison to be a compliment, but other times, it is criticism. Consider the apostle Paul's warning in Ephesians chapter 4. Paul urged believers in Ephesus to act differently than non-believers. For their minds and hearts were being hardened against God as they pursued their personal pleasures. So Paul reminded the Ephesians about the truths they had learned when they placed their faith in Christ.

He encouraged them to turn away from their former way of living and instead, put on their new nature since they were created to be like God. Paul's letter pointed out some of the sins the Ephesians needed to leave behind, such as lying, anger, stealing, and using abusive language. Instead, believers are expected to be kind, tenderhearted, and forgiving of one another, just as God, through Jesus, has forgiven us.

COURAGE FOR TODAY

Do you find it difficult to stay away from old habits, attitudes, and behaviors? Read the verse from Romans below and vow today to courageously walk in the newness of life that is found only in Christ.

We died and were buried with Christ by baptism. And just as Christ was raised from the dead by the glorious power of the Father, now we also may live new lives.
ROMANS 6:4

THE COURAGE TO
Endure Consequences

When Jacob woke up in the morning—it was Leah! "What have you done to me?"
Jacob raged at Laban. "I worked seven years for Rachel! Why have you tricked me?"
GENESIS 29:25

Father, you taught me that I reap what I sow. Help me consider consequences when I am tempted to do something morally or ethically wrong.

Do you consider the consequences before making decisions and choices? Consider Jacob's predicament recorded in Genesis chapter 29. Jacob was the son of Isaac and the grandson of Abraham. Even before their birth, Jacob and his twin brother Esau struggled with one another in their mother's womb. Though Esau was entitled to the family's firstborn rights, Jacob convinced him to trade those rights for a pot of stew. In time, when their father was elderly and in poor health, Jacob stole Esau's blessing by disguising himself as his brother.

But Jacob, who had deceived both his brother and father, would soon be deceived himself. When he fled to a relative's home to escape his brother's wrath, Jacob fell in love with his uncle's daughter Rachel. So he worked for his uncle Laban for seven years for the right to marry her. Yet when the time came for them to wed, Jacob's uncle deceived him and secretly gave him Rachel's older sister Leah instead of Rachel.

COURAGE FOR TODAY

Do you ever get discouraged or frustrated by the undesirable outcomes of your questionable choices? Meditate on the verse below and vow today to courageously maintain a positive attitude in the face of any consequences you endure.

No discipline is enjoyable while it is happening—it's painful! But afterward there
will be a peaceful harvest of right living for those who are trained in this way.
HEBREWS 12:11

THE COURAGE TO
Speak Life

*"What I tell you now in the darkness, shout abroad when daybreak comes.
What I whisper in your ear, shout from the housetops for all to hear!"*

MATTHEW 10:27

Father, thank you for giving me your Holy Spirit that gives me wisdom,
guides me toward truth, and equips me with just the right words at just
the right time. Please speak through me so I can speak life into other
people's lives every day.

How often do you speak life into other people's lives? Let Jesus' instructions in
Matthew chapter 10 motivate you to look for people you can encourage. After
Jesus gathered his twelve disciples, taught them, and allowed them to witness
miraculous healings, he instructed them to share his message of true life with
other Israelites. After telling the disciples what to say and do, Jesus warned
them about people who would reject, oppose, and even persecute them
because of their message.

But this shouldn't have discouraged Jesus' disciples from their
assignment because such hardships gave them the opportunity to tell even
more unbelievers about their Savior. When they didn't know what to say, Jesus
promised that God would give them the right words at just the right time. For it
would not be them but God's Spirit speaking through them to open the hearts
and minds of those they encountered.

COURAGE FOR TODAY

Do you sometimes hesitate to share words of encouragement with people
you don't know? Let the following verse inspire you to courageously speak
life into many people's lives today.

*Don't use foul or abusive language. Let everything you say be good and helpful,
so that your words will be an encouragement to those who hear them.*

EPHESIANS 4:29

THE COURAGE TO
Revere God's Holiness

All around him was a glowing halo, like a rainbow shining in the clouds on a rainy day. This is what the glory of the LORD looked like to me. When I saw it, I fell face down on the ground, and I heard someone's voice speaking to me.

EZEKIEL 1:28

Father, you are all-knowing, all-powerful, ever-present, and in complete control. Give me an unquenchable desire to consistently revere and honor your holiness.

How often do you think about the magnificence and majesty of almighty God? Consider the great prophet's vision in Ezekiel chapter 1. Ezekiel was in exile in Babylon in approximately 593 BC when the word of the Lord and a vision came upon him. Ezekiel saw four living beings that he described in great detail. The beings had both human and animal features, massive wings, and wheels on each that allowed them to go in any direction without ever turning around.

Above the beings sat a throne made of bright and beautiful jewels, and on the throne appeared the glory of the Lord, resembling a man yet glowing like a radiant flame. When Ezekiel saw God's glory, he fell face down on the ground in awe.

COURAGE FOR TODAY

Are you truly in awe of God's glory? Meditate on the verse below from the Gospel of John and describe how the glory of the Lord gives you more courage and confidence for today.

The Word became human and made his home among us.
He was full of unfailing love and faithfulness.
And we have seen his glory, the glory of the Father's one and only Son.

JOHN 1:14

THE COURAGE TO
Teach Others

Let the message about Christ, in all its richness, fill your lives.
Teach and counsel each other with all the wisdom he gives.
Sing psalms and hymns and spiritual songs to God with thankful hearts.
COLOSSIANS 3:16

Father, you call me to be a disciple and to disciple others.
Give me the courage to teach and counsel others according to
your perfect will and truth.

Are you ever reluctant to share biblical truth? Do you ever feel unqualified, under-educated, or hesitant to speak out about God and his Word? Let the apostle Paul's encouragement in Colossians chapter 3 inspire you to set aside your reservations and educate others. Paul urged believers in Colossae to teach and counsel one another. Even if their knowledge was limited, God would give them the wisdom they needed to share. Paul stated that God's Word was rich and capable of filling their lives. Therefore, out of this overflow, they should inspire and teach it to others. With the psalms, spiritual songs, and thankful hearts, Colossian believers would be capable of providing godly instruction and counsel.

But they also needed to speak and act as representatives of Christ. Since Jesus is the perfect model of grace and kindness, the Colossian Christians had all the motivation they needed. The only thing left was for them to choose to be courageous and obedient to their assignment.

COURAGE FOR TODAY

Teaching and counseling others require preparation, perseverance, and courage. Read the verse below and describe how you will put any reservations aside today and courageously commit to teaching others about God.

Brothers and sisters, we urge you to warn those who are lazy. Encourage those who are timid. Take tender care of those who are weak. Be patient with everyone.
1 THESSALONIANS 5:14

THE COURAGE TO
Seek God's Wisdom

The Lord was pleased that Solomon had asked for wisdom. So God replied, "Because you have asked for wisdom in governing my people with justice and have not asked for a long life or wealth or the death of your enemies—I will give you what you asked for! I will give you a wise and understanding heart such as no one else has had or ever will have!"

1 KINGS 3:10–12

Father, you know and control all things. Help me avoid costly mistakes by leading me to seek your wisdom before making important decisions.

Where do you turn for advice? How often do you seek wisdom and understanding from God? Consider the attributes King Solomon held in high regard in 1 Kings chapter 3, when God offered to give him whatever he asked for. In this passage from Scripture, God appeared to Solomon in a dream. When God asked Solomon what he wanted, Solomon first acknowledged God's love and faithfulness, and then he chose to ask for the one thing he truly needed: wisdom to govern God's people.

God was pleased with Solomon's request, and he not only gave the king sound judgment, but he also rewarded Solomon with riches and a long life. After celebrating before the Lord, Solomon put his God-given gift to work and began settling disputes among the people God had place under his care.

COURAGE FOR TODAY

How often do you stop to ask God for wisdom and understanding before making important decisions? Memorize the verse below and write a prayer asking God to give you supernatural discernment regarding a current situation or for a courageous decision you need to make today.

"True wisdom and power are found in God; counsel and understanding are his."

JOB 12:13

THE COURAGE TO
Embrace Freedom

"The Spirit of the LORD is upon me, for he has anointed me to bring Good News to the poor. He has sent me to proclaim that captives will be released, that the blind will see, that the oppressed will be set free."

LUKE 4:18

Father, you sent Jesus to earth to set me free from sin and shame. Help me genuinely embrace my freedom in Christ and inspire me to encourage others to do the same.

Do you need to be set free from your fears, failures, or frustrations? Let Jesus' prophetic fulfillment in Luke chapter 4 encourage you to fully embrace your salvation and freedom in Christ. After being filled with God's Holy Spirit and experiencing a time of fasting, temptation, and preparation, Jesus returned to Galilee and began teaching in a synagogue. During the Sabbath, he read from the book of Isaiah and acknowledged that the prophecy was fulfilled in him that very day.

Through Jesus, God's favor had come to the people of Israel to set them free from their sin, shame, and the oppressive rules of the religious leaders. Yet instead of embracing their freedom and welcoming their Savior, the people listening to Jesus became furious and tried to push him off a cliff. But Jesus easily escaped their grip and went on his way.

COURAGE FOR TODAY

What does it mean to you to truly be set free? Consider the apostle Paul's declaration below and describe the ways you currently engage in your new life in Christ. Then list the courageous changes you will make today to more fully embrace your freedom.

Christ has truly set us free. Now make sure that you stay free, and don't get tied up again in slavery to the law.

GALATIANS 5:1

THE COURAGE TO
Accept Consequences

All Israel was listed in the genealogical records in The Book of the Kings of Israel. The people of Judah were exiled to Babylon because they were unfaithful to the LORD.

1 CHRONICLES 9:1

Father, Satan is a liar. He tries to convince me that my sin has no consequences. Help me recognize this lie and accept the consequences of my sins. And give me the wisdom and courage to resist temptation in the future.

When you choose to sin, are you tempted to believe you won't face consequences? Consider 1 Chronicles. The first eight chapters of 1 Chronicles list Israel's genealogy leading up to Saul, Israel's first earthly king. But 1 Chronicles chapter 9 begins by recalling how the people of the Southern Kingdom of Judah would give in to temptation and follow sinful practices. However, they suffered consequences for their relentless pattern of evil and unfaithfulness to God, who allowed them to fall into enemy hands and be held captive for seventy-five years.

Yet after the people of Judah had endured their consequences, God, as promised, brought them back to their homeland so that they could choose a more righteous path and build a new life.

COURAGE FOR TODAY

Are you willing to own your sin and accept responsibility for its consequences? Read the verse below and describe how consequences inspire you to be more faithful to God. What courageous changes will you make today that can help you resist temptation?

No discipline is enjoyable while it is happening—it's painful! But afterward there will be a peaceful harvest of right living for those who are trained in this way.

HEBREWS 12:11

THE COURAGE TO
Pray at All Times

*Confess your sins to each other and pray for each other so that you may be healed.
The earnest prayer of a righteous person has great power
and produces wonderful results.*

JAMES 5:16

Father, thank you for always hearing my prayers and caring not only for my needs but for the needs of others as well. Help me remember that prayers are powerful and that you will answer them in your perfect timing and perfect ways.

Do you regularly communicate with God? And do you honor him for who he is while sharing your concerns and addressing the needs of others? Let the message of Jesus' faithful disciple James encourage you to make your prayer time with the Lord more consistent. As he concluded his letter, James warned believers about the disadvantages and distractions of seeking wealth. He reminded them to "be patient" and to "take courage" while awaiting God's return (vv. 7–8). For although suffering was a normal experience for Christ followers, they needed extra encouragement to not lose hope or falter in their faith.

James then reminded believers about the importance and effectiveness of prayer. He encouraged them to pray and sing praises in both good times and bad. And he urged them to call on godly mentors to join them in seeking God's deliverance when they needed it. For when they confessed their sins to one another and prayed earnestly for healing, God would certainly answer their prayers and bring about wonderful results.

COURAGE FOR TODAY

How often do you pray? Memorize and heed the short verse below and describe how you will make courageous and necessary changes to your prayer life today.

Never stop praying.
1 THESSALONIANS 5:17

THE COURAGE TO
Love God's Law

*God gave the people all these instructions: "I am the L*ORD *your God, who rescued you from the land of Egypt, the place of your slavery. You must not have any other god but me."*

EXODUS 20:1–3

Father, many people in our culture today view your commandments as oppressive. Yet without boundaries, we are susceptible to all types of destructive behaviors. Place within me a courageous desire to honor, obey, and love your commands.

God established his law to provide protection, order, and harmony in our lives. Without laws we are prone to disorganization, chaos, and violence, both personally and as a society. Consider God's Ten Commandments in Exodus chapter 20 that provide important behavioral boundaries.

In Matthew 22:36, when Jesus' disciples asked him about the most important commandment, Jesus responded by saying, "'You must love the LORD your God with all your heart, all your soul, and all your mind.' This is the first and greatest commandment. A second is equally important: 'Love your neighbor as yourself.' The entire law and all the demands of the prophets are based on these two commandments" (vv. 37–40). When we embrace a true love for God and others, courageously obeying God's remaining commandments comes easily.

COURAGE FOR TODAY

Read the following verse and note the apostle Paul's words regarding the purpose of God's law. Do God's commands reveal any sin in your life? Write a prayer asking God to give you the courage today to turn away from sin and make obedience to him a priority.

Am I suggesting that the law of God is sinful? Of course not! In fact, it was the law that showed me my sin. I would never have known that coveting is wrong if the law had not said, "You must not covet."

ROMANS 7:7

THE COURAGE TO
Be Led by God

I say, let the Holy Spirit guide your lives.
Then you won't be doing what your sinful nature craves.
GALATIANS 5:16

Father, I struggle with temptation. Let your spirit lead me so I can overcome my selfish desires.

How often do you hurt someone else because you've been hurt? Do you ever misuse God's love to condone your behavior? Be challenged by the apostle Paul's reprimand recorded in Galatians chapter 5. Paul chose to rebuke the believers in Galatia who had fallen away from God's grace. The Galatians had turned from God's mercy and were trying to live by the old laws. They were battling their "sinful nature" and were walking according to their flesh. But Paul knew that, when guided by God's Spirit, believers could avoid their sinful cravings. So he compared the natural cravings of one's flesh—sexual sins, idolatry, hostility, quarreling, jealousy, division, drunkenness, and other sins— to the fruits of the Holy Spirit—love, joy, peace, patience, kindness, goodness, faithfulness, gentleness, and self-control. Paul urged believers to live by God's Holy Spirit and follow its guidance in every area of their lives.

COURAGE FOR TODAY

Do you find that satisfying your own needs is easier than following God's will? Meditate on the passage below and vow to courageously follow God's guidance today.

Dear brothers and sisters, you have no obligation to do what your sinful nature urges you to do. For if you live by its dictates, you will die. But if through the power of the Spirit you put to death the deeds of your sinful nature, you will live. For all who are led by the Spirit of God are children of God.
ROMANS 8:12–14

THE COURAGE TO
Face Resistance

The local residents tried to discourage and frighten the people of Judah to keep them from their work.

Ezra 4:4

Father, some people try to discourage my faith and distract me from your will. Help me respond to them in godly ways and give me courage to resist their persuasive tactics.

When you encounter resistance to your God-given calling, how do you respond? Consider the Israelites' response in the book of Ezra, which records the Israelites' return to Jerusalem after seventy-five years of captivity in Babylon.

In Ezra chapter 4, we learn that unbelieving locals opposed the Israelites' project to rebuild God's temple. When the unbelievers asked the king to stop the project, he agreed and halted its reconstruction. Yet when a new king came into power many years later, God's people courageously petitioned him, and he granted them permission to resume their work. The Israelites were committed to rebuilding their house of worship, and when their enemies opposed their work, they respectfully waited until they could secure permission and complete their work.

COURAGE FOR TODAY

How do you respond to opposition? Read the following verses and list specific and courageous ways you will respond to any conflict you are facing today.

You yourself must be an example to them by doing good works of every kind. Let everything you do reflect the integrity and seriousness of your teaching. Teach the truth so that your teaching can't be criticized. Then those who oppose us will be ashamed and have nothing bad to say about us.

Titus 2:7–8

THE COURAGE TO
Prepare the Way

Just as the prophet Isaiah had written: "Look, I am sending my messenger ahead of you, and he will prepare your way. He is a voice shouting in the wilderness, 'Prepare the way for the LORD's coming! Clear the road for him!'"

MARK 1:2–3

Father, I am eternally grateful for my salvation and for your presence in my life. Give me endless opportunities to share my faith with others in ways that prepare them to surrender their lives to you too.

How important is it to you to plant seeds and prepare others to receive Jesus? Be inspired by the account of John the Baptist in Mark chapter 1. Before Jesus arrived, John the Baptist was preaching and urging people to repent and be baptized. John was a man of few resources, but his passion for his calling was all he needed to prepare the way for people to receive Jesus.

Once Jesus began his ministry, he began calling his disciples and preparing them for their roles in his mission. Jesus taught in synagogues, cast out demons, and preformed miracles in their midst. All of this prepared the way for many more women and men to learn about, see, receive, and follow their long-awaited Messiah.

COURAGE FOR TODAY

Are you doing your part to prepare others to follow Jesus? Let the verses below compel you to courageously plant seeds of faith in the lives of others today.

"Everyone who calls on the name of the LORD will be saved." But how can they call on him to save them unless they believe in him? And how can they believe in him if they have never heard about him? And how can they hear about him unless someone tells them?

ROMANS 10:13–14

THE COURAGE TO
Embrace Conviction

"Are they ashamed of their disgusting actions?
Not at all—they don't even know how to blush!"
JEREMIAH 6:15

Father, give me the courage to see and know in my spirit when there is something wrong in and around me. Help me turn away from destructive thoughts and behaviors so I can keep purity as a priority in my life.

Are you disturbed by what society has made common and acceptable behavior today? Consider Jeremiah chapter 6, which reveals God's judgment against his people who refused to admit their wrongdoings. God had a case against Israel. Numerous times the Lord begged the Israelites to repent and return to him, but they refused to listen.

While the great prophet and priest Jeremiah was grieved over their sin, the people of Israel were completely callous and "refused to be corrected" (5:3). Jeremiah stated, they had "eyes that do not see and ears that do not hear" (v. 21). Their hearts were hardened; they had no conviction, no emotion, and no courage to confront their own sin. Even the priests lacked discernment and courage to address the disobedience of the people. For when God's people ignore their convictions and refuse to move toward repentance, judgment is inevitable, leaving anguish in its wake.

COURAGE FOR TODAY

Does your conscience consistently measure what is acceptable and what is not? When you are convicted in your spirit, do you promptly address your issues and strive to make changes? Read the verse below and vow today to courageously live your life according to God's values.

Dear brothers and sisters, one final thing. Fix your thoughts on what is true, and honorable, and right, and pure, and lovely, and admirable. Think about things that are excellent and worthy of praise.
PHILIPPIANS 4:8

THE COURAGE TO
Revere God's Word

Work hard so you can present yourself to God and receive his approval.
Be a good worker, one who does not need to be ashamed and who correctly
explains the word of truth.

2 TIMOTHY 2:15

Father, your Word gives me encouragement, guidance, and hope while helping me recognize my mistakes. Give me great respect for your truth and a burning desire to share it with others.

Do you cherish God's Word, and are you willing to teach it to others? Let the apostle Paul's message in 2 Timothy chapter 2 challenge you to make sharing God's truth a regular practice. Paul consistently encouraged Timothy to be strong and teach others. But in this letter, Paul also reminded him to entrust God's message to women and men who would be faithful to pass it on.

Paul knew from personal experience that suffering for one's faith was common, for he was "chained like a criminal" at the time he wrote his second letter to Timothy (v. 9). So in light of the fact that he was "willing to endure anything" to share his faith (v. 10), Paul urged Timothy to never be ashamed but to work hard, avoid arguments, and then gently and correctly explain God's truth every chance he could.

COURAGE FOR TODAY

Do you strive to honor Scripture and share it accurately? Consider the apostle John's warning below and vow today to revere God's Word by courageously and carefully teaching it to others.

I solemnly declare to everyone who hears the words of prophecy written in this
book: If anyone adds anything to what is written here, God will add to that person
the plagues described in this book.

REVELATION 22:18

THE COURAGE TO
Confront Unfaithfulness

When I arrived back in Jerusalem, I learned about Eliashib's evil deed in providing Tobiah with a room in the courtyards of the Temple of God. I became very upset and threw all of Tobiah's belongings out of the room.

NEHEMIAH 13:7–8

Father, you command me to be not only strong and courageous but also kind and gentle. Help me incorporate each of these attributes as I confront my own sin and address the sins of others.

When you recognize unfaithfulness, are you quick to confront it? Consider Nehemiah's response when he discovered Eliashib's sin, recorded in Nehemiah chapter 13. After having journeyed to Jerusalem to oversee the rebuilding of its walls, Nehemiah returned to his position as cup-bearer to the king of Babylon. Nehemiah then requested another leave from his duties to the king so he could go back to Jerusalem.

When he arrived, he found that Eliashib the priest had given a friend permission to store personal items in a room that was dedicated to housing the sacred temple utensils. Other acts of unfaithfulness that Nehemiah also realized included that the people of Jerusalem had neglected to provide support for the temple workers. So he scolded the officials and the congregation and helped them restore order and faithfulness to their worship.

COURAGE FOR TODAY

Do you humbly respond when others confront your sin? Are you willing to gently approach others about their unfaithfulness? Read the following verses and commit today to courageously and appropriately confront all unfaithfulness.

My dear brothers and sisters, if someone among you wanders away from the truth and is brought back, you can be sure that whoever brings the sinner back from wandering will save that person from death and bring about the forgiveness of many sins.

JAMES 5:19–20

THE COURAGE TO
Remain Strong

These trials will show that your faith is genuine. It is being tested as fire tests and purifies gold—though your faith is far more precious than mere gold. So when your faith remains strong through many trials, it will bring you much praise and glory and honor on the day when Jesus Christ is revealed to the whole world.

1 PETER 1:7

Father, you promise to be with me wherever I go. Give me the courage to remain strong in the midst of my trials. Help me never give up but instead to look up, knowing you are where my help comes from.

Do you give up at the first sign of adversity, or do you persevere, growing ever stronger through your trials? Let the apostle's words in 1 Peter chapter 1 challenge you to remain strong in hard times. Peter knew adversity. He had seen Jesus tortured and crucified, and he had witnessed his Savior's death, burial, and resurrection. He knew the heartache of denying Christ and the beauty of being loved unconditionally afterward.

Peter understood that persecution was a part of identifying as one of Jesus' followers. So he wrote this letter to strengthen believers while they were suffering for their faith. Peter used the analogy of being "tested as fire tests and purifies gold" to further illustrate his point (v. 7). A believer's tested faith will make them stronger, proving them worthy when Jesus Christ returns to claim them as his own.

COURAGE FOR TODAY

Do you accept that you are growing stronger though your trials? Meditate on the verse below and describe how you will commit today to courageously remain hopeful, patient, and prayerful amidst life's daily challenges.

Rejoice in our confident hope.
Be patient in trouble and keep on praying.
ROMANS 12:12

THE COURAGE TO
Pray Humble Prayers

*That night God appeared to Solomon and said, "What do you want? Ask, and I
will give it to you!" Solomon replied to God, "You showed great and faithful love
to David, my father, and now you have made me king in his place...Give me the
wisdom and knowledge to lead them properly, for who could possibly govern this
great people of yours?"*

2 CHRONICLES 1:7–8, 10

Father, it is easy to be captivated by the desires of this world. Give me the
ability to focus on the things that are truly important, things that honor
you and equip me for your service.

When you pray, are you primarily concerned about your wants and needs?
Recall Solomon's prayer in 2 Chronicles chapter 1 and be inspired to ask
God for the graces that will help you accomplish his will. Second Chronicles
chapters 1–9 provide a historical account of King Solomon's reign over Israel.

In chapter 1, Solomon's reign was established, and he addressed the
people. Further on in this passage, God appeared to Solomon and asked him
to state his desires. Instead of asking for comfort, prosperity, and a long life, he
requested only what he truly needed to accomplish God's calling: "wisdom and
knowledge." (v. 10). Just as God was pleased with Solomon's humble request,
God is also pleased when we seek his guidance, ability, and provisions that
help us achieve his purposes and calling.

COURAGE FOR TODAY

What have you asked God for lately? Are your requests directed more
toward personal pleasures or authentic needs? Read the verse below and
write a courageous prayer asking God to accomplish his will in your life,
giving you only what you truly need for today.

*"Those who exalt themselves will be humbled,
and those who humble themselves will be exalted."*

MATTHEW 23:12

THE COURAGE TO
See and Speak

"Go wash yourself in the pool of Siloam" (Siloam means "sent").
So the man went and washed and came back seeing!

JOHN 9:7

Father, open my eyes so I can see you at work in my life and give me the courage to share your life-giving truth with others.

How do you respond when others criticize you, embarrass you, or put you on the spot? Consider the account of the blind man whom Jesus healed in John chapter 9. He'd been blind since birth and only knew of Jesus by name. When the Messiah's disciples asked him why the man had been blind from birth, Jesus took the initiative to heal him in order to reveal God's great power. No sin had caused this man's blindness. Rather, it was a display of God's grace and an opportunity for hearts to be changed.

The contemptuous religious leaders wanted to trap Jesus and the healed man by interrogating them with challenging questions and accusations. The Pharisees, who believed they could see, refused to believe in Christ, who offered both physical and spiritual sight. When the Jewish leaders continued their interrogation, the healed man replied in exasperation and with great courage saying, "I told you once. Didn't you listen?" (v. 27). The blind man could see clearly who Jesus was, and he was unafraid to speak the truth.

COURAGE FOR TODAY

Has your faith ever been questioned or ridiculed? Standing up for God can require great courage. Meditate on the verse below and let God's light and hope give you more courage to speak up for him today.

I pray that your hearts will be flooded with light so that you can understand the confident hope he has given to those he called—his holy people who are his rich and glorious inheritance.

EPHESIANS 1:18

THE COURAGE TO

Depend on God

I love you, LORD; you are my strength. The LORD is my rock, my fortress, and my savior; my God is my rock, in whom I find protection. He is my shield, the power that saves me, and my place of safety.

PSALM 18:1–2

Father, throughout life I encounter seasons of difficulty and opposition. When I am in trouble and when others turn against me, help me remember that you are my source of courage and shelter and that with you, I can overcome every storm in life.

Do you depend on God in both good times and bad? Do you count on him to help you manage the challenges and decisions of everyday life? Take into account how David relied on God when he was pursued by a sinful king who hated him. Psalm 18 records David's beautiful song of deliverance.

Israel's future king, David, begins his psalm by expressing his love for and confidence in God. The following verses describe David's dire circumstances and deliverance as he fought against King Saul. Though his life was far from flawless, David describes his rescue as God's reward to David for "doing right" and his "innocence" in his dealings with King Saul (v. 20). To those who are humble and faithful, God will provide guidance, protection, and deliverance.

COURAGE FOR TODAY

How often do you turn to God for help? Is he your first source of aid or your last resort? Memorize the following verse and commit today to trust God completely and to courageously depend on him to guide, protect, and deliver you from your troubles.

The LORD is good, a strong refuge when trouble comes. He is close to those who trust in him.

NAHUM 1:7

THE COURAGE TO

Overcome Your Past

No, dear brothers and sisters, I have not achieved it, but I focus on this one thing:
Forgetting the past and looking forward to what lies ahead.

PHILIPPIANS 3:13

Father, my past failures sometimes haunt me. Give me the courage to set aside self-doubt so I can live with great hope for the future.

Do past hurts or failures keep you from moving forward? Consider the apostle Paul's wise words in Philippians chapter 3. Prior to salvation, Paul's resume as a strict and obedient Jewish leader was impressive. While he could have boasted about his heritage and obedience to Jewish law, Paul refused to let either interfere with his mind or ministry. He counted everything as "worthless" when compared to the infinite value of knowing Christ (v. 8).

Instead of looking backward, Paul chose to look ahead. He knew that God had plans not only for his life but also for the church. So Paul called the Philippians to finish strong so that they would "receive the heavenly prize" (v. 14). Four experiences Paul desired for himself and others were to become one with Christ, to know Christ well, to experience Christ's power, and to suffer with Jesus and share in his resurrection. Putting your past behind you, like Paul did, allows you to look ahead and focus on cultivating these same experiences.

COURAGE FOR TODAY

Do you need more courage to put your past behind and press forward? Read the following passage and decide today to courageously set aside any self-doubt or reservations and embrace God's plans for your future.

"Forget all that—it is nothing compared to what I am going to do. For I am about to do something new. See, I have already begun! Do you not see it? I will make a pathway through the wilderness. I will create rivers in the dry wasteland."

ISAIAH 43:18–19

THE COURAGE TO
Give Back to God

She made this vow: "O LORD of Heaven's Armies, if you will look upon my sorrow and answer my prayer and give me a son, then I will give him back to you. He will be yours for his entire lifetime, and as a sign that he has been dedicated to the LORD, his hair will never be cut."

1 SAMUEL 1:11

Father, you are generous to me. Give me patience as I await your answer to my prayers and grant me a willingness to dedicate to you all the blessings I receive.

When you receive a blessing, are you willing to dedicate it to the Lord? Reflect on Hannah's longing for a son recorded in 1 Samuel chapter 1. In the first eight verses of this book of Scripture, we discover that Hannah was greatly distressed because she is unable to have children. Burdened by her sorrows, she went to the Hebrew temple and poured her heart out to God.

In her heartfelt plea, Hannah promised the Lord, "If you will...give me a son, then I will give him back to you" (v. 11). And that is exactly what she did. When her son was born, she named him Samuel, and as soon as he was weaned, she took him to the temple and gave him to the priest to be raised as a servant to the Lord.

COURAGE FOR TODAY

Are you willing to surrender your blessings back to God? Read the verse below and list the people and things you treasure. Describe ways you will courageously allow God to use your blessings to further his kingdom work today.

"Who am I, and who are my people, that we could give anything to you? Everything we have has come from you, and we give you only what you first gave us!"

1 CHRONICLES 29:14

THE COURAGE TO
Be Passionate

"I know all the things you do, that you are neither hot nor cold. I wish that you were one or the other! But since you are like lukewarm water, neither hot nor cold, I will spit you out of my mouth!"

REVELATION 3:15–16

Father, you are passionate about me, and you offer me forgiveness, salvation, and unconditional love. Protect my faith and help me maintain great love for and devotion to you so I can be a more godly example for others to follow.

Are you ever lukewarm when it comes to your faith? Consider Jesus' message to the church of Laodicea in Revelation chapter 3. Church members in Laodicea lived in an area known for its prosperity in banking, manufacturing, and medicine. Therefore, they felt as if they had everything they needed and didn't really believe that God's presence was essential for their success.

Since these believers didn't realize how "wretched and miserable and poor and blind and naked" their faith really was (v. 17), Jesus rebuked them and labeled them "lukewarm" (v. 16). He advised them to acquire from him what was truly valuable: "white garments" to cover their nakedness and "ointment" to open their eyes (v. 18). For if they repented and turned away from their indifference toward God, they could be victorious and sit with him on his throne.

COURAGE FOR TODAY

Have you taken inventory of your faith lately? Meditate on the verse below and examine your affection and dedication to God. What courageous steps will you take today to avoid falling into a lukewarm faith?

Examine yourselves to see if your faith is genuine. Test yourselves. Surely you know that Jesus Christ is among you; if not, you have failed the test of genuine faith.

2 CORINTHIANS 13:5

THE COURAGE TO
Be a Whistleblower

Sound the trumpet in Jerusalem! Raise the alarm on my holy mountain!
Let everyone tremble in fear because the day of the LORD is upon us.

JOEL 2:1

Father, I desire to appropriately confront people whose behavior causes chaos and harm. Give me the courage to speak your truth in ways that inspire positive changes in the lives of my family, community, and country.

Do you have the courage to confront the people in your life who are causing chaos? While most of us would rather not, God calls on all believers to carefully confront sinful situations. Take for example Joel chapters 1–3. During the days of the prophet Joel, Israel's land had been stripped by locusts and weakened by outside military invasions. Its condition was the result of its people's rebellion.

So once again, God allowed their hardship to encourage the people of Israel to turn back to him. In the book of Joel, "The day of the Lord" is a major theme. This is a time of destruction and chastisement from the Lord. Because God desires a personal relationship with everyone he creates, he allows our dark days to turn into praying nights. Yet through it all, his ultimate desire is to bless us and remind us that he alone is God.

COURAGE FOR TODAY

Do you need more courage to speak in a bad situation or to a certain group of people? Read the verse below and ask God today to prepare the hearts of those who need to hear the truth—even if it's you—and to give you wisdom to speak truth in appropriate, loving, and courageous ways.

"Be strong and courageous!
Do not be afraid and do not panic before them.
For the LORD your God will personally go ahead of you.
He will neither fail you nor abandon you."

DEUTERONOMY 31:6

THE COURAGE TO
Protect Your Reputation

Kings from every nation came to consult him and to hear the wisdom God had given him. Year after year everyone who visited brought him gifts of silver and gold, clothing, weapons, spices, horses, and mules.

2 CHRONICLES 9:23–24

Father, I want to follow you faithfully and represent you honorably. Help me turn away from the world's lure and remain steadfast in my obedience to you.

How important is your reputation to you? Consider King Solomon's character revealed in 2 Chronicles chapter 9. We are introduced to Solomon in 2 Samuel 12:24. Then in 1 Kings 1:28, King David chose Solomon, his son, to succeed him as king. In the early years of his reign, King Solomon was humble, responsible, and faithful to God. His words, wisdom, fortune, and fame were legendary. Yet, it all became meaningless when Solomon failed to maintain his promises to God as he grew older.

Solomon's heart turned away from God as he allowed pagan women, possessions, and pleasure to distract him from his covenant with the Lord. We, like King Solomon, can fall prey to temptation if we don't intentionally put safeguards in place.

COURAGE FOR TODAY

Do you value your reputation? Read the verses below and heed their warning. What safeguards will you courageously put into place today to protect you from falling prey to temptation?

Dear friends, I warn you as "temporary residents and foreigners" to keep away from worldly desires that wage war against your very souls. Be careful to live properly among your unbelieving neighbors. Then even if they accuse you of doing wrong, they will see your honorable behavior, and they will give honor to God when he judges the world.

1 PETER 2:11–12

THE COURAGE TO
Honor Your Family

The LORD said to Moses, "Give the following instructions to the people of Israel. I am the LORD your God. So do not act like the people in Egypt, where you used to live, or like the people of Canaan, where I am taking you. You must not imitate their way of life."

LEVITICUS 18:1–3

Father, you created families to be the building block of our society. Give me that desire and courage to honor my loved ones and relatives and help me avoid hurting those who are closest to me.

Are you convinced that healthy relationships with God and others improve your quality of life? Do you agree that healthy marriages and intact families lead to a stronger society and greater physical health? Note God's passion to protect the family unit in Leviticus chapter 18. In these verses, God urged his people to avoid the immoral behaviors unbelieving nations regularly practiced.

It's easy to see that sexual sin causes pain and destroys happy homes. While healthy homes nurture feelings of stability and security in children, broken homes leave children feeling vulnerable and insecure. When we incorporate wise boundaries in our lives and when we choose to courageously celebrate, cherish, and protect our spouses and loved ones, we create healthy families and legacies that positively impact our communities, nation, and world for generations to come.

COURAGE FOR TODAY

Read the following verse and describe the boundaries you will put in place to protect your family from suffering or destruction. Name ways you will intentionally celebrate, cherish, and courageously protect your loved ones today, tomorrow, and for years to come.

Those who bring trouble on their families inherit the wind. The fool will be a servant to the wise.

PROVERBS 11:29

THE COURAGE TO
Live by Faith

My old self has been crucified with Christ.
It is no longer I who live, but Christ lives in me.
So I live in this earthly body by trusting in the Son of God,
who loved me and gave himself for me.

GALATIANS 2:20

Father, since I became a believer, you assure me that I am a new person. Help me live by faith in you and not by faith in what I do.

Do you sometimes think your good works impress God? Or do you ever fall short of God's commands and feel inadequate? Consider Galatians chapter 2 and the life of the apostle Paul, who was an ambassador for Christ who was born into a religion that was solely focused on the law. Paul was also a Pharisee. The Pharisees were a strict group of Jews who tried to please God by following countless rules.

After Paul's conversion in Acts 9, his life dramatically changed. His zeal for God and others led him to passionately preach about living "by faith in Jesus Christ, not by obeying the law" (v. 16). Paul learned that by trying to keep the law, he felt condemned. But when he lived for Christ and allowed Christ to live through him, he embraced and understood true grace. For if rule following could make a person right with God, there would be no need for Christ's sacrifice.

COURAGE FOR TODAY

Do you need more courage to truly trust God and live by faith alone? Memorize the verse below and make a commitment today to maintain a more courageous faith.

This Good News tells us how God makes us right in his sight. This is accomplished from start to finish by faith. As the Scriptures say, "It is through faith that a righteous person has life."

ROMANS 1:17

THE COURAGE TO
Give Generously

"Because of my devotion to the Temple of my God, I am giving all of my own private treasures of gold and silver to help in the construction. This is in addition to the building materials I have already collected for his holy Temple."

1 CHRONICLES 29:3

Father, you are the giver of all things. Remind me that everything I have has come from you and help me to keep an open hand, giving unselfishly to you and others.

Do you live as if everything you have belongs to you or that it belongs to God? Be inspired and challenged by King David's words in 1 Chronicles chapter 29. In this passage of Scripture, David described his commitment and generosity toward the construction of God's temple. Then he challenged the rulers, princes, commanders, and overseers to follow his example—and they willingly did so.

David acknowledged that everything comes from God, belongs to God, and is allocated by God. He affirmed that God will "examine our hearts and rejoice" over those with integrity (v. 17). He then led the Israelites to praise God for his generosity. As King David's life came to an end, his farewell speech set the stage for his son Solomon to follow in his footsteps.

COURAGE FOR TODAY

Are you a generous giver? Do you consider it a privilege to help someone in need or further God's ministry here on earth? Read the verse below and list specific ways you will be courageously generous in your giving today.

You must each decide in your heart how much to give. And don't give reluctantly or in response to pressure. "For God loves a person who gives cheerfully."

2 CORINTHIANS 9:7

THE COURAGE TO
Know Truth from Error

Some people may contradict our teaching, but these are the wholesome teachings of the Lord Jesus Christ. These teachings promote a godly life.

1 TIMOTHY 6:3

Father, I desire to know the difference between true and false teachings. Give me the desire and ability to know your Word and the courage to speak its truth.

Have you listened to someone teach the Bible and felt as if something wasn't right? If so, did you take the time to search for the truth? Consider the apostle Paul's warning in 1 Timothy chapter 6. Paul urged Timothy to watch out for false teachers, for they were spreading lies and leading people away from God's truth. Their motive to mislead was evident by their sinful behaviors, such as pride, "arguments…, jealousy, division, slander, and evil suspicions" (v. 4).

These false teachers were troublemakers who foolishly pursued wealth over integrity and only looked out for themselves. Their fake display of godliness was only a way to gain wealth. Paul advised that Timothy and other believers needed to prepare themselves to recognize the truth. Therefore, it was imperative for them—and for us—to study and know God's Word. That way, we can contradict and avoid any teaching that denies, ignores, or misrepresents the truth of Scripture.

COURAGE FOR TODAY

What courageous steps do you need to take to recognize God's truth from worldly lies? Read the following verse, describe your current prayer and Bible study routine, and list the courageous changes you will make beginning today so you can know truth from error.

Dear friends, do not believe everyone who claims to speak by the Spirit. You must test them to see if the spirit they have comes from God. For there are many false prophets in the world.

1 JOHN 4:1

THE COURAGE TO
Embrace Difficulty

When the LORD first began speaking to Israel through Hosea, he said to him, "Go and marry a prostitute, so that some of her children will be conceived in prostitution. This will illustrate how Israel has acted like a prostitute by turning against the LORD and worshiping other gods."

HOSEA 1:2

Father, I want to be faithful to you even when you ask me to accomplish difficult tasks. Let my yes be confident and more frequent than my hesitation to follow your promptings.

When was the last time you were given a difficult assignment? Has God asked you to accomplish something you feel unqualified to take on? Be influenced by the prophet Hosea, who may outshine any of us in executing unpleasant assignments. In Hosea chapter 1, God commanded his prophet to marry a prostitute to demonstrate God's own heartache over Israel's rejection and disobedience.

When Hosea married a woman who ultimately refused his love and returned to her former lovers, he fully identified with God's sorrow. The recipients of Hosea's message had rejected the God who loved and provided for them. Instead they chose to worship other gods. Although his obedience to God caused him great heartache, Hosea courageously vowed to love and even bear children with the unfaithful wife God commanded him to marry.

COURAGE FOR TODAY

Do you need courage to execute a challenging assignment from God? Be motivated by the verses below and let them inspire you to take courageous steps today to pursue God's calling.

Work willingly at whatever you do, as though you were working for the Lord rather than for people. Remember that the Lord will give you an inheritance as your reward, and that the Master you are serving is Christ.

COLOSSIANS 3:23–24

THE COURAGE TO
Love Others

If I gave everything I have to the poor and even sacrificed my body,
I could boast about it; but if I didn't love others, I would have gained nothing.

1 CORINTHIANS 13:3

Father, you call me to love others in the same way you love me. Give me courage to love in ways that please you and to not withhold my love from those who need it most.

Do you consider yourself a loving person? Would others identify you as one who loves unconditionally? Consider the apostle Paul's letter, in 1 Corinthians chapter 13, in which he speaks about love. The people of Corinth were not only misusing their spiritual gifts, but they had also missed the main goal of their gifting, which was to love.

So Paul reminded them that if they were using their gifts but not loving other people, there was no real profit. The Greek word Paul used for the word "love" was *agape*, a sacrificial and unselfish love. The motive of love is to be pure and selfless. Love will outlive all other gifts and will never fail. While all spiritual gifts are important, "the greatest of these is love" (v. 13).

COURAGE FOR TODAY

Do you love others the way God desires? Meditate on the verses below and describe at least three ways you can courageously show love to others today.

"I am giving you a new commandment: Love each other. Just as I have loved you,
you should love each other. Your love for one another will prove to the world that
you are my disciples."

JOHN 13:34–35

THE COURAGE TO
Let God Revive You

"This is what the Sovereign Lord says:
Look! I am going to put breath into you and make you live again!"

Ezekiel 37:5

Father, at times, I feel like giving up. Help me remember that you are with me both in good times and in bad and that I can rely on your promise to revive me in your perfect timing and way.

Have you ever felt spiritually or emotionally dead? Do you know someone who feels that way now? Let God's words in Ezekiel chapter 37 encourage you and inspire you to minister to someone who is hurting today. God called Ezekiel to deliver words of judgment and hope to the people of Israel who were exiled in Babylon.

In this chapter, God transported the great prophet in a vision to a valley of dry bones. He then asked Ezekiel, "Can these bones become living people again?" (v. 3). The deteriorating bones represented God's people, the Israelites, who had lost all hope, and the restoration of life to these bones represented their revival. While God's people suffered as a result of societal sin, all hope was not lost. For God is full of mercy and grace, and he revives all people who seek his forgiveness and restoration.

COURAGE FOR TODAY

Do you need revival? Or do you know someone who does? Read the verse below and ask God to revive your courage and restore your hope today. Then think of others whom you can also encourage.

The high and lofty one who lives in eternity, the Holy One, says this: "I live in the high and holy place with those whose spirits are contrite and humble. I restore the crushed spirit of the humble and revive the courage of those with repentant hearts."

Isaiah 57:15

THE COURAGE TO
Pray for God's Will

"Don't be like them, for your Father knows exactly what you need even before you ask him! Pray like this: Our Father in heaven, may your name be kept holy. May your Kingdom come soon. May your will be done on earth, as it is in heaven."

MATTHEW 6:8–10

Father, it is easy for me to pray for the things I want in life. But I need you to help me surrender my wants and needs to you so I can persistently pursue your will in my life.

Do you sometimes find it difficult to pray for God's will over your life? Let Jesus' words in Matthew chapter 6 inspire you to entrust your hopes and dreams to God. In the midst of his Sermon on the Mount, Jesus spoke to the crowd about prayer.

First, Jesus discussed the importance of humility and sincerity when praying. Then he urged his audience to avoid using repetitive and meaningless words like many religious leaders did at this time. Instead, Jesus taught his followers to acknowledge God and to pray for his kingdom to come and his will to be done. Then Jesus encouraged followers to pray for provisions, forgiveness of their sins, the ability to forgive others, and help in resisting temptation and wrongdoing. When we pray for God's will over ours, we profess our belief and faith in his sovereign ability to lead us in the best direction or to the best solution.

COURAGE FOR TODAY

Do you pray for God's kingdom and his will over your personal wants and needs? Describe how you will let John's words below inspire you to courageously pray God's will for your life today.

We are confident that he hears us whenever we ask for anything that pleases him.

1 JOHN 5:14

THE COURAGE TO
Celebrate Your Savior

Rejoice, O people of Zion! Shout in triumph, O people of Jerusalem!
Look, your king is coming to you. He is righteous and victorious,
yet he is humble, riding on a donkey—riding on a donkey's colt.

ZECHARIAH 9:9

Father, thank you for sending Jesus to pay my sin-debt in full. Remind me
to celebrate my Savior and find joy in my salvation every day.

Do you delight in your salvation and in the existence of your savior? Let
Zechariah chapter 9 prompt you to celebrate Jesus today. In approximately
520 BC, God called Zechariah to prophesy to a remnant of Israelites who
had returned to Jerusalem from exile in Babylon. The first half of this book of
Scripture describes visions that God gave to Zechariah to inspire the people of
Israel to repent and rebuild God's temple.

Chapter 9, on the other hand, begins Zechariah's prophecies about
a future time when Israel's enemies would be conquered and their Savior
would reign. Zechariah's prophecies detail God's judgment against Israel's
enemies, including God's personal protection over Israel's new temple and
the announcement of the Messiah's first coming. The specific details of this
prophecy were fulfilled when Jesus arrived in Jerusalem, humble and "riding on
a donkey's colt" (v. 9; see also Matthew 21:2–7 and John 12:12–15).

COURAGE FOR TODAY

Describe how you celebrate your relationship with God. Meditate on the
verses below and identify courageous ways you can rejoice over your
salvation and your Savior today.

Since our friendship with God was restored by the death of his Son while we were
still his enemies, we will certainly be saved through the life of his Son. So now we
can rejoice in our wonderful new relationship with God because our Lord Jesus
Christ has made us friends of God.

ROMANS 5:10–11

THE COURAGE TO
Mind Your Business

Make it your goal to live a quiet life, minding your own business
and working with your hands, just as we instructed you before.

1 THESSALONIANS 4:11

Father, help me to keep quiet and mind my own business rather than
interfering in the lives of others when I shouldn't.

Are you ever tempted to meddle in other people's affairs? Do you frequently
fight the urge to impose your point of view? Consider the apostle Paul's
advice in 1 Thessalonians chapter 4. Paul understood that in order to promote
healthy relationships, believers need to "live a quiet life, minding your own
business" (v. 11).

To achieve a quiet life, one must pursue true peace, which only comes
from a close and personal relationship with God. A quiet and peaceful life
means listening to God and learning his ways. Rather than being obsessed
with the lives and issues of others, Paul urged believers to balance their
concern for other people with their own responsibilities. By being respectful
and responsible, Christ followers will encourage more people to pursue the
Christian faith.

COURAGE FOR TODAY

Do you need to be more careful with your comments and more respectful
of other people's opinions? Read the verses below and vow today to
courageously speak words that uplift, encourage, and inspire others rather
than regularly challenging their points of view.

Live wisely among those who are not believers, and make the most of every
opportunity. Let your conversation be gracious and attractive so that you will have
the right response for everyone.

COLOSSIANS 4:5–6

THE COURAGE TO
Welcome God's Wisdom

Trust in the LORD with all your heart; do not depend on your own understanding. Seek his will in all you do, and he will show you which path to take.

PROVERBS 3:5–6

Father, thank you for offering me wisdom. Help me overcome self-sufficiency and pride so I will rely more on you for knowledge, discernment, and direction.

Do you read your Bible regularly, welcome God's wisdom, and consistently apply it to your life? Be inspired by King Solomon's words in Proverbs chapter 3. Wisdom is not something we simply acquire; rather, it is something we choose to embrace. When we remember God's teaching and strive to keep his commandments, our lives are fruitful, satisfying, and longer lasting.

When we ask God for understanding and honor him in our decisions, he will lead us away from evil and give us all we truly need. God uses his Holy Spirit and his Word to give us wisdom and to guide us toward his will. Nothing compares to the wisdom of God. So let us welcome, value, and apply God's wisdom above everything else we see and hear.

COURAGE FOR TODAY

How often do you turn to prayer or the Bible when making important decisions? Meditate on the verse below and vow today to stop trusting in your own judgment and courageously commit to trusting God with every aspect of your life.

The wisdom from above is first of all pure. It is also peace loving, gentle at all times, and willing to yield to others. It is full of mercy and the fruit of good deeds. It shows no favoritism and is always sincere.

JAMES 3:17

THE COURAGE TO
Embrace God's Pardon

There is no condemnation for those who belong to Christ Jesus.
And because you belong to him, the power of the life-giving Spirit
has freed you from the power of sin that leads to death.

ROMANS 8:1–2

Father, thank you for sending Jesus. Give me courage to fully embrace your
pardon and wisdom to honor your sacrifice in everything I do and say.

Do you let negative self-talk discourage you or cause you to doubt your
relationship with God? Let the apostle Paul's words of encouragement in
Romans chapter 8 inspire you to fully embrace God's pardon. In his letter to
the Roman church, Paul shared his struggle with his sinful nature. Right after
writing about his enslavement to sin, Paul reassured believers that because of
their relationship with Jesus, his "life-giving Spirit has freed you from the power
of sin that leads to death" (v. 2).

On the other hand, people who surrender to evil thoughts and ways are
controlled by their "sinful nature" (v. 9). Those who strive to maintain thoughts
and behaviors that honor the Lord are being guided by the Holy Spirit. Nothing
can separate a believer from God's love, and judgment and condemnation
have been removed. However, Christ followers must still resist the desires of
their flesh so that the Spirit of God, which lives within them, can lead them
toward a wholesome lifestyle that reflects our status as children of God.

COURAGE FOR TODAY

God knows everything about us, including our thoughts. Does your lifestyle
reflect your pardon by God? Be encouraged by the following verse and
vow today to courageously allow your attitudes and behaviors to display
God's Holy Spirit living within you.

Even if we feel guilty, God is greater than our feelings,
and he knows everything.

1 JOHN 3:20

THE COURAGE TO
Defend Your Mission

When Sanballat and Tobiah and the Arabs, Ammonites, and Ashdodites heard that the work was going ahead and that the gaps in the wall of Jerusalem were being repaired, they were furious. They all made plans to come and fight against Jerusalem and throw us into confusion.

NEHEMIAH 4:7–8

Father, I trust you with every challenge. Yet you do not call me to sit idly by. Help me discern what courageous action to take when others attempt to hinder the work you've called me to accomplish.

Do you defend your God-given calling when rejected, ridiculed, or criticized? Consider Nehemiah's response to his enemies' anger, mocking, and threats in Nehemiah chapter 4. The prophet had gotten word that his homeland was in ruins and that his native people were in distress. In response, Nehemiah asked the king of Babylon for permission to return to Judah. After receiving permission, Nehemiah returned to Jerusalem, inspected its boundaries, and encouraged God's people to restore the city walls.

In Nehemiah chapter 4, we learn that the Arabs, Ammonites, Ashdodites, and other officials were furious and fought against the Jewish people's progress. In response to the opposition, Nehemiah and the people of Jerusalem prayed and stationed guards throughout the city so that their work could continue.

COURAGE FOR TODAY

Are you willing to persevere when unbelievers oppose you? Is someone else's opinion currently hindering your God-given calling? Read the verse below, seek God's wisdom and guidance, and write your commitment to courageously and appropriately protect yourself as you move forward in God's calling today.

Prepare your minds for action and exercise self-control. Put all your hope in the gracious salvation that will come to you when Jesus Christ is revealed to the world.

1 PETER 1:13

THE COURAGE TO

Wish Salvation for Others

Paul replied, "Whether quickly or not, I pray to God that both you and everyone here in this audience might become the same as I am, except for these chains."

ACTS 26:29

Father, your primary calling on my life is for me to share the great news of your forgiveness and salvation with others. Give me a burning desire and great courage to inspire and lead others to saving faith in you.

Are you passionate about sharing Jesus with others? Be inspired by the account of the apostle Paul's dedication to the gospel in Acts chapter 26. After having incited an uproar among the religious elite in Jerusalem, Paul was taken to Caesarea and imprisoned in Herod's headquarters.

Following his bold, passionate, and thorough defense before King Agrippa and the crowd, Paul made it known that his primary objective and greatest prayer was for everyone who heard him to become a believer and follower of Christ. Yet rather than receiving his passionate plea, accepting his invitation to become a Christian, or setting him free, the Roman leaders decided to keep Paul in custody and send him to Caesar for further interrogation. Even this hardship did not deter Paul from following through with his mission.

COURAGE FOR TODAY

How often do you share God's good news with family members, friends, or acquaintances? Meditate on the verse below and vow to lean into the Holy Spirit's prompting and courageously tell others about Jesus and his saving grace today.

"You will receive power when the Holy Spirit comes upon you. And you will be my witnesses, telling people about me everywhere—in Jerusalem, throughout Judea, in Samaria, and to the ends of the earth."

ACTS 1:8

THE COURAGE TO
Trust God with Your Future

Boaz took Ruth into his home, and she became his wife. When he slept with her, the LORD enabled her to become pregnant, and she gave birth to a son.

RUTH 4:13

Father, you are the source of hope, healing, and restoration. Help me to always trust you with my future and give me supernatural courage to take any necessary steps along the way.

Have you ever experienced a life-altering loss? A loss can be devastating, leaving you feeling hopeless, helpless, and uncertain about the future. The book of Ruth begins with great tragedy but concludes with significant success. Reflect on Ruth chapter 4 and consider how God restored both Ruth and Naomi's lives.

The first twelve verses of this chapter describe how Boaz respectfully sought to redeem Naomi's deceased husband's property. In doing so, Boaz not only inherited the remaining assets of the family, but he also took on the responsibility of both Ruth and Naomi. Through Boaz, God lovingly cared for Naomi and Ruth. Through their son, Boaz and Ruth became the great-grandparents of Israel's most beloved king, David, which ultimately included them in the lineage of Jesus Christ.

COURAGE FOR TODAY

Do you trust God to heal your hurts and restore your future? Read the passage below and note God's promises to Israel. How do God's words inspire you to courageously trust him with your future today?

This is what the LORD says: "When I bring Israel home again from captivity and restore their fortunes, Jerusalem will be rebuilt on its ruins, and the palace reconstructed as before. There will be joy and songs of thanksgiving, and I will multiply my people, not diminish them; I will honor them, not despise them."

JEREMIAH 30:18–19

THE COURAGE TO
Support Godly Messengers

*We ourselves should support them so that we can be their partners
as they teach the truth.*

3 John 1:8

Father, you give me resources to use in helping spread your gospel message. Give me wisdom, discernment, and the desire to do all I can to support your godly messengers.

Do you support believers who speak and teach God's truth? Let the apostle John's words in his third letter inspire you to help further the ministries of faithful believers. John wrote to his friend and brother in the faith to discuss his support of godly teachers. He first commended Gaius for his faithfulness and expressed great joy in knowing that his friend was following God's truth. For Gaius had lovingly cared for traveling teachers as they were passing through.

John then discussed his concerns about a leader who "refuses to have anything to do with" God's servants (v. 9). While John encouraged Gaius to continue caring for faithful teachers, he rebuked the unsupportive leader's actions and even said the way he was behaving was evil (vv. 10–11).

COURAGE FOR TODAY

Explain how you currently help support ministries. Then consider the passage below that illustrates the support Jesus received from his followers. Describe how you will embrace your God-given courage today and support godly messengers.

Jesus began a tour of the nearby towns and villages, preaching and announcing the Good News about the Kingdom of God. He took his twelve disciples with him, along with some women who had been cured of evil spirits and diseases. Among them were Mary Magdalene, from whom he had cast out seven demons; Joanna, the wife of Chuza, Herod's business manager; Susanna; and many others who were contributing from their own resources to support Jesus and his disciples.

Luke 8:1–3

THE COURAGE TO
End Family Feuding

*"Because of the violence you did to your close relatives in Israel,
you will be filled with shame and destroyed forever."*

OBADIAH 1:10

Father, family wounds can be painful. Help me establish appropriate boundaries with those who've mistreated me. But above all, give me unconditional love and compassion for my family, and help me honor you in all my relationships.

Have you experienced a family feud? Or have you been mistreated by a close relative or other loved one? Take into consideration how the prophet Obadiah pronounced judgment on the Edomites, the descendants of Esau. Esau and his twin brother Jacob struggled in their relationship even before they were born. Generations later, their descendants, the Israelites and Edomites, continued their conflict.

Because Edom gloated over the destruction of Israel, God pronounced judgment on them, promising that the same destruction that befell Israel would happen to Edom. Despite its dire warning, Obadiah faithfully and courageously delivered God's harsh message, finally putting an end to their family feud.

COURAGE FOR TODAY

Are you currently at odds with a family member? Are you waiting for the other person to make the first move toward reconciliation? Meditate on the following verses and let them stir your heart toward healing. Then vow today to make a courageous effort to forgive and resolve your differences.

Do all that you can to live in peace with everyone. Dear friends, never take revenge. Leave that to the righteous anger of God. For the Scriptures say, "I will take revenge; I will pay them back," says the LORD.

ROMANS 12:18–19

THE COURAGE TO
Live a Worthy Life

I, a prisoner for serving the Lord, beg you to lead a life worthy of your calling,
for you have been called by God.

EPHESIANS 4:1

Father, this life is filled with temptations and challenges. Help me
persevere, overcome, and behave in ways that are worthy of your calling
on my life.

Do you accept that God's calling requires greater accountability? Be challenged
by the apostle Paul's words in Ephesians chapter 4. Paul reminded the Ephesian
church of the importance of living "a life worthy of your calling" (v. 1). To be
identified as a Christ follower meant—and still means—living for God in both
word and behavior. So Paul urged Ephesian believers to "always be humble and
gentle…[and] patient with each other" (v. 2). And he encouraged them to be
united in God's Spirit so they could live together in peace. For as believers, the
Ephesians were connected in many ways.

Paul expressed his theme of unity by his use of the word *one*: "One body
and one Spirit…one glorious hope…one Lord, one faith, one baptism, one
God and Father of all, who is over all, in all, and living through all" (vv. 4–6). Paul
then listed gifts that Christ had given to believers for the building up of others,
such as prophets, pastors, and teachers. As each person lived and worked out
their gifting, the whole body of believers would be "healthy and growing and
full of love" (v. 16).

COURAGE FOR TODAY

Do you need more courage to live an upright and moral life? Read the
verse below and ask God to give you more courage to make any necessary
life changes today.

"If you are faithful in little things, you will be faithful in large ones. But if you are
dishonest in little things, you won't be honest with greater responsibilities."

LUKE 16:10

THE COURAGE TO
Be Prepared

"On that day I will make Jerusalem an immovable rock. All the nations will gather against it to try to move it, but they will only hurt themselves."

ZECHARIAH 12:1, 3

Father, thank you for sending Jesus to be my Savior. Help me to always be prepared for his triumphant return.

Are you prepared to meet your Savior? Let Zechariah chapters 12–14 encourage you to always be prepared for Christ's return. In approximately 520 BC, God commissioned Zechariah to prophesy to his people who had returned to Jerusalem from their captivity in Babylon. These final three chapters record Zechariah's Messianic prophecies. Seventeen times, Zechariah repeated the phrase "on that day," meaning "one day in the future," in his closing message.

In these chapters, Zechariah's description of Israel's Savior includes a prediction of him being "pierced" by the very people he was sent to save (12:10). Zechariah's prophecy also states that the Messiah would provide cleansing for sin and would "refine them like silver and purify them like gold" (13:9). The prophet's message also indicates that the Messiah would be killed and that his followers would be scattered—all of which precisely took place when Christ was crucified. Zechariah wanted God's people to be prepared for their Savior, and the same holds true for us today regarding his second coming.

COURAGE FOR TODAY

What does it mean to you to be prepared for Christ's return? Meditate on the familiar verse below and describe ways you will courageously be ready today for Jesus' return.

"You also must be ready all the time, for the Son of Man will come when least expected."

MATTHEW 24:44

THE COURAGE TO
Rescue Others

Rescue others by snatching them from the flames of judgment. Show mercy to still others, but do so with great caution, hating the sins that contaminate their lives.

JUDE 1:23

Father, you command me to love and lift others up. Give me wisdom and courage to help those who are sinning to faithfully return to you.

Do you know someone who has fallen into sin? Are you willing to reach out and encourage them to repent? Be motivated by Jude's letter. Jude was a half brother to Jesus. Like his brother James, Jude had initially denied that Jesus was the Messiah (see John 7:5). Yet later, Jude became a confident believer and encouraged others to join him in defending their faith against ungodly teachers.

In his letter to believers, Jude explained that some people were spreading false prophecies and "creating divisions" among Christ followers (Jude 1:19). Therefore, he urged believers to build one another up in their faith, pray in the power of the Holy Spirit, and keep themselves "safe in God's love" (v. 21). While courage and compassion are necessary to witness to unbelievers, caution is also a must to keep Christ followers from falling prey to the sin that contaminates the lives of the lost.

COURAGE FOR TODAY

Are you willing to help rescue a friend or loved one who has fallen into sin? Read the verse below and describe how you will courageously and gently encourage someone to repent and return to God today.

Dear brothers and sisters, if another believer is overcome by some sin, you who are godly should gently and humbly help that person back onto the right path. And be careful not to fall into the same temptation yourself.

GALATIANS 6:1

THE COURAGE TO
Walk Humbly

No, O people, the LORD has told you what is good, and this is what he requires of you: to do what is right, to love mercy, and to walk humbly with your God.

MICAH 6:8

Father, you call me to live in ways that honor and exemplify my relationship with you. Help me be faithful to do right, love mercy, and walk humbly with you.

Do you faithfully fulfill God's everyday calling on your life? Be challenged by God's words in Micah chapter 6. While every believer has a responsibility to use their talents and abilities to serve God and others, there are basic standards of behavior that God calls believers to live by. In this chapter, the prophet Micah began his third message to Israel and presented God's case against his unfaithful people.

First God asked, "What have I done to you...to make you tired of me?" (v. 3). God did everything he could to teach the Israelites about faithfulness; he had delivered them from Egypt, rescued them from slavery, and sent great leaders to guide them. In return, his people had questioned their sacrifices and had been wicked, dishonest, and violent. Therefore, God clarified what he required from them: "To do what is right, to love mercy, and to walk humbly with your God" (v. 8). These same requirements remain for every believer today.

COURAGE FOR TODAY

How important is it to you to remain humble and kind, regardless of your circumstances? Meditate on the following verse and vow today to courageously clothe yourself in the attributes it advocates.

Since God chose you to be the holy people he loves, you must clothe yourselves with tenderhearted mercy, kindness, humility, gentleness, and patience.

COLOSSIANS 3:12

THE COURAGE TO
Take Thoughts Captive

We use God's mighty weapons, not worldly weapons, to knock down the strongholds of human reasoning and to destroy false arguments. We destroy every proud obstacle that keeps people from knowing God. We capture their rebellious thoughts and teach them to obey Christ.

2 CORINTHIANS 10:4–5

Father, my thoughts control my emotions, and my emotions are sometimes out of control. Help me take my thoughts captive so I can replace any that are negative with the truth that comes from you.

Do negative thoughts ever discourage you or keep you from living a godly life? Let the apostle Paul's teaching in 2 Corinthians chapter 10 encourage you to take inventory of your thoughts. In his letter to the church in Corinth, Paul begged believers to "wage war" against all things that interfere with their faith (v. 3). But he also reminded them that they could not win a battle with their minds by employing worldly weapons.

The only way to eliminate emotional strongholds and destroy false beliefs was by taking their thoughts captive. Paul urged the believers to pay close attention to the way they thought and to make their thoughts obey the Lord so that they could overcome any false teaching and maintain a strong faith and godly obedience.

COURAGE FOR TODAY

When your thoughts head down a negative path, are you able to redirect them toward hope and advice from God? Memorize the verse below and decide today that you will fix your thoughts on Jesus, who offers courage, confidence, and guidance for everyday life.

You will keep in perfect peace all who trust in you,
all whose thoughts are fixed on you!

ISAIAH 26:3

THE COURAGE TO
Step Out in Faith

The LORD said to Moses, "Gather before me seventy men who are recognized as elders and leaders of Israel. Bring them to the Tabernacle to stand there with you. I will come down and talk to you there. I will take some of the Spirit that is upon you, and I will put the Spirit upon them also. They will bear the burden of the people along with you, so you will not have to carry it alone."

NUMBERS 11:16–17

Father, I sometimes allow apprehension to keep me from your calling. Give me courage every day to pursue your will for my life.

Rarely does God call the equipped. Most often he equips those he calls. Consider how God empowered the seventy elders in Numbers chapter 11. Throughout the Bible, we meet countless women and men who, without God's presence and power, could not have accomplished the tasks he gave them.

In the first nine verses of Numbers 11, we discover that the Israelites angered God by their selfish and ungrateful attitudes. In verses 10–15, Moses expressed his frustration and asked for God's help. In response, God told Moses to gather seventy elders and leaders for God's Spirit to empower. The remaining verses describe God empowering the leaders, providing meat for the people, and implementing consequences for those who selfishly overindulged. Today, at all times, God's Spirit resides within us who are believers to equip and empower us to accomplish his calling.

COURAGE FOR TODAY

Ask God to reveal his calling on your life. Write it down, confess any hesitancy, and recite the following verse. Commit to overcome your reluctance and list the courageous steps you will take today to accomplish God's will.

I can do everything through Christ, who gives me strength.
PHILIPPIANS 4:13

THE COURAGE TO
Run with Endurance

Since we are surrounded by such a huge crowd of witnesses to the life of faith, let us strip off every weight that slows us down, especially the sin that so easily trips us up. And let us run with endurance the race God has set before us.

HEBREWS 12:1

Father, I long to finish well. Give me more courage and help me remove anything that hinders my ability to achieve your purpose and will for my life.

Are you inundated with distractions, weighed down by problems, or obsessed with possessions and pleasure? Let Hebrews chapter 12 motivate you to set life's temporary satisfactions aside so you can focus on achievements that make an eternal impact. In the previous chapter, the writer of this letter to the Hebrews had listed the names of men and women who could have easily been deterred from their God-given calling. Yet they kept their faith and completed their assignments with great courage.

These faithful believers uncovered the secret to finishing well: to remove the things that would slow them down, "especially the sin that so easily trips us up" (v. 1). By keeping their eyes on Jesus, their faith would be perfected. For Christ was their champion, and his life was their example. A disciplined life reinforces the endurance needed to please God and finish well.

COURAGE FOR TODAY

Do you need more courage to run with endurance as you pursue God's will? Meditate on the verse below and describe how you plan to rely on God's strength today for the ability and courage to finish well.

We also pray that you will be strengthened with all his glorious power so you will have all the endurance and patience you need. May you be filled with joy.

COLOSSIANS 1:11

THE COURAGE TO
Choose Godly Leaders

Whenever the LORD raised up a judge over Israel, he was with that judge and rescued the people from their enemies throughout the judge's lifetime. For the LORD took pity on his people, who were burdened by oppression and suffering.

JUDGES 2:18

Father, leadership is vital within every society, community, and group of people. Yet too often, we take these positions for granted. Help me to always value godly leadership when leading others and when choosing those whom I will follow.

How careful are you when choosing leaders? Reflect on Judges chapter 2 and discover how the people of Israel broke their promises to God once they no longer had an honorable leader to follow. After Joshua and the elders died, the Israelites abandoned God and began worshiping Canaanite idols. Therefore, God allowed them to experience the consequences of their unfaithfulness, including the invasion of enemy nations and defeat in battle.

When Israel became distressed and cried out to God, he compassionately raised up a faithful leader to rescue them. Each time God sent a judge to deliver them, the people of Israel prospered. Yet as soon as each judge died, the Israelites returned to their wicked ways. This pattern became a vicious cycle that chronically repeats itself, even throughout our society today.

COURAGE FOR TODAY

What process do you go through when choosing leaders in your community, state, or nation? Read the verse below and describe your responsibility to carefully choose, honor, and respect your leaders. List ways you can demonstrate more courage when leading others and when choosing the leaders you will follow.

Obey your spiritual leaders, and do what they say. Their work is to watch over your souls, and they are accountable to God. Give them reason to do this with joy and not with sorrow. That would certainly not be for your benefit.

HEBREWS 13:17

THE COURAGE TO
End Division

If people are causing divisions among you, give a first and second warning.
After that, have nothing more to do with them.

TITUS 3:10

Father, I sometimes encounter divisive people who insist that
I adhere to man-made rules and false teaching. Keep me grounded in
your truth and give me the courage to speak lovingly and
truthfully according to your Word.

Do you shy away from confrontation, or do you respectfully address
misunderstandings and errors when they arise? Be challenged by the apostle
Paul's words in Titus chapter 3. Earlier in his letter, Paul had warned Titus to
avoid foolish disputes. There were false teachers who insisted that believers in
Christ, who were justified by grace through faith, must also adhere to Jewish
laws. Paul firmly urged Titus to reject such teachers, for he knew that arguing
with them would be "useless and a waste of time" (v. 9). So he instructed Titus
to warn the misguided leaders twice, then to "have nothing more to do with
them" (v. 10).

Paul confessed that before knowing Christ, he and other believers were
also foolish and disobedient. They had lived lives full of evil, envy, and hatred.
But God, in his grace-filled love, had forgiven their sins and given them a new
life. Now, they were determined to help other believers be unified in God's truth.

COURAGE FOR TODAY

Do you need more courage to help end quarrels or stop divisions? Be
challenged by the verses below and describe how you will compassionately
and courageously confront misunderstandings and disputes today.

Do everything without complaining and arguing, so that no one can criticize you.
Live clean, innocent lives as children of God, shining like bright lights in a world full
of crooked and perverse people.

PHILIPPIANS 2:14–15

THE COURAGE TO
Believe God

Abram believed the Lord, and the Lord counted him as righteous because of his faith.

GENESIS 15:6

Father, I believe in you, and I believe in your Word. Give me a faith that is keenly aware and overpowers any temptation, distraction, or lie.

Are you convinced that God's greatest desire is for his people to believe in him? From the very beginning, God has based humankind's righteousness on faith alone. Consider God's covenant with Abram in Genesis chapter 15. The account of Abraham's life began with the record of his family in Genesis 11. In Genesis chapter 12, God told Abram to leave his father's home and go to an unknown land. Abram believed God and did exactly "as the Lord had instructed" (Genesis 12:4).

After an adventurous and treacherous journey that included a detour both to and from Egypt, Abram and his wife settled in the land of Canaan. Sometime later, God spoke to Abram and promised that he would be the father of many nations through a son that God would give to him and his wife Sarai. Abram "believed the Lord, and the Lord counted him as righteous because of his faith" (15:6).

COURAGE FOR TODAY

Do you accept that, as a believer, you are counted as righteous and that God calls you his friend? Read the familiar passage below and describe how you will courageously protect your faith and honor your relationship with God today.

It happened just as the Scriptures say: "Abraham believed God, and God counted him as righteous because of his faith." He was even called the friend of God. So you see, we are shown to be right with God by what we do, not by faith alone.

JAMES 2:23–24

THE COURAGE TO
Share without Reservation

Living means living for Christ, and dying is even better.
PHILIPPIANS 1:21

Father, I often fear being ridiculed or excluded for sharing my faith. Give me the courage to share without any reservation.

Are you confident when sharing your faith? Or do you fear criticism for your beliefs? Be comforted by the apostle Paul's words in Philippians chapter 1. Paul wrote to the Philippian church from a prison cell, yet his letter conveyed his love, joy, and gratefulness for the members of the church in Philippi. He urged believers to share God's good news no matter the cost. And rather than complaining about his circumstances, Paul celebrated his imprisonment, for it had given him a new audience to witness to.

As a result of his boldness, others were also emboldened to "speak God's message without fear" (v. 14). Paul pointed out that some believers were sharing the gospel with ulterior motives, such as rivalry. Yet, he rejoiced that Christ's message was being preached, regardless of the reason behind it. Because Philippian believers were faithfully praying, Paul was confident he would be set free. But regardless of his circumstances, Paul was never ashamed of his faith. Paul's reason for living was for Christ, and his willingness to die unashamedly was for Christ as well.

COURAGE FOR TODAY

Do you ever hesitate to share your faith because you fear that friends, loved ones, acquaintances, or authority figures may get upset? Meditate on the verses below and rely on your God-given courage to share your faith with confidence today.

When I am afraid, I will put my trust in you. I praise God for what he has promised. I trust in God, so why should I be afraid? What can mere mortals do to me?
PSALM 56:3–4

THE COURAGE TO

Do What God Asks

*The kings joined forces and established their camp around the water near Merom to fight against Israel. Then the L*ORD *said to Joshua, "Do not be afraid of them. By this time tomorrow I will hand all of them over to Israel as dead men. Then you must cripple their horses and burn their chariots."*

JOSHUA 11:5–6

Father, I admit I often try to manage my challenges alone before coming to you for help. Remind me to let go of the need to control my circumstances and to seek your guidance first.

Just as the Israelites needed God's help to prevail in battle, so we, too, need God's help to succeed in life. Take into account Joshua's battles in Joshua chapter 11. A large portion of this book of Scripture is dedicated to relating how God allowed Joshua and the people of Israel to successfully capture each territory within the land of Canaan. Throughout these chapters, we repeatedly discover that "the LORD was with Joshua" and the people of Israel (6:27). God fought their battles and gave them victory. Not only did Joshua listen for God's instructions, but he also obeyed them. Because of Joshua's faithfulness to God, he was successful in every battle he fought.

COURAGE FOR TODAY

Are you currently facing a challenging situation or decision? Have you asked God for help? Read the familiar passage below and write a prayer asking God to guide your steps. Now listen carefully for God to speak to your heart and commit to courageously heed his guidance today.

*Trust in the L*ORD *with all your heart; do not depend on your own understanding. Seek his will in all you do, and he will show you which path to take.*

PROVERBS 3:5–6

THE COURAGE TO

Experience New Life

Put on your new nature, and be renewed as you learn to know your Creator and become like him.

COLOSSIANS 3:10

Father, I desire to become more like you. Help me eliminate the sins that were part of my past life so I can fully experience my new life with you.

Do you believe sinning is a choice or something that simply sneaks into your life? Let the apostle Paul's words in Colossians chapter 3 remind you of your new life in Christ. When the Colossians trusted God for salvation, they were reborn. Therefore, they needed to discard their old habits, such as sexual sins, evil desires, greed, anger, malicious behavior, dirty language, and lying. And Paul urged them instead to put on their new nature since they had been renewed by Christ and were becoming intimately acquainted with Jesus and his ways.

In a loving manner, Paul explained that believers were to display "tenderhearted mercy, kindness, humility, gentleness, and patience" as well as forgiveness. And, "above all," he told them to "clothe yourselves with love, which binds us all together in perfect harmony" (vv. 12–14). By letting peace permeate their lives, they would experience an outpouring of Christ's presence.

COURAGE FOR TODAY

Do you truly desire to be a new person? To be changed by your new life in Christ? Meditate on the verse below and describe how your relationship with Jesus inspires you to experience a new and more courageous life today.

We died and were buried with Christ by baptism. And just as Christ was raised from the dead by the glorious power of the Father, now we also may live new lives.

ROMANS 6:4

THE COURAGE TO
Read God's Word

When I discovered your words, I devoured them. They are my joy and my heart's delight, for I bear your name, O LORD God of Heaven's Armies.

JEREMIAH 15:16

Father, thank you for your Word. Give me a consistent desire to read my Bible for comfort, conviction, and as guide for daily living.

Without truly knowing what the Bible says, many people consider it outdated, hard to understand, and even boring. But nothing could be further from the truth. Consider Jeremiah chapter 15 and how the great prophet dealt with the people's rejection of God's Word.

In desperation, Jeremiah pleaded his case before the Lord. He reminded God that he'd been faithful to his calling, yet he had endured rejection and alienation for doing so. Jeremiah also affirmed that when he found God's words, he devoured them and called them "my joy and my heart's delight" (v. 16). He didn't take God's words for granted or neglect them. So in response to Jeremiah's loyalty, God assured him that he would rescue, protect, strengthen, and restore the devoted prophet so he could continue to be a faithful spokesman.

COURAGE FOR TODAY

Are you sometimes too busy to read, study, and apply Scripture to your life? Do you genuinely believe the Bible is the most valuable resource you own? Read the verse below and let God's words give you the courage to meet today's challenges with clarity and great confidence.

The word of God is alive and powerful. It is sharper than the sharpest two-edged sword, cutting between soul and spirit, between joint and marrow. It exposes our innermost thoughts and desires.

HEBREWS 4:12

THE COURAGE TO

Abide in God's Joy

"I am coming to you. I told them many things while I was with them in this world so they would be filled with my joy."

JOHN 17:13

Father, I want to be filled with your joy at all times. Help me remain positive, cheerful, and full of hope even when my circumstances don't justify it.

Does God's joy prevail in your life even when you are experiencing hurt, loss, or hardship? Let Jesus' message in John chapter 17 motivate you to delight in his presence and promises at all times. Just before he prayed his final prayer, Jesus encouraged his disciples to have peace in him. Although his followers would grieve when he was arrested, convicted, and crucified, Jesus assured them that God would answer their prayer requests, meet their needs, and give them joy. He also promised that the Holy Spirit would strengthen them, lead them, and help them hold on to God's truth.

During his prayer, before going to accept his cross on Calvary, Jesus declared that the many things he had told his followers were to prepare them to be filled with his joy. For he had given believers God's Word, and very soon, he would give himself as a sacrifice for their salvation.

COURAGE FOR TODAY

List the ways God's joy is currently manifested in your life. Then meditate on King David's conviction below and vow today to let God's presence and promises empower you to courageously abide in his joy.

You will show me the way of life, granting me the joy of your presence and the pleasures of living with you forever.

PSALM 16:11

THE COURAGE TO
Pray for Deliverance

Jonah prayed to the LORD his God from inside the fish. He said, "I cried out to the LORD in my great trouble, and he answered me. I called to you from the land of the dead, and LORD, you heard me!"

JONAH 2:1–2

Father, I sometimes rebel and stray from you. Help me realize my need for forgiveness and give me the courage to believe you still love me and desire my presence.

When you find yourself trapped in sin, are you reluctant to cry out to God? Or are you unsure if forgiveness is even still possible? Consider how God's prophet responded to his entrapment in Jonah chapter 2.

After being swallowed by a great fish, Jonah cried out to God for help. When he realized his life was at stake, he remembered the Lord, and God rescued him. Jonah longed to offer a sacrifice to God from the belly of the fish, but the only offering he had was a broken and remorseful heart. After realizing God had spared his life despite his disobedience, Jonah praised the Lord and promised to fulfill his vows, acknowledging that "salvation comes from the LORD alone" (v. 9).

COURAGE FOR TODAY

Have you ever doubted God's willingness to forgive you? Read the psalm below, written by King David when he was in great distress. Just as Jonah sought God in prayer, commit to fall at God's feet today and courageously ask him for forgiveness and redirection.

In my distress I cried out to the LORD; yes, I prayed to my God for help. He heard me from his sanctuary; my cry to him reached his ears.

PSALM 18:6

THE COURAGE TO
Stop Fearing People

"But Lord," exclaimed Ananias, "I've heard many people talk about the terrible things this man has done to the believers in Jerusalem! And he is authorized by the leading priests to arrest everyone who calls upon your name."

ACTS 9:13–14

Father, you command me to revere you and not be afraid of other people. Help me to trust you more and to fear people less.

Do you shy away from certain people? Has society's opinion caused you to avoid particular groups or individuals? Be inspired by the courageous faith of a new believer named Ananias in Acts chapter 9. After Jesus' death and resurrection, fear, hatred, and prejudice were commonplace. One of the leading Christian persecutors was a man named Saul. Like a terrorist, Saul sought to rid the world of all Christians. But God had other plans for this oppressor.

After Saul's miraculous conversion in Acts 9, the Lord asked Ananias to find his new convert and "[lay] hands on him so he can see again" (v. 12). But Saul's reputation as a murderer frightened Ananias, and he urged God to reconsider. Instead, God told him to go to Saul anyway. So in obedience and with great courage, Ananias set aside his fear, went to Saul, and did as God requested.

COURAGE FOR TODAY

Has God given you an assignment you are hesitant to take on? Are you willing to let go of fear and embrace the courage God will give you? Memorize the verse below and take steps today to courageously pursue God's calling.

Fearing people is a dangerous trap, but trusting the LORD means safety.

PROVERBS 29:25

THE COURAGE TO
Love Your Enemies

David and his men tore their clothes in sorrow when they heard the news.
2 SAMUEL 1:11

Father, I find it hard sometimes to let go of bitterness and unforgiveness toward those who have hurt me. Help me see the brokenness within the people who have mistreated me and soften my heart so I can have compassion for them when they, too, are struggling.

It can be difficult to have sympathy for someone who has hurt us. Could you ever have compassion for an enemy who is suffering? Or would you be more likely to celebrate their misfortune? Consider 2 Samuel chapter 1 and note how David responded when he heard of King Saul's demise.

In the book of 1 Samuel, we learn about the rise and fall of Israel's first king, Saul, and his relationship with God's chosen replacement for him, David. Although Saul was insanely jealous of David, pursued him relentlessly, and tried countless times to kill him, David still mourned Saul's death and honored him by composing a song that paid homage to his life.

COURAGE FOR TODAY

Are you willing to truly love your enemies? Read the passage below and write a commitment to God promising to courageously view others through his eyes of compassion today, including those who have hurt you.

"To you who are willing to listen, I say, love your enemies! Do good to those who hate you. Bless those who curse you. Pray for those who hurt you...Give to anyone who asks; and when things are taken away from you, don't try to get them back. Do to others as you would like them to do to you."
LUKE 6:27–28, 30–31

THE COURAGE TO

Be Fully Alive

"Write this letter to the angel of the church in Sardis. This is the message from the one who has the sevenfold Spirit of God and the seven stars: 'I know all the things you do, and that you have a reputation for being alive—but you are dead.'"

REVELATION 3:1

Father, sometimes in life I feel like my relationship with you is strong, and other times, I sense my commitment to you needs improvement. Give me wisdom and understanding to know when I need to strengthen my faith so I can be fully alive in my love and devotion to you.

Is your love for the Lord truly alive? Be motivated by Jesus' critique of the church at Sardis in Revelation chapter 3. While he praised some believers for their dedication to the Lord, Jesus found the majority of Sardis' congregation unworthy.

Although they had fooled others into believing their faith in God was alive, it was actually dead. If they didn't wake up, repent, and return to the zeal and commitment to God that they had when they first believed, they would be left behind. The ones who remained faithful, along with those who turned away from evil and rededicated their lives to the Lord, would be victorious, clothed in white, and presented before the Almighty as Jesus' personal possessions.

COURAGE FOR TODAY

Explain how your life gives evidence of your love and devotion to God. Then memorize the verse below and describe how you will make courageous changes, beginning today, to become more fully alive in your relationship with the Lord.

If we live, it's to honor the Lord. And if we die, it's to honor the Lord. So whether we live or die, we belong to the Lord.

ROMANS 14:8

THE COURAGE TO
Do Good

"Learn to do good. Seek justice. Help the oppressed.
Defend the cause of orphans. Fight for the rights of widows."

ISAIAH 1:17

Father, it's easy to get caught up in work, distractions, errands, and my own needs. Help me set aside time in my day to pray and genuinely care for the needs of others.

How often do you concern yourself with the needs of others? Let God's message in Isaiah chapter 1 motivate you to think of ways you can help those who are disadvantaged. Isaiah was an educated poet and prophet who received challenging messages from God and delivered them to the people living in the Southern Kingdom of Israel. In this first chapter of his prophecies, God gives the great prophet a vision of the corrupt condition of Judah and its capital city, Jerusalem.

After explaining how the people had turned away from true worship and were offering God only insincere religious practices, the Lord urged the Israelites to repent. If they would rid themselves of wicked behaviors, "learn to do good [and] seek justice" (v. 17), God would forgive their sins and tend to their needs.

COURAGE FOR TODAY

Are you so wrapped up in your own world that you rarely consider the anxiety and hardship of others? Meditate on the verse below and name at least one person you know who is in need. How will you courageously alter your schedule today so you can do good and care for them?

Don't look out only for your own interests,
but take an interest in others, too.

PHILIPPIANS 2:4

THE COURAGE TO
Accept God's Purposes

We know that God causes everything to work together for the good of those who love God and are called according to his purpose for them.

ROMANS 8:28

Father, you always know best, and even when bad things happen, you can make something good come from them. Help me accept your purpose in allowing misfortune or suffering to take place, and give me great faith that trusts you completely even when I don't understand.

Do you accept that God knows and controls everything? Allow the apostle Paul's teaching in Romans chapter 8 to strengthen your ability to persevere when life gets difficult. Paul knew what it was like to suffer and yet to trust God in every circumstance. After he surrendered his life to Jesus, Paul was rejected by the religious elite, who were his former friends and colleagues. And he was threatened, beaten, regularly imprisoned for sharing his faith, and even abandoned by ministry friends and partners near the end of his life.

Therefore, when he spoke about trusting God to make something good come out of something bad, he spoke from personal experiences to affirm this truth. Paul encouraged Christ followers by assuring them that the Holy Spirit gives strength in times of weakness and even pleads with God on their behalf when they are too distressed to pray.

COURAGE FOR TODAY

Do you truly trust God with your life, your family, and your future? Meditate on the following verse, name the people and circumstances that concern you, then courageously rely on God for hope, help, and guidance today.

I look up to the mountains—does my help come from there?
My help comes from the LORD,
who made heaven and earth!

PSALM 121:1–2

THE COURAGE TO
Be Different

Hezekiah trusted in the LORD, the God of Israel.
There was no one like him among all the kings of Judah,
either before or after his time.

2 KINGS 18:5

Father, I sometimes face pressure to follow the crowd, and I am rejected when I choose not to do so. Give me courage to be noticeably different so I can honor you in everything I do.

Are you willing to be different? Or do you follow the crowd? Consider 2 Kings chapters 18 and 19, in which King Hezekiah chose to honor God despite his predecessors' dreadful legacies. The books of 1 and 2 Kings record the history of the rulers of Israel. In 931 BC, God divided Israel into two kingdoms, the Northern Kingdom (Israel) and Southern Kingdom (Judah). Every king of the Northern Kingdom chose evil over good.

Of the eleven kings of the Southern Kingdom, leading up to King Hezekiah, six chose obedience to God while the rest were ungodly. King Ahaz of Judah chose to disobey God. But in contrast, his son Hezekiah pursued faithfulness. In 2 Kings 18:1–7, we learn that King Hezekiah "trusted in the LORD…and he carefully obeyed all the commands the LORD had given Moses" (vv. 5–6). The book of 2 Kings remarks that "There was no one like him among all the kings of Judah" (v. 5), and God rewarded his faithfulness.

COURAGE FOR TODAY

Are you willing to be different? Read the verses below and describe your commitment to courageously stand out in a crowd by choosing godly speech and behavior today.

Get rid of anger, rage, malicious behavior, slander, and dirty language…
Put on your new nature, and be renewed as you learn to know your Creator
and become like him.

COLOSSIANS 3:8, 10

THE COURAGE TO
Examine Your Heart

"You brood of snakes! How could evil men like you speak what is good and right? For whatever is in your heart determines what you say. A good person produces good things from the treasury of a good heart, and an evil person produces evil things from the treasury of an evil heart."

MATTHEW 12:34–35

Father, you aren't concerned with outward appearances. Instead, you examine our hearts. Help me keep a close eye on the condition of my heart and give me the wisdom and courage to correct any areas that aren't pleasing to you.

Have you done a thorough examination of your heart lately? Let Jesus' words in Matthew chapter 12 inspire you to question your motives, opinions, and ways of thinking today. As Jesus and his disciples were gathering food on the Sabbath, religious leaders were criticizing them for breaking the law. So Jesus challenged the Pharisees' beliefs with truth from God's Word.

When Jesus entered their synagogue and healed a man's hand, the religious leaders condemned him again for working on God's holy day. Once more, Jesus disputed their way of thinking, saying, "Yes, the law permits a person to do good on the Sabbath" (v. 12). Yet instead of considering Christ's perspective, they refused to examine their hearts and instead plotted to kill him.

COURAGE FOR TODAY

How often do you examine your heart? Meditate on the verse below and vow to courageously guard your heart from stubbornness and pride today.

The LORD said to Samuel, "Don't judge by his appearance or height, for I have rejected him. The LORD doesn't see things the way you see them. People judge by outward appearance, but the LORD looks at the heart."

1 SAMUEL 16:7

THE COURAGE TO
Honor Your Body

"I will live among the people of Israel and be their God, and they will know that I am the Lord their God. I am the one who brought them out of the land of Egypt so that I could live among them. I am the Lord their God."

Exodus 29:45–46

Father, your presence brings me courage, comfort, and joy. I am eternally grateful that you made a way for me to be in your holy presence forever.

Do you sense God's presence? From the moment he created humankind, God has desired a close and personal relationship with us. But Adam and Eve's sin restricted our ability to be in God's presence for a period of time. Note how, in Exodus chapters 25–29, God once again made a way to be in the presence of his people. These chapters record God's instructions for the Israelites to prepare a physical dwelling place for him that would allow him to once again live among his people.

The tabernacle provided a process by which God's people could be made right with God temporarily through a sacrificial system. Today, because God made a way through Jesus Christ, we have the privilege, through salvation and the Holy Spirit, to personally be in God's presence every single day.

COURAGE FOR TODAY

Do you honor your body as God's temple? Read the following passage. Considering God's perfect sacrifice and presence in your life, what courageous changes will you commit to making today?

Don't you realize that your body is the temple of the Holy Spirit, who lives in you and was given to you by God? You do not belong to yourself, for God bought you with a high price. So you must honor God with your body.

1 Corinthians 6:19–20

THE COURAGE TO
Call on God

Jesus was sleeping at the back of the boat with his head on a cushion.
The disciples woke him up, shouting,
"Teacher, don't you care that we're going to drown?"

MARK 4:38

Father, life is filled with ups and downs. Help me remember that you are present and ready in every circumstance and that you desire to comfort me when I call.

When you experience difficult times, do you fixate on your problems or call on God for help? Consider the disciples predicament recorded in Mark chapter 4. After teaching his followers about the importance of letting their faith shine and planting seeds of faith, Jesus got on a boat with his disciples and headed across the Sea of Galilee. When a fierce storm arose that threatened to break apart their boat, the disciples called on Jesus.

The storm didn't wake their Savior, but the disciples did, and when Jesus rebuked the winds and ordered the waves to be silent, immediately the storm stopped. However, then his disciples were terrified of him. God doesn't promise to always remove our storms, but he does promise to hold our hand as we walk through them. Therefore, we should always call on God and praise him in the storm.

COURAGE FOR TODAY

Do you let fear, doubt, and worry take over in troubling times? Let the verse below inspire you to set aside your concerns and courageously call on Jesus for hope and help today.

The LORD hears his people when they call to him for help.
He rescues them from all their troubles.

PSALM 34:17

THE COURAGE TO
Embrace the Seasons

For everything there is a season,
a time for every activity under heaven.
ECCLESIASTES 3:1

Father, in life, we experience times of prosperity and seasons of loss. Give me the courage to persevere and help me remember that you walk with me no matter what season I am in.

Are you currently in a season of confidence and success or a time of trials and discouragement? Meditate on King Solomon's words in Ecclesiastes chapter 3 and consider how your current circumstances can prepare you for your next season. In the first eight verses of this chapter, Solomon reminds us that throughout our lives we will experience both good times and bad. From new beginnings to times for hard work, from periods of progress to interims of hardship.

Yet through it all, God's presence and power remain reliable and consistent. Therefore, Solomon concludes that while every season in life has its issues, the way we handle each occasion determines how we will enter the next one. So we should make the most of every circumstance, seek joy in all seasons, and trust in the Lord because life on earth is brief and eternity is our greatest reward.

COURAGE FOR TODAY

What season of life are you currently in? Read Jesus' words of encouragement below, ask God for wisdom and divine direction, and make a courageous commitment today to embrace your current season, pursue God's will, and always walk in Christ's light.

Jesus spoke to the people once more and said, "I am the light of the world.
If you follow me, you won't have to walk in darkness,
because you will have the light that leads to life."
JOHN 8:12

THE COURAGE TO
Stand Out

Of course, your former friends are surprised when you no longer plunge into the flood of wild and destructive things they do. So they slander you. But remember that they will have to face God, who stands ready to judge everyone, both the living and the dead.

1 PETER 4:4–5

Father, there are times when I hesitate to stand out in a crowd. Give me courage and confidence to be in this world but not of it.

What is more important to you, your faith or your friends? Consider 1 Peter chapter 4. A primary theme throughout the book of 1 Peter is suffering. Peter's letter not only affirms the certainty of adversity here on earth, but it also challenges believers to stand out among the crowd, to be different, distinct, and unique.

In the first six verses of this chapter, Peter urged Christ followers to leave their old ways behind and live for God. While verses 7 through 11 outline ways in which believers can live for the Lord, the rest of the chapter makes it clear that Christians are to expect pushback for choosing a godly life. When followers of Jesus suffer, they are "partners with Christ in his suffering" (v. 13). Therefore, Peter urged believers to choose wisely in the midst of pain, stand firm in the midst of rejection, and always persevere when their faith is challenged.

COURAGE FOR TODAY

Describe how your faith factors into your everyday life. Are there changes God is calling you to make? Read the following verses and explain the steps you will take today to courageously stand out as a believer.

Do everything without complaining and arguing, so that no one can criticize you. Live clean, innocent lives as children of God, shining like bright lights in a world full of crooked and perverse people.

PHILIPPIANS 2:14–15

THE COURAGE TO
Watch Your Words

A gentle answer deflects anger, but harsh words make tempers flare.
The tongue of the wise makes knowledge appealing,
but the mouth of a fool belches out foolishness.

PROVERBS 15:1–2

Father, you have taught me that what I say can build people up or tear them down. Help me choose my words carefully so I can honor you in everything I say.

How good are you at controlling your tongue? Be challenged by King Solomon's words in Proverbs chapter 15. Solomon begins his teaching by reminding us that God "is watching everywhere, keeping his eye on both the evil and the good" (v. 3). Our heavenly Father is fully aware of our kindness and our cruelty.

Throughout this chapter Solomon points out the positive influence kind conversations create as well as the negative effects hateful dialogue can have. While gentle words curtail anger, promote peace, delight God, and lead to life, harsh words dampen one's spirit, inspire foolishness, start fights, and bring about judgment and consequences. As God's children, we represent him to the world; therefore, we should always be quick to hear and careful when we speak.

COURAGE FOR TODAY

Have you recently been the recipient of someone's hurtful words? Or have you been the one making unkind remarks? Meditate on the verse below and vow today to courageously set aside any cruel comments from others and commit to carefully choosing your words before you speak or respond.

Don't use foul or abusive language. Let everything you say be good and helpful,
so that your words will be an encouragement to those who hear them.

EPHESIANS 4:29

THE COURAGE TO

Follow Jesus' Example

"Since I, your Lord and Teacher, have washed your feet, you ought to wash each other's feet. I have given you an example to follow. Do as I have done to you."

JOHN 13:14–15

Father, you love unconditionally, forgive continuously, and offer endless blessings to those who believe in and follow you. Help me love, forgive, and care for others like you do.

Do you follow Jesus' example by loving and treating others well? Be inspired by Jesus' lesson in John chapter 13. After gathering with his disciples to celebrate his last Passover meal, Jesus clothed himself like a servant and began washing his disciples' feet. When he came to Simon Peter, his friend and follower protested, "'You will never ever wash my feet!' Jesus replied, 'Unless I wash you, you won't belong to me'" (v. 8).

After he finished cleaning their feet, Jesus explained to his disciples what he had done. Jesus' cleansing not only represented washing one's sins away, but it also demonstrated an act of a true godly leader, one who humbles himself and serves others well. To further encourage his disciples to humbly care for others, Jesus assured them that "God will bless you" for doing so (v. 17).

COURAGE FOR TODAY

Explain the ways you love, forgive, and care for others like Jesus does. Then meditate on the verses below and describe how you will be more courageous in following Jesus' example today.

God called you to do good, even if it means suffering, just as Christ suffered for you. He is your example, and you must follow in his steps...He did not retaliate when he was insulted, nor threaten revenge when he suffered. He left his case in the hands of God, who always judges fairly.

1 PETER 2:21, 23

THE COURAGE TO
Give God Your Concerns

The LORD said to Elijah, "Go to the east and hide by Kerith Brook, near where it enters the Jordan River. Drink from the brook and eat what the ravens bring you, for I have commanded them to bring you food."

1 KINGS 17:2–4

Father, during seasons of difficulty I am tempted to worry and embrace doubt. At times like these, give me the desire to draw closer to you and the courage to entrust you with my problems.

Have you ever experienced a wilderness season? Are you in one now? Consider 1 Kings chapter 17. In Elijah's early life, God prepared him for his future by allowing him to go through a challenging season. In the first verse of chapter 17, we meet Elijah who was sent by God to warn King Ahab of a coming drought. The remaining twenty-three verses describe how God sent Elijah into the wilderness and cared for him as he prepared him for his future calling.

When God sent him to live off the land, Elijah obeyed and trusted God for all his needs. Every difficulty Elijah's faced allowed God to demonstrate his power as he miraculously cared for every need of his faithful servant.

COURAGE FOR TODAY

How do you respond to challenging seasons? Do you trust God to prepare and care for you? Read the verses below and list your current concerns. Make a commitment today to courageously lay your worries at the feet of Jesus where his peace, comfort, and promises will always see you through.

"Seek the Kingdom of God above all else, and live righteously, and he will give you everything you need. So don't worry about tomorrow, for tomorrow will bring its own worries. Today's trouble is enough for today."

MATTHEW 6:33–34

THE COURAGE TO
Choose God's Wisdom

When we tell you these things, we do not use words that come from human wisdom. Instead, we speak words given to us by the Spirit, using the Spirit's words to explain spiritual truths.

1 CORINTHIANS 2:13

Father, you are the giver of knowledge and understanding. Remind me to value and seek your wisdom over worldly guidance and inspire me to consistently share my knowledge of you and your truth with others.

Do you value godly advice over worldly opinions or knowledge? Let the apostle Paul's message in 1 Corinthians chapter 2 inspire you to choose God's wisdom today. Even though Paul had been well educated in Jewish laws and had been a student of a great rabbi named Gamaliel, he considered no education more important than the knowledge of Jesus Christ. For he knew that being wise according to the world was of no value without knowing how to receive eternal life.

Instead of honoring worldly wisdom, God chose what some consider to be foolish, weak, and despised to bewilder those who think they are wise. "As a result, no one can ever boast in the presence of God" about saving themselves (1 Corinthians 1:29). Therefore, when believers need true wisdom and guidance, they must seek it from God, who will provide it through his Holy Spirit.

COURAGE FOR TODAY

When you need guidance, where do you turn? Let King Solomon's wise saying below challenge you to seek knowledge and understanding from God today so you he can guide you to courageously and faithfully walk in honesty and integrity.

The LORD grants wisdom! From his mouth come knowledge and understanding.
He grants a treasure of common sense to the honest.
He is a shield to those who walk with integrity.

PROVERBS 2:6–7

THE COURAGE TO
Worship God

Let the godly sing for joy to the LORD; it is fitting for the pure to praise him. Praise the LORD with melodies on the lyre; make music for him on the ten-stringed harp. Sing a new song of praise to him; play skillfully on the harp, and sing with joy. For the word of the LORD holds true, and we can trust everything he does.

PSALM 33:1–4

Father, you are worthy of my worship. Give me a joyful heart that desires to worship you and a courageous spirit that longs to honor you.

How often do you privately and publicly worship God? Be motivated by the words of the author of Psalm 33. In this psalm, God's followers worship him in song and with musical instruments. God is worthy of worship because of his character, he is to be honored for his creative power, and his authority over nations and people warrants adoration and respect.

God fashioned the earth, understands those he created, knows and sees all things, and protects and provides due to his infinite loving-kindness. Therefore, let your confidence, faith, and hope be in almighty God who is worthy to be worshiped.

COURAGE FOR TODAY

Do you worship success, prosperity, or possessions over God? Meditate on the following conversation between Jesus and Satan and commit today to courageously deny the temptation to worship anything other than God.

"I will give you the glory of these kingdoms and authority over them," the devil said, "because they are mine to give to anyone I please. I will give it all to you if you will worship me." Jesus replied, "The Scriptures say, 'You must worship the LORD your God and serve only him.'"

LUKE 4:6–8

THE COURAGE TO
Testify

*The woman left her water jar beside the well and ran back to the village,
telling everyone, "Come and see a man who told me everything I ever did!
Could he possibly be the Messiah?"*

JOHN 4:28–29

Father, sharing my testimony with others can sometimes be difficult. Give
me the courage to speak of the marvelous work you've done in my life so
that I may encourage others to draw closer to you.

Are you willing to share the truth about your past with others to draw them
closer to Christ? While tell-all talk shows draw viewers and increase ratings,
Christ gets all the glory when someone shares a transformational testimony.
Consider the story of the Samaritan woman at the well in John chapter 4. The
woman from Samaria had experienced one failed relationship after another.
So at the time Jesus came to her, she was living in adultery. As her Savior spoke
with her, he relayed events in her life that a stranger would not have known.

Once the woman realized who Jesus was, her life was changed by her
belief. One minute she was fetching water at a time when no one would be
around to cast condemning glances. Then shortly after, she courageously ran
back to town, "telling everyone, 'Come and see a man who told me everything
I ever did! Could he possibly be the Messiah?'" (vv. 28–29). Because of her
courageous testimony, others followed her to meet Jesus, and many were
saved. One dramatically changed life changed the lives of many others.

COURAGE FOR TODAY

Are you hesitant to share your testimony with others? Draw strength
from the verse below and decide how you will courageously share your
testimony today.

Never be ashamed to tell others about our Lord.

2 TIMOTHY 1:8

THE COURAGE TO
Give God Credit

"Praise the name of God forever and ever, for he has all wisdom and power.
He controls the course of world events; he removes kings and sets up other kings.
He gives wisdom to the wise and knowledge to the scholars."

DANIEL 2:20–21

Father, you are Creator of all and the giver of everything good. Give me a heart that longs to acknowledge you for everything I have.

Do you thank God for your many blessings and abilities? Let Daniel chapter 2 inspire you to give God credit. Daniel was taken into captivity in 605 BC. Blessed by God with great favor, knowledge, and intelligence, he was quickly trained and installed into the Babylonian king's personal service. In the second year of Nebuchadnezzar's reign, the king had a disturbing dream, and he demanded that his sorcerers and enchanters interpret for him. But none of his astrologers could fulfill his demand. Furious over their failure, Nebuchadnezzar ordered all wise men in the country to be executed, including Daniel.

But when Daniel learned of the king's decree, he went to see the king and requested more time to understand the dream. After Daniel gathered his friends and bowed before the Lord, God answered Daniel's prayer and revealed the meaning of the king's dream to him. So Daniel quickly presented himself to the king. Yet when the king asked Daniel if he understood the meaning of the dream, Daniel quickly gave God all the credit.

COURAGE FOR TODAY

Do you give God credit for your possessions, resources, opportunities, and hope? Read the verse below and vow today to courageously acknowledge God for all you have.

You must worship Christ as Lord of your life.
And if someone asks about your hope as a believer,
always be ready to explain it.

1 PETER 3:15

THE COURAGE TO
Give Another Chance

"We had to celebrate this happy day.
For your brother was dead and has come back to life!
He was lost, but now he is found!"

LUKE 15:32

Father, thank you for being a God of second chances. Help me offer forgiveness to everyone, set boundaries when necessary, and give second chances to those who genuinely seek them.

Do you need a second chance? Or do you know someone who does? Consider the parable of the lost son in Luke chapter 15. As Jesus spoke to the crowds about God's passion for lost sinners, he told several parables to illustrate God's mercy. After teaching about the recovery of a shepherd's lost sheep and a woman's missing coin, Jesus told a story about a lost son.

A man with two sons gave them both their inheritance. While the older son remained faithful and hardworking, the younger son moved away and "wasted all his money in wild living" (v. 13). When the younger son came to his senses, he headed home to confess his sins to his father and ask to become a hired servant. But when his father saw the boy coming, he immediately rejoiced, ordered his servants to bring fine clothes for his son, and planned a party. When the older son got upset out of jealousy, his father explained why he had given his brother a second chance: "He was lost, but now he is found!" (v. 32).

COURAGE FOR TODAY

How often do you give and seek second chances? Meditate on the following verse and courageously offer forgiveness unconditionally and second chances to those who are genuinely seeking them today.

Peter came to him and asked, "Lord, how often should I forgive someone
who sins against me? Seven times?" "No, not seven times," Jesus replied,
"but seventy times seven!"

MATTHEW 18:21–22

THE COURAGE TO
Resist Peer Pressure

The LORD has given me a strong warning not to think like everyone else does.
ISAIAH 8:11

Father, every day I am inundated with opportunities to adopt humanity's perspective and engage in worldly behaviors. Give me the desire and courage to resist society's influence.

Do you have the willpower to withstand the temptation to follow the crowd? Let God's words in Isaiah chapter 8 inspire you to be unique. The first six chapters of the book of Isaiah pronounce God's judgment against his people for their unfaithfulness. Chapters 7 through 12 remind the Israelites that God is faithful and would stand by them if they only repented and turned back to him.

In chapter 8, God asked the great prophet Isaiah to deliver his message of judgment not only in words but also by example. So he told Isaiah to have a child and name him *Maher-shalal-hash-baz*, meaning swift to plunder and quick to carry away (v. 3). Further in this passage, God reminded the people that he will fight their battles for them. Then he commanded Isaiah "not to think like everyone else does" (v. 11). For it is God and his teachings that they should respect, honor, obey, and turn to for help.

COURAGE FOR TODAY

Are you able to resist peer pressure from non-believers? Are you willing to stand out in a crowd? Meditate on the verse below and vow today to pursue God's will above all other opportunities.

Oh, the joys of those who do not follow the advice of the wicked, or stand around with sinners, or join in with mockers. But they delight in the law of the LORD, meditating on it day and night.
PSALM 1:1–2

THE COURAGE TO
Examine Your Life

Examine yourselves to see if your faith is genuine. Test yourselves. Surely you know that Jesus Christ is among you; if not, you have failed the test of genuine faith.

2 CORINTHIANS 13:5

Father, give me the courage to look within and examine my life. Help me realize the changes I need to make and give me the ability to begin making them today.

How often do you examine your life? Are you more apt to scrutinize the lives of others while making excuses for yourself? Ponder the apostle Paul's words in 2 Corinthians chapter 13. Paul wanted the believers in Corinth to know God and to walk with him in a more mature faith. He wanted them to test their faith so they could determine if it was truly genuine. Paul had previously warned the Corinthians by pointing out their inappropriate behaviors. Now he urged them to walk in truth by examining their ways.

Paul planned to visit the Corinthian church, and he prayed the members would receive his correction. Instead of dealing with them harshly, Paul longed to use the authority of the Lord to lovingly strengthen them. As Paul concluded his letter, he encouraged believers to be joyful, to grow mature in their faith, to support each other, and to live in harmony and peace.

COURAGE FOR TODAY

Are you willing to regularly examine your life? Read the verses below and ask God to reveal any changes you need to make to your circumstances, behaviors, attitudes, or relationships. Describe the courageous changes you will begin making today.

Why should we, mere humans, complain when we are punished for our sins? Instead, let us test and examine our ways. Let us turn back to the LORD.

LAMENTATIONS 3:39–40

THE COURAGE TO
Remember God's Faithfulness

"You saw the misery of our ancestors in Egypt, and you heard their cries from beside the Red Sea. You displayed miraculous signs and wonders against Pharaoh, his officials, and all his people, for you knew how arrogantly they were treating our ancestors. You have a glorious reputation that has never been forgotten."

NEHEMIAH 9:9–10

Father, you are trustworthy and true even when I fail you. Thank you for your unending love and presence in my life. Help me to always remember and celebrate your faithfulness.

Is God's ongoing faithfulness a source of courage and confidence in your life? How often do you intentionally recall the many things God has done for you? Consider the prayer recorded in Nehemiah chapter 9. Having been moved by God's Word, the people of Judah had celebrated God and his faithfulness. Then they gathered again in a spirit of repentance to confess their sins and remember God's faithfulness.

The prayer recorded in Nehemiah chapter 9 details how God established, saved, forgave, and provided for the people of Israel throughout a troubled history that vacillated between faithfulness, infidelity, captivity, and salvation. As the people recalled God's presence, provision, and unconditional love, they were motivated to take an oath to faithfully abide by God's commands.

COURAGE FOR TODAY

Do you regularly reflect on the goodness of God? Meditate on the verse below and praise God today for his unconditional love and faithfulness. Describe ways you will courageously celebrate him today.

Let all that I am praise the LORD; with my whole heart, I will praise his holy name. Let all that I am praise the LORD; may I never forget the good things he does for me.

PSALM 103:1–2

THE COURAGE TO

Compliment Others

I commend to you our sister Phoebe, who is a deacon in the church in Cenchrea.
Welcome her in the Lord as one who is worthy of honor among God's people. Help
her in whatever she needs, for she has been helpful to many, and especially to me.

ROMANS 16:1–2

Father, you encourage me to encourage others. Remind me to give credit
where credit is due, to cheer others on, and to compliment those who put
forth great effort.

Are you quick to commend others for a job well done? Consider how the
apostle Paul bragged on his coworkers in Romans chapter 4. Paul had a
monumental task of ministering to many churches. Often when he was unable
to visit believers in person, he engaged helpers to carry his messages and
minister to church members.

Rather than highlighting the great work he was doing for the Lord, Paul
regularly concluded his letters by complimenting the many men and women
who had helped him. He described these women and men as leaders and
coworkers who labored alongside him and who were also often persecuted as a
result. Paul routinely recognized and complimented those who served with him
and wanted others to assist them, imitate them, and delight in them as well.

COURAGE FOR TODAY

How often do you compliment others? Let the passage below inspire
you to find courageous ways you can encourage and build up those with
whom you come in contact today.

Encourage each other and build each other up, just as you are already doing.
Dear brothers and sisters, honor those who are your leaders in the Lord's work.
They work hard among you and give you spiritual guidance.

1 THESSALONIANS 5:11–12

THE COURAGE TO
Lead Others to God

Jehoshaphat lived in Jerusalem, but he went out among the people, traveling from Beersheba to the hill country of Ephraim, encouraging the people to return to the LORD, the God of their ancestors.

2 CHRONICLES 19:4

Father, as a believer, I am your disciple. Give me courage and confidence every day to share my love for you with others and help me lead the people around me toward a more personal relationship with you.

In what ways do you lead others toward a closer relationship with God? Be inspired by King Jehoshaphat's intentional efforts to compel the people of Judah to draw closer to God in 2 Chronicles chapter 19. King Jehoshaphat was a godly king in the Southern Kingdom, Judah. He honored, respected, and followed God's commands.

However, in chapter 19, a prophet of God scolded Jehoshaphat for aligning himself with King Ahab, the wicked king of Israel. As the prophet continued, he acknowledged that Jehoshaphat had good in him and that he was faithful in seeking the Lord. In the remaining verses of this chapter, King Jehoshaphat appointed leaders and established guidelines to intentionally lead the people of Judah back to God.

COURAGE FOR TODAY

Do you intentionally lead others to God? Read the following command and describe the courageous changes you will make to share your faith with others more often. How will you courageously share God with someone today?

Preach the word of God. Be prepared, whether the time is favorable or not. Patiently correct, rebuke, and encourage your people with good teaching.

2 TIMOTHY 4:2

THE COURAGE TO
Pray for All People

I urge you, first of all, to pray for all people.
Ask God to help them; intercede on their behalf,
and give thanks for them.

1 TIMOTHY 2:1

Father, prayer is a vital component of my relationship with you. Remind me to pray for people in my life, those whom I love and even those whom I struggle with.

Do you find it difficult to pray for certain people? Have hurt feelings or bitterness caused you to leave them off your prayer list? Consider the apostle Paul's instructions in 1 Timothy chapter 2. Paul taught his ministry partner, Timothy, "to pray for all people" (v. 1). This included "kings and all who are in authority" (v. 2).

At the time of Paul's writing, a wicked ruler by the name of Nero was the emperor of Rome. Under Nero's leadership, Paul was imprisoned and ultimately beheaded. By praying for those in authority, Paul showed that he desired a nation marked with peace, godliness, and dignity. Such prayers please God, "who wants everyone to be saved and to understand the truth" (v. 4). So Paul reminded Timothy to teach believers that they are to also lift up all people in holiness and to pray free from anger and controversy.

COURAGE FOR TODAY

Are you willing to pray for all people? Let the verse below challenge you to make a list of individuals who have hurt you and courageously petition God on their behalf today.

"Bless those who curse you.
Pray for those who hurt you."

LUKE 6:28

THE COURAGE TO
Take Responsibility

Ruth the Moabite said to Naomi, "Let me go out into the harvest fields to pick up the stalks of grain left behind by anyone who is kind enough to let me do it."

RUTH 2:2

Father, you've given me everything I need to succeed, including your guidance and presence. Inspire me to take on the challenges before me and give me strength to accomplish the task at hand.

There will be moments, days, and even seasons in life when we will find ourselves needing to work a little harder. Ponder the account of Ruth's eagerness to provide for herself and her mother-in-law, Naomi, in Ruth chapter 2. Ruth was not afraid of hard work. She was willing to do whatever it took to meet their needs.

Although she was a foreigner and the locals might have rejected her, Ruth asked Naomi if she could go to gather scraps of grain that were left behind by field workers. God had a plan for Ruth and Naomi's future, and he rewarded Ruth's hard labor and faithfulness to Naomi. When Ruth came to a field owned by a godly man and relative of Naomi's, she found favor with him and continued working throughout the entire barley and wheat harvests.

COURAGE FOR TODAY

Are you willing to do whatever it takes to accomplish the duties or tasks that are put before you? What task are you currently facing? Read the verse below and describe the courageous steps you will take today to carry out your responsibilities.

Work willingly at whatever you do,
as though you were working for the Lord
rather than for people.

COLOSSIANS 3:23

THE COURAGE TO

Hold Fast to Faith

"God knows people's hearts, and he confirmed that he accepts Gentiles by giving them the Holy Spirit, just as he did to us. He made no distinction between us and them, for he cleansed their hearts through faith."

ACTS 15:8–9

Father, thank you for offering me salvation from my sins. Help me always hold fast to my faith, especially when I am discouraged or feel as if I have failed you.

Do you ever get discouraged and feel as if your faith is weak? Be encouraged by Paul's response to the Pharisees in Acts chapter 15. The apostle Paul and his missionary partner, Barnabas, arrived back in Jerusalem, where members of the Christian church greeted them.

When some of the religious leaders began debating whether gentile Christ followers in Antioch also needed to adhere to Jewish laws, Paul objected. He explained that believers had received the Holy Spirit, who had "cleansed their hearts through faith" (v. 9), and that they were all "saved the same way, by the undeserved grace of the Lord Jesus" (v. 11) and not by following any set of rules, laws, or traditions. After hearing Paul's response, the other apostles, elders, and church members agreed to send a letter to the church in Antioch removing the burden of Jewish laws from gentile believers.

COURAGE FOR TODAY

Is your faith only based on what Jesus has done and not on a set of rules, laws, or traditions? Meditate on the familiar verse below and describe how you will allow your faith in God to give you more courage for life today.

God saved you by his grace when you believed.
And you can't take credit for this; it is a gift from God.

EPHESIANS 2:8

THE COURAGE TO
Await God's Timing

Sarai, Abram's wife, had not been able to bear children for him.
But she had an Egyptian servant named Hagar.
GENESIS 16:1

Father, I am often impatient and choose my own way rather than waiting for your ideal timing and will. Reassure me and help me to courageously trust that your ways are superior and your timing is perfect.

Are you concerned that God won't keep his promises or answer your prayers? Consider the story of Hagar and Ishmael in Genesis chapter 16. In this chapter, God reveals what can happen when we take matters into our own hands. Earlier in the book of Genesis, we learn of God's promises to Abram, and we discover Abram's struggle between faith and fear. God promised to make Abram a great nation and that his descendants would be vast in number.

But at this point, Abram, now advanced in years, and Sarai, who was barren, were unsure how God could make good on his promise. Therefore, Abram and Sarai attempted to achieve God's promise by arranging for Sarai's servant to conceive Abram's son. The consequences of their decision not only affected their immediate family, but it also impacted the lives of everyone around them—even future generations.

COURAGE FOR TODAY

Memorize the following verse. What situation or prayer request do you need to courageously entrust to God? Make a commitment to set aside your worry and impatience today. Instead, embrace God's peace while you rely on his perfect will and timing.

Don't worry about anything; instead, pray about everything.
Tell God what you need, and thank him for all he has done.
PHILIPPIANS 4:6

THE COURAGE TO
Die to Self

Jesus said to his disciples, "If any of you wants to be my follower,
you must give up your own way, take up your cross, and follow me."
MATTHEW 16:24

Father, in this world filled with temptation, it is easy to be consumed by my desires. Help me accept that you know what I truly need and understand that what I think best isn't always the case.

Are you so preoccupied by worldly wants that you neglect your relationship with God? Be inspired by Matthew chapter 16, in which Jesus confronted religious leaders and prepared his disciples for his death. While the Pharisees and Sadducees demanded miraculous signs, Jesus refused their request, saying their teaching was deceptive and their demands were sinful. So when he spoke to his disciples about the suffering he would endure at the hands of these leaders, he assured them that, even though he would be killed, he would be raised to life again on the third day.

When Peter tried to stop Jesus from speaking about his death, Jesus rebuked Peter, saying, "You are seeing things merely from a human point of view, not from God's" (v. 23). Therefore, Jesus explained that in order to be his follower, one must die to self. For "if you try to hang on to your life, you will lose it. But if you give up your life for my sake, you will save it" (v. 25).

COURAGE FOR TODAY

Are you willing to let your selfish desires die? Meditate on the verse below and describe how you will set aside your own passions to courageously pursue God's will for your life today.

Those who belong to Christ Jesus have nailed the passions and desires of their
sinful nature to his cross and crucified them there.
GALATIANS 5:24

THE COURAGE TO

Seek God's Safety

God is our refuge and strength,
always ready to help in times of trouble.

PSALM 46:1

Father, thank you for promising to always be with me, no matter where I go. Your loving arms bring me comfort, and your powerful presence delivers reassurance. Help me always to remember that I can find real safety only in you.

Whom do you turn to in times of trouble? Anxiety can usher in depression, but confidence in God settles our spirit and restores our hope. Be encouraged by Psalm 46 and its reminder to us that God promises his closeness, assures his protection, and guarantees that he will provide us with all we need. Therefore, we should set aside our fears, seek safety in God, and allow him to be our armor and protection.

COURAGE FOR TODAY

Do you currently feel vulnerable? Or do you know someone who does? Read the following passages from Psalm 91 and ask God to give you divine wisdom and guidance regarding the situation. Then take intentional steps to courageously heed God's guidance today regarding your protection or that of your hurting friend.

If you make the LORD your refuge, if you make the Most High your shelter, no evil will conquer you; no plague will come near your home. For he will order his angels to protect you wherever you go. They will hold you up with their hands so you won't even hurt your foot on a stone…The LORD says, "I will rescue those who love me. I will protect those who trust in my name. When they call on me, I will answer; I will be with them in trouble. I will rescue and honor them. I will reward them with a long life and give them my salvation."

PSALM 91:9–12, 14–16

THE COURAGE TO
Warn Others

You must warn each other every day, while it is still "today,"
so that none of you will be deceived by sin and hardened against God.

HEBREWS 3:13

Father, you command me to love others and care for their needs. Give me courage and a tender heart that is willing to warn others when I see them walking away from your truth.

Have you ever stood idly by while someone veers from God's truth or is careless in their walk with the Lord? Consider the wise words of warning in Hebrews chapter 3. The author of this letter urged believers to "warn each other every day" to avoid any rebelling against God (v. 13).

Paul wrote that because of their love and compassion for one another, Christ followers were first to make sure their own hearts were loyal and protected. Then, they were to courageously speak up and caution other Christians who may have been drifting away from the Lord. There was also a sense of urgency in the author's advice; brothers and sisters needed to warn vulnerable believers "every day" and right away (v. 13). For history had shown that God's people were entirely capable of rebelling against God and suffering the consequences as a result.

COURAGE FOR TODAY

Are you willing to lovingly warn other believers when you see them rebelling against God? Is God encouraging you to speak into someone's life today? Draw inspiration from the verse below and describe how you plan to courageously confront those who are walking away from God's truth.

Dear brothers and sisters, if another believer is overcome by some sin, you who are godly should gently and humbly help that person back onto the right path. And be careful not to fall into the same temptation yourself.

GALATIANS 6:1

THE COURAGE TO
Dismiss Rejection

Korah son of Izhar, a descendant of Kohath son of Levi, conspired with Dathan and Abiram, the sons of Eliab, and On son of Peleth, from the tribe of Reuben. They incited a rebellion against Moses, along with 250 other leaders of the community, all prominent members of the assembly.

NUMBERS 16:1–2

Father, you will always be my comforter and protector. Help me to live a more courageous and confident life no matter what personal or professional complications I face.

Rejection is a part of life, but it can cause feelings of doubt, frustration, insecurity, and even hopelessness if we allow it to. In Numbers chapter 16, we learn that three leaders from the tribes of Israel united and instigated a rebellion against Moses and Aaron. While this constant rejection could have enraged God's faithful servants or even discouraged them from continuing to serve God, instead it drove Moses to his knees in prayer.

Moses then challenged his opponents to test God's will regarding his leadership. When God's anger burned against their rivals so that he threatened to destroy the rebellious tribes, Moses and Aaron repeatedly prayed for the safety of the people who were innocent. "Must you be angry with all the people when only one man sins?" (v. 22). And God relented. God defended the authority of Aaron and Moses among the people that day, and he defends us as well.

COURAGE FOR TODAY

Are you distressed because you feel overlooked, undervalued, or rejected? Read the verse below and note God's promises. What changes will you make today to live a more courageous and confident life?

Let all who take refuge in you rejoice; let them sing joyful praises forever. Spread your protection over them, that all who love your name may be filled with joy.

PSALM 5:11

THE COURAGE TO
Grow in Knowledge

May God give you more and more grace and peace as you grow in your knowledge of God and Jesus our Lord.

2 PETER 1:2

Father, you desire a close relationship with me. Give me the courage to grow in my faith so I can truly know you and your Word.

Do you know a lot about God? Or do you personally know him? Consider the apostle's encouragement in 2 Peter chapter 1. The apostle Peter followed Jesus and believed he was God's Son. Yet it wasn't until after Peter denied knowing his Savior that his faith grew even stronger. From then on, Peter's relationship with Jesus completely defined his life.

In his first letter to believers, Peter urged them to persevere through trials outside the church. In this second letter, he warned them of the dangers of sin within the church. Knowing about God would never be enough to overcome the trials of this life. But "by coming to know him, the one who called us to himself" (v. 3), believers could recognize and courageously stand firm against any false teaching or destructive behaviors.

COURAGE FOR TODAY

Do you know God intimately? Meditate on the following verses and determine the steps you need to take today to courageously grow in your knowledge of God and his Word.

"Don't let the wise boast in their wisdom, or the powerful boast in their power, or the rich boast in their riches. But those who wish to boast should boast in this alone: that they truly know me and understand that I am the LORD who demonstrates unfailing love and who brings justice and righteousness to the earth, and that I delight in these things. I, the LORD, have spoken!"

JEREMIAH 9:23–24

THE COURAGE TO
Give God Control

When she could no longer hide him, she got a basket made of papyrus reeds and waterproofed it with tar and pitch. She put the baby in the basket and laid it among the reeds along the bank of the Nile River.

EXODUS 2:3

Father, my life experiences prepare me to do your will. Help me understand your will and calling and give me courage to pursue it.

Do you trust that God is in control and uses all things to accomplish his perfect will? In Exodus chapter 1 we learn that the king of Egypt feared the strength and population of the people from Israel. So he ordered his people to enslave the Israelites and kill all newborn Hebrew boys.

In Exodus chapter 2, we read about Moses' birth and how God protected, provided for, and prepared Moses for his future leadership. God was aware of the Hebrew's suffering, and he "heard their cries of distress" (3:7), so he protected and prepared Moses to lead them out of Egypt. Despite Moses' reluctance and his feelings of inadequacy, God chose him to be Israel's leader. In preparation for his great purpose, God spared Moses' life. Forty years later, God commissioned Moses to save the Israelites, and he led them safely out of Egypt.

COURAGE FOR TODAY

Memorize the following verse about God's sovereignty. Ask God to reveal his calling on your life. What courageous steps will you take today to pursue God's invitation?

*We can make our plans,
but the LORD determines our steps.*

PROVERBS 16:9

THE COURAGE TO
Lead Wisely

I urge you to imitate me.
1 CORINTHIANS 4:16

Father, being a courageous leader requires wisdom and dedication. Lord, please lead me so, in turn, I can effectively lead others.

Are you a leader at home, at work, in your church, or in your community? Do you live and behave in ways that inspire others to emulate you? Examine the apostle Paul's life in the book of 1 Corinthians. As an unbeliever, Paul embraced self-righteousness and promoted pride and arrogance. But after his encounter with Jesus on the road to Damascus, he dedicated his life to leading people to the Lord.

Paul's passion was fueled by his love for Christ. He desired to grow in his faith and see others grow too. With courage, he urged those he led to "imitate" his dedication to the gospel (v. 16). Paul even sent Timothy to remind believers of how Paul faithfully followed Christ. In his letter, Paul explained that, as a servant who had been "put in charge of explaining God's mysteries" (v. 1), he must be faithful. In Paul's day, the world watched God's people with great scrutiny, and they still do today. With the privilege of representing almighty God comes the great responsibility of leading wisely.

COURAGE FOR TODAY

Leadership requires selflessness and dedication. Be encouraged by the verse below and let God's words inspire you to be a courageous and exemplary leader today.

Don't let anyone think less of you because you are young.
Be an example to all believers in what you say, in the way you live,
in your love, your faith, and your purity.
1 TIMOTHY 4:12

THE COURAGE TO

Set Aside Pride

"What sorrow awaits my rebellious children," says the Lord.
"You make plans that are contrary to mine.
You make alliances not directed by my Spirit, thus piling up your sins."

ISAIAH 30:1

Father, you warn me that pride will lead me to destruction while humility will reap rewards. Give me the desire and ability to set aside my ego and independence so I can faithfully rely on you.

Do you trust in your own solutions more than in God's will and ways? Let the prophetic words in Isaiah chapter 30 inspire you to set aside your pride and turn to the Lord for protection. The great prophet Isaiah warned the people of Israel about the sorrows that would result from their egotistic and rebellious behavior. At the time of Isaiah's prophecy, Israel's king sought Egypt's unreliable alliance instead of clinging to God's trustworthy promise of provisions and protection. By trusting in humankind instead of the Lord, Israel would suffer consequences that included being "humiliated…disgraced… [and] ashamed" (vv. 3–5).

Isaiah then relayed a few more details of God's judgment against the Israelites. Calamity would come upon them suddenly, and their enemies would attack and destroy them. Yet if God's people wholeheartedly returned to him, they would receive his unconditional love, salvation, guidance, and many blessings.

COURAGE FOR TODAY

Do you struggle with pride and self-sufficiency? Meditate on the verse below and vow today to courageously set aside your pride and rely wholeheartedly on God for wisdom, guidance, provisions, and protection.

He gives grace generously. As the Scriptures say,
"God opposes the proud but gives grace to the humble."

JAMES 4:6

THE COURAGE TO
Protect Your Faith

"I have told you these things so that you won't abandon your faith."
JOHN 16:1

Father, people, places, and things in this world often tempt me to walk away from my faith and devotion to you. When my faith is under attack, give me the ability to protect it and the courage to stand firm so I can faithfully defend my love and commitment to you.

Are you prepared to maintain your faith when hardships arise? Be comforted by Jesus' encouraging message in John chapter 15. Before he was to be arrested, beaten, and crucified, Jesus prepared his disciples for his departure. He told them that they would also be hated, rejected, and persecuted. They would be thrown out of synagogues and even killed for sharing their beliefs.

But God would give them wisdom, power, and peace through his Holy Spirit to protect their faith and remind them of everything Jesus had said and done. Jesus told his followers these things in advance so they would believe and not abandon their faith.

COURAGE FOR TODAY

Describe ways you are currently prepared to defend your faith. Read the apostle Paul's important advice and prayer below and let his message inspire you today to courageously prepare to maintain your love and dedication to God.

With all these things in mind, dear brothers and sisters, stand firm and keep a strong grip on the teaching we passed on to you both in person and by letter. Now may our Lord Jesus Christ himself and God our Father, who loved us and by his grace gave us eternal comfort and a wonderful hope, comfort you and strengthen you in every good thing you do and say.

2 THESSALONIANS 2:15–17

THE COURAGE TO
Have Hope

As the deer longs for streams of water, so I long for you, O God. I thirst for God, the living God. When can I go and stand before him?…Why am I discouraged? Why is my heart so sad? I will put my hope in God! I will praise him again— my Savior and my God!

PSALM 42:1–2, 11

Father, you are my hope and my salvation. Give me the courage and confidence to stand firm when I am discouraged and face adversity, knowing that with your help, I can endure and overcome any challenge.

Where do you find hope? Do you look for it in your circumstances, loved ones, possessions, or wealth? Consider the wise words in Psalm 42 that encourage us to acquire hope in God alone. The writer of this psalm lamented his circumstances while his accusers ridiculed his faith. He recalled a time when his life was full of joy and thanksgiving, and he longed to be rescued from his suffering.

Yet through it all, the psalmist remembered where real hope comes from: the God whose "unfailing love" pours out upon him and gives him life (v. 8). Therefore, when we are in despair, we must remember to praise the Lord in whom our hope can be found.

COURAGE FOR TODAY

What is your greatest source of hope? Embrace the words of the apostle Paul below and courageously choose joy and peace today, knowing that, because of the power and presence of almighty God, you do have hope.

I pray that God, the source of hope, will fill you completely with joy and peace because you trust in him. Then you will overflow with confident hope through the power of the Holy Spirit.

ROMANS 15:13

THE COURAGE TO
Be Intolerant of Sin

"I have a few complaints against you. You tolerate some among you whose teaching is like that of Balaam, who showed Balak how to trip up the people of Israel. He taught them to sin by eating food offered to idols and by committing sexual sin."

REVELATION 2:14

Father, in a world that promotes the tolerance of almost everything, I am tempted to look the other way regarding sin. Give me wisdom and courage to lovingly lead myself and others toward true repentance and a closer relationship with you.

Are you tolerant or intolerant of sin? Let Jesus' warning in Revelation chapter 2 motivate you to repent of your sins and lead others toward repentance too. In his message to the church at Pergamum, Jesus complimented those members who remained loyal in the midst of persecution.

But he also complained that they were tolerating false worship and eating sinful foods that had been sacrificed to false gods. So Jesus instructed the church to repent and stop engaging in ungodly practices. For if they did, he would bless them. But if they didn't, he would personally fight against them.

COURAGE FOR TODAY

When you see someone sinning, do you attempt to lovingly lead them back to God, or do you tolerate your sin and theirs as if nothing is wrong? Read the passage below and decide today to courageously and lovingly lead yourself and others toward true confession and repentance.

My dear brothers and sisters, if someone among you wanders away from the truth and is brought back, you can be sure that whoever brings the sinner back from wandering will save that person from death and bring about the forgiveness of many sins.

JAMES 5:19–20

THE COURAGE TO
Serve God Enthusiastically

"Solomon, my son, learn to know the God of your ancestors intimately. Worship and serve him with your whole heart and a willing mind. For the L<small>ORD</small> sees every heart and knows every plan and thought. If you seek him, you will find him. But if you forsake him, he will reject you forever."

1 C<small>HRONICLES</small> 28:9

Father, you deserve my full attention and commitment. Give me a longing to achieve your will and the courage to pursue your calling on my life with determination.

Do you serve God half-heartedly? Or do you courageously pursue his calling? Consider King David's words in 1 Chronicles chapter 28 when he informed the Israelites and instructed his son Solomon to serve God passionately. In this chapter, we learn that David told the people of Israel that God had chosen Solomon to succeed him as king and that Solomon had also been chosen by God to build the temple.

David then urged Solomon to "learn to know the God of your ancestors intimately…worship and serve him with your whole heart and a willing mind" because God searches hearts and knows all intentions (v. 9). After David reveals to his son every detail of God's specific plans for the temple, he boldly reminds Solomon to "be strong and courageous, and do the work" (v. 20).

COURAGE FOR TODAY

How enthusiastic are you about serving God? Memorize the verse below and describe God's current calling on your life. What courageous steps will you take today to serve God faithfully?

Be strong and immovable. Always work enthusiastically for the Lord, for you know that nothing you do for the Lord is ever useless.

1 C<small>ORINTHIANS</small> 15:58

THE COURAGE TO
Acknowledge Obstacles

"What do you mean, 'If I can'?" Jesus asked.
"Anything is possible if a person believes." The father instantly cried out,
"I do believe, but help me overcome my unbelief!"

MARK 9:23–24

Father, I sometimes struggle with doubt, discouragement, and even despair. Give me the courage to acknowledge every obstacle that interferes with my faith and to confidently trust in your promises and ways.

Are there circumstances or situations in your life that cause your faith to waver? Be inspired by Jesus' conversation with a desperate father in Mark chapter 9. After his transfiguration, Jesus and several of his disciples came down the mountain and noticed a large crowd arguing with religious leaders. When the group ran to meet Jesus, he asked about their dispute.

A man spoke up to say that his son was possessed by an evil spirit, and the other disciples had not been able to cure him. So the father asked Jesus to "have mercy on us and help us, if you can" (v. 22). Jesus replied, "What do you mean, 'If I can'?…Anything is possible if a person believes" (v. 23). The boy's father immediately responded and confessed his obstacle of unbelief (v. 24).

COURAGE FOR TODAY

Do you sometimes struggle with discouragement or doubt? Are you willing to believe in God's power and accept his promises even when they don't occur how or when you expect them to? Meditate on the following verses and courageously trust God with all your obstacles today.

Dear brothers and sisters, when troubles of any kind come your way, consider it an opportunity for great joy. For you know that when your faith is tested, your endurance has a chance to grow. So let it grow, for when your endurance is fully developed, you will be perfect and complete, needing nothing.

JAMES 1:2–4

THE COURAGE TO
Seek God's Comfort

The angel of the LORD came again and touched him and said,
"Get up and eat some more, or the journey ahead will be too much for you."

1 KINGS 19:7

Father, there are times when I am discouraged and tempted to doubt your ability to rescue me. Help me overcome moments of despair by empowering me to focus on your voice of reason and your words of encouragement.

Do you ever doubt God's ability or faithfulness? Consider how God's great prophet Elijah struggled with overwhelming fear and doubt in 1 Kings chapter 19. In the previous chapter, 1 Kings 18, Elijah's faith was so strong that he courageously challenged 850 false prophets to a contest in order to prove that the Lord was the only true God. But in chapter 19, we discover that Elijah's faith quickly wavered when he embraced his fears. Elijah heard Jezebel's threatening message and allowed his fears to overwhelm his faith. He ran for his life and, likely in a state of exhaustion, even prayed that God would take his life.

The hand of God had always been upon Elijah, giving him great spiritual strength and physical ability. Yet now he cowered in the wilderness alone. But God, in his great mercy and compassion, comforted and cared for the anguished prophet, gently speaking to him words of great encouragement and instruction in order to restore him physically and emotionally.

COURAGE FOR TODAY

How often do you struggle with doubt or discouragement? Memorize the passage below and choose today to courageously overcome any feelings of disbelief or hopelessness by wholeheartedly trusting God.

Trust in the LORD with all your heart; do not depend on your own understanding.
Seek his will in all you do, and he will show you which path to take.

PROVERBS 3:5–6

THE COURAGE TO

Make Jesus Your Lord

You must worship Christ as Lord of Your life.
And if someone asks about your hope as a believer,
always be ready to explain it.

1 PETER 3:15

Father, my flesh wants to be in charge of all the details of my life. Give me the courage to submit to you as Lord over everything in my life.

How do you make life-changing decisions? Do you consult your inner circle, write down the pros and cons, test the waters, or drop to your knees and seek God's help? Consider the apostle's wise words in 1 Peter chapter 3. Peter knew from experience the consequences of making hasty and harmful decisions. So he learned the key to wise choices: submit everything to the Lord.

Instead of controlling every situation, Peter advised believers, "You must worship Christ as Lord of your life" (v. 15). He knew that selfish desires, the opinions of others, the ways of the world, and outside pressures can sway a believer's life. But by surrendering to Jesus, their consciences would remain clear. Even if they suffered for following the Lord, it would be better than the consequences for following their own will and ways.

COURAGE FOR TODAY

Are you willing to relinquish control of your decisions and outcomes to God? Read the following verse and courageously make Jesus Lord over your life today.

"The LORD will guide you continually, giving you water when you are dry
and restoring your strength. You will be like a well-watered garden,
like an ever-flowing spring."

ISAIAH 58:11

THE COURAGE TO
Admit Your Need

"This is what the LORD says to Zerubbabel: It is not by force nor by strength,
but by my Spirit, says the LORD of Heaven's Armies."

ZECHARIAH 4:6

Father, I often need advice for making important decisions or knowing which way to go. Give me the ability to set aside my pride and the courage to ask you and godly friends for help.

When you need help to complete a project or assignment, where and to whom do you turn? Be inspired by Zechariah chapter 4. God gave the great prophet Zechariah visions regarding rebuilding the temple and encouraging God's people, yet Zechariah needed help to understand them.

Even though the prophet came from a priestly background and the symbols in his vision represented priestly duties, Zechariah couldn't comprehend God's prophecy. So he asked God's angel for help. In response, the angel relayed that the task of rebuilding the temple would require more than the strength of the prophet and the people. In fact, it would take more than even the collective power of the team. The temple would be completed "not by force nor by strength, but by my Spirit, says the LORD" (v. 6).

COURAGE FOR TODAY

True humility sets aside all pride and is willing to ask for assistance. Do you currently need encouragement or help with a situation or assignment? Memorize the following verse and ask God to help you today by giving you wisdom, courage, guidance, and godly friends.

"For I hold you by your right hand—I, the LORD your God.
And I say to you, 'Don't be afraid. I am here to help you.'"

ISAIAH 41:13

THE COURAGE TO
Be Ready

Preach the word of God. Be prepared, whether the time is favorable or not. Patiently correct, rebuke, and encourage your people with good teaching. For a time is coming when people will no longer listen to sound and wholesome teaching. They will follow their own desires and will look for teachers who will tell them whatever their itching ears want to hear.

2 TIMOTHY 4:2–3

Father, you call me to be your disciple. Help me always be prepared to share my faith in you.

Are you prepared to tell people you know—and even those you don't know—about your love and devotion to God? Let the apostle Paul's instructions in 2 Timothy chapter 4 inspire you to always "be ready" to share your faith.

At the time Paul wrote this second letter to Timothy, he was being held in chains for boldly declaring God's truth. Paul knew that there would be a time when people would turn away from faith in God to pursue teachings that would only tell them "whatever their itching ears want to hear" (v. 3). Therefore, he urged his ministry partner and son in the faith to keep a clear mind and set aside any fear so he could continue to preach, patiently correct, and encourage believers to hold fast to their faith.

COURAGE FOR TODAY

Are you passionate about sharing your knowledge of God and his Word with others? Meditate on the verse below and describe how you will courageously tell and teach others about Jesus today.

He must have a strong belief in the trustworthy message he was taught; then he will be able to encourage others with wholesome teaching and show those who oppose it where they are wrong.

TITUS 1:9

THE COURAGE TO
Delight in God's Presence

What joy for those who can live in your house, always singing your praises.
What joy for those whose strength comes from the LORD,
who have set their minds on a pilgrimage to Jerusalem.

PSALM 84:4–5

Father, I find true joy in your presence and comfort in your promises. Help me focus on the joy, strength, and courage that comes from a close and personal relationship with you.

Does your relationship with God give you courage and bring you joy? Reflect on the psalmist's perspective in Psalm 84. In writing this psalm, the author expresses his longing to be in the house of God, the temple where God's people worship, serve, and celebrate their closeness with the Lord.

In the presence of the Almighty, the psalmist's entire being is filled with joy. He points out that the truly blessed are those "whose strength comes from the LORD" and who make their relationship with him a priority (v. 5). The psalmist confidently states that there is no comparison between walking with God and walking with the wicked; a truly blessed life is found in God's light, joy, grace, and favor.

COURAGE FOR TODAY

Do you experience delight in God, his presence, and his Word? Read the following verses and decide today to courageously set boundaries with people who are toxic and direct your attention instead toward your relationship with the Lord.

Oh, the joys of those who do not follow the advice of the wicked, or stand around with sinners, or join in with mockers. But they delight in the law of the LORD, meditating on it day and night.

PSALM 1:1–2

THE COURAGE TO
Love, Not Hate

Anyone who hates a fellow believer is still living and walking in darkness.
Such a person does not know the way to go, having been blinded by the darkness.
1 JOHN 2:11

Father, I need courage to release feelings of hurt or hatred that I have
tucked away in my heart. Fill me with your love and forgiveness today so I
can let go of my bitterness.

When you think of certain people, is your first emotion hurt or hatred?
Consider the apostle's challenging words in 1 John chapter 2. The apostle John
identified himself as "the disciple Jesus loved" (John 13:23). He wrote this letter
to remind believers of some basic truths of Christianity. John encouraged
Christ followers to "love one another" (1 John 2:7). He claimed this was both a
new and an old commandment since Jesus illustrated self-sacrificing love and
commanded his followers to do the same.

Anyone claiming to live like Jesus while holding hatred in their heart
"is still living in darkness" and may "cause others to stumble" (vv. 9–10). But
by allowing Christ's love to infiltrate their hearts and lives, believers can be
shining lights in a darkened world. Hatred stems from unforgiveness. So John
reminded believers that their "sins have been forgiven through Jesus" (v. 12).
Therefore, if they lived in light of their forgiveness, there should be no room in
their hearts for hatred.

COURAGE FOR TODAY

Do you need to forgive someone and let go of hurt and hatred? Read the
verse below and let God's love motivate you today to courageously pardon
and pray for those who have offended you.

Dear friends, let us continue to love one another, for love comes from God.
Anyone who loves is a child of God and knows God.
1 JOHN 4:7

THE COURAGE TO
Complete a Task

The LORD sent this message through the prophet Haggai:
"Why are you living in luxurious houses while my house lies in ruins?"
HAGGAI 1:3–4

Father, my heart needs encouragement to finish the tasks at hand. Help me complete all that you put before me by getting rid of any distractions.

Are you hindered by distractions or unable to finish what you start? Be inspired by the prophet Haggai's message as he motivated God's people to finish rebuilding their holy temple. After seventy years captive in Babylon, the Israelites had returned to their homeland. Their enemies had destroyed their once magnificent place of worship. So the monumental task before them was to rebuild the house of the Lord.

But as they began the project, distractions arose in the forms of a small construction crew, opposition from neighbors, indifference, and misplaced spiritual priorities. So they abandoned their temple project and launched into building fine houses for themselves. In response, God sent economic and social hardship, such as drought, poverty, and physical suffering. But Haggai's blunt message reminded them of the primary purpose for returning to Jerusalem— to rebuild God's house of worship. As the people revived their devotion to the Lord, God sent a message of encouragement saying, "I am with you" (v. 13). Filled with enthusiasm, the Israelites got back to work to complete their assignment.

COURAGE FOR TODAY

When a job, project, or assignment becomes too difficult, do you sometimes procrastinate or give up? Meditate on the verse below and make a commitment today to courageously finish what you've started. Describe how God's presence inspires you to get back to work.

"What is impossible for people is possible with God."
LUKE 18:27

THE COURAGE TO
Be Fearless

One night the Lord spoke to Paul in a vision and told him, "Don't be afraid! Speak out! Don't be silent! For I am with you, and no one will attack and harm you, for many people in this city belong to me."

ACTS 18:9–10

Father, you give me hope, inspiration, and guidance. Help me overcome any fear or hesitation so I can freely, frequently, and confidently share my testimony and faith with others.

How often does the Holy Spirit prompt you to speak up about your faith? Do you listen each time? Or do you second guess the opportunity and remain silent? Let God's words of encouragement to the apostle Paul in Acts chapter 18 inspire you to speak out. On one of his missionary journeys, Paul traveled to Corinth. When he arrived, he stayed with a local couple, named Aquila and Priscilla, who were believers, and he openly preached in the synagogue each Sabbath.

While Paul was sharing his testimony about Jesus being the Messiah, some in the Jewish community opposed his message and insulted him. So Paul decided to leave them to their ignorance and go elsewhere to preach. But one night, God spoke to Paul and told him, "Don't be afraid! Speak out! Don't be silent! For I am with you, and no one will attack and harm you, for many people in this city belong to me" (vv. 9–10).

COURAGE FOR TODAY

Does fear ever keep you from sharing your faith with others? Memorize the verse below and vow to courageously speak up today about your love for the Lord and your close relationship with him.

The LORD is my light and my salvation—so why should I be afraid?
The LORD is my fortress, protecting me from danger, so why should I tremble?

PSALM 27:1

THE COURAGE TO
Endure Loss

Elimelech died, and Naomi was left with her two sons. The two sons married Moabite women. One married a woman named Orpah, and the other a woman named Ruth. But about ten years later, both Mahlon and Kilion died. This left Naomi alone, without her two sons or her husband.

RUTH 1:3–5

Father, at times, I feel alone and hopeless. Help me to always trust you to restore my future and lead me to trustworthy friends and loved ones for encouragement and support.

Have you recently experienced a loss? Do you know someone who has? Consider Ruth chapter 1 and note how Naomi and Ruth coped with their tragic loss. In the first five verses of Ruth chapter 1, we learn that Naomi lost her husband and both sons within a ten-year period. While her daughter-in-law, Ruth, was also grieving the loss of her husband, she obviously cared deeply for Naomi because she chose to stay with her mother-in-law rather than return to her biological family for support.

Ruth and Naomi found comfort in one another's company, and they courageously trusted God with their futures. While trials and sorrows will come, we can cope with them when we rely on God and reach out to trustworthy friends and loved ones for support.

COURAGE FOR TODAY

When you face a loss, are you more apt to isolate yourself or reach out for comfort and encouragement? Read the verse below and embrace Jesus' peace. What courageous step will you take today to seek comfort in your time of need?

"I have told you all this so that you may have peace in me. Here on earth you will have many trials and sorrows. But take heart, because I have overcome the world."

JOHN 16:33

THE COURAGE TO
Trust God's Strength

All glory to God, who is able, through his mighty power at work within us, to accomplish infinitely more than we might ask or think.

EPHESIANS 3:20

Father, I sometimes wonder how I fit into your overall plan. Give me guidance and help me access your strength so I can accomplish the many wonderful assignments you have prepared for me.

How confident are you in God's plan for your life? Do you see yourself as a courageous contributor or an insignificant and reluctant participant? Draw inspiration and courage from the apostle Paul's words in Ephesians chapter 3. While Paul could have been hindered by his former cruelty, he instead chose to overcome his prior reputation and fully embrace his role as a faithful believer, teacher, and encourager.

Paul celebrated the life-changing grace that God gave to him at the moment of his salvation. So with courage, he boldly shared his faith and experiences with all who would listen. For if the believers in Ephesus chose to also grasp the greatness of God's grace and salvation, they, too, would be "made complete with all the fullness of life and power" that can only come from a personal relationship with almighty God (v. 19).

COURAGE FOR TODAY

Do you need more strength to pursue God's plans for your life? Embrace God's character described in the verses below and vow to take intentional and courageous steps toward God's will and calling today.

He never grows weak or weary. No one can measure the depths of his understanding. He gives power to the weak and strength to the powerless.

ISAIAH 40:28–29

THE COURAGE TO
Sow Good Seeds

These disasters happened to Judah because of the LORD's command. He had decided to banish Judah from his presence because of the many sins of Manasseh, who had filled Jerusalem with innocent blood. The LORD would not forgive this.

2 KINGS 24:3–4

Father, while I cannot control what others around me do, I can govern my behavior and be an example for others to follow. Help me to sow good seeds of faith and faithfulness that inspire others to do the same.

Do you ever take advantage of God's patience, mercy, and kindness by dismissing your sin as not so serious? Consider the trouble the people of Israel's Southern Kingdom, Judah, brought upon themselves when they disregarded God's covenant and ignored his warnings.

King Josiah was a good king who respected God, followed God's law, and led the people to do the same. Yet many other kings, both before and after him, chose to pursue evil in God's sight. The account of the wickedness of one such king, Manasseh, is recorded in 2 Kings 21:1–18. Manasseh renewed many pagan practices and built shrines for pagan worship. Because of Manasseh's offense, God pronounced judgment on the people of Judah, saying, "I will bring such disaster…that the ears of those who hear about it will tingle with horror" (v. 12). While Josiah's faithful leadership had postponed God's punishment, the evil behavior of future kings prompted God to act on his promised punishments.

COURAGE FOR TODAY

Do you accept the reality that you reap what you sow? Read aloud the verse below and describe how the promise of consequences inspires you to begin making courageous changes to your attitudes and behaviors today.

Don't be misled—you cannot mock the justice of God. You will always harvest what you plant.

GALATIANS 6:7

THE COURAGE TO

Be a Good Steward

"If you are faithful in little things, you will be faithful in large ones. But if you are dishonest in little things, you won't be honest with greater responsibilities. And if you are untrustworthy about worldly wealth, who will trust you with the true riches of heaven?"

LUKE 16:10–11

Father, you have given me many possessions and relationships. Help me recognize my many blessings and steward them in ways that honor you, demonstrate honesty and integrity, and help others.

Are you a good steward of your money, relationships, and possessions? Consider Jesus' lesson in Luke chapter 16. After teaching about a wayward son, Jesus told the story of the rich man and his manager. When the wealthy man entrusted his money to his employee, the worker was unfaithful and mishandled his employer's riches. Once the employee realized he would soon be fired, he began preparing for his future by nurturing relationships with potential new employers.

The moral of Jesus' parable was that believers should use their earthly possessions "to benefit others and make friends. Then…they will welcome you to an eternal home" (v. 9). Because if Christ followers cannot be trusted with their worldly wealth, how can the Lord trust them with the riches of heaven?

COURAGE FOR TODAY

List the ways you currently manage your finances, possessions, and relationships. Do you care for them in ways that demonstrate your love for God and others? Read the following verses and describe the courageous steps you will take today to be a better steward of all God has entrusted to you.

Honor the LORD with your wealth and with the best part of everything you produce. Then he will fill your barns with grain, and your vats will overflow with good wine.

PROVERBS 3:9–10

THE COURAGE TO
Accept God's Character

The LORD is good, a strong refuge when trouble comes. He is close to those who trust in him. But he will sweep away his enemies in an overwhelming flood. He will pursue his foes into the darkness of night.

NAHUM 1:7–8

Father, when my adversaries appear to have the upper hand, remind me that you get the last word and will work all things together for my good and for your glory.

Do you believe God is jealous? Not that he is possessive of us but loving and protective over us? Allow the words of the prophet Nahum and his message to Nineveh to open your eyes to the full character of God. The city of Nineveh had once surrendered to God under the prophet Jonah's preaching. But a century later, they had returned to their wicked ways. So God called Nahum to boldly reveal the Lord's character and pronounce judgment against the people of Nineveh.

Nahum explained that while God is a patient, compassionate, and forgiving father, he will also "sweep away his enemies" and "pursue his foes into the darkness of night" (v. 8). Sadly, the Ninevites refused to change their ways, so Nahum's prophecy ended with Nineveh's enemies rejoicing over their destruction.

COURAGE FOR TODAY

Do you believe God is both loving and just? That he is slow to anger but not willing to ignore sin forever? Meditate on the following verse and describe how you will courageously allow your life to reflect your full acceptance of God's character today.

If we confess our sins to him, he is faithful and just to forgive us our sins and to cleanse us from all wickedness.

1 JOHN 1:9

THE COURAGE TO

Refrain from Revenge

See that no one pays back evil for evil,
but always try to do good to each other and to all people.

1 Thessalonians 5:15

Father, when I am hurt, I want to fight back. Give me the desire and courage to rise above my pain and release my offender to you.

Have you ever wanted to get even with someone who has hurt you? Be motivated by the apostle Paul's words in 1 Thessalonians chapter 5. In Paul's letter to the church at Thessalonica, he instructed believers to build and nurture their relationships, not tear them down.

Paul prompted believers to honor their leaders, warn those who are lazy, encourage those who are timid, take care of the weak, and be patient with everyone. And he also urged them to "see that no one pays back evil for evil, but always try to do good to each other and to all people" (v. 15). Lastly, Paul closed his first letter to the church members by telling them to be joyful and thankful, and to "never stop praying" (v. 17). Because with the Holy Spirit and God's peace, God-honoring behavior is always achievable.

COURAGE FOR TODAY

Are you willing to let go of your need for revenge? Let the verse below inspire you today to set aside any bitterness and instead to courageously entrust your offenders' future to God.

Don't repay evil for evil. Don't retaliate with insults when people insult you.
Instead, pay them back with a blessing. That is what God has called you to do,
and he will grant you his blessing.

1 Peter 3:9

THE COURAGE TO
Change Your Plans

We can make our plans,
but the LORD determines our steps.

PROVERBS 16:9

Father, you know all things, past, present, and future. Give me the wisdom to seek your will and guidance and the courage to set my own plans aside so I can confidently follow yours.

Do you insist on proceeding with your plans even when there are roadblocks? Consider the wise words of King Solomon in Proverbs chapter 16. In this chapter, Solomon teaches that while our plans seem right to us, it is God's plans for our lives that truly matter and are truly best.

Solomon's wise sayings remind us that God "has made everything for his own purposes" (v. 4), that he considers our motives and always knows what is best. Therefore, if we will trust and respect God, commit all our efforts to him, treasure his wisdom, and seek to please only him, he will direct our steps, establish our plans, keep us from harm, and give us peace.

COURAGE FOR TODAY

Are you willing to trust God with your plans and future? Read the passage below and describe how you will courageously entrust your life to the Lord today and let him override your plans for his better purposes.

Look here, you who say, "Today or tomorrow we are going to a certain town and will stay there a year. We will do business there and make a profit." How do you know what your life will be like tomorrow? Your life is like the morning fog—it's here a little while, then it's gone. What you ought to say is, "If the Lord wants us to, we will live and do this or that."

JAMES 4:13–15

THE COURAGE TO

Rely on Your Helper

"I will ask the Father, and he will give you another Advocate, who will never leave you. He is the Holy Spirit, who leads into all truth. The world cannot receive him, because it isn't looking for him and doesn't recognize him. But you know him, because he lives with you now and later will be in you."

JOHN 14:16–17

Father, when I surrendered my life to you, you placed your Spirit within me to lead me to your truth. Remind me to continuously rely on the Holy Spirit for wisdom and guidance every day.

How often do you depend on God's Holy Spirit to help you navigate life's daily decisions and challenges? Let Jesus' message in John chapter 14 inspire you to rely on God's assistance every day. As Jesus prepared for his death and ascension back to heaven, he told his followers that God would be sending them another Advocate, the Holy Spirit, who would assist them and never leave them.

God's Spirit leads Christ followers "into all truth" (v. 17) and reminds them of everything Jesus has said. He gives strength when believers are weak and provides power, knowledge, wisdom, and understanding to those who receive him. And the Holy Spirit provides peace, joy, and hope to all believers at all times.

COURAGE FOR TODAY

Do you regularly seek truth and guidance from God? Meditate on the verse below and vow today to courageously follow the Holy Spirit's counsel.

"When the Spirit of truth comes, he will guide you into all truth. He will not speak on his own but will tell you what he has heard. He will tell you about the future."

JOHN 16:13

THE COURAGE TO
Believe the Impossible

"This is what the LORD of Heaven's Armies says: All this may seem impossible to you now, a small remnant of God's people. But is it impossible for me? says the LORD of Heaven's Armies."

ZECHARIAH 8:6

Father, there are times when I struggle to believe that my situation will change for the better. Give me the courage to truly believe that with you, all things are possible.

Have you ever believed that something you longed for was impossible? Did you give up hope for brighter days and for your joy to return? Consider the book of Zechariah and his words of encouragement. When the Israelites returned from Babylon to Jerusalem, their city was in ruins and no longer safe for elderly citizens or children. While God proclaimed everything would once again "be his own city" (2:12), the people who returned still had their doubts. God said of those struggling with unbelief that "they will be my people, and I will be...their God" (8:8). So Zechariah encouraged and urged the people of Jerusalem to live in truth and peace so that the days ahead would be filled with "festivals of joy and celebration" (v. 19). For God had promised that people from other nations and cities around the world would again travel to Jerusalem to worship and be blessed. Now God's people needed to believe.

COURAGE FOR TODAY

Is there a situation in your life you believe is "impossible"? Isn't it time for you to embrace a new outlook, one filled with hope? Take hold of the following verse and vow to courageously believe in God and his Word today.

*Jesus looked at them intently and said,
"Humanly speaking, it is impossible.
But with God everything is possible."*

MATTHEW 19:26

THE COURAGE TO
Soften Your Heart

"Moses permitted divorce only as a concession to your hard hearts,
but it was not what God had originally intended."
MATTHEW 19:8

Father, some relationships are hard, and sometimes boundaries are necessary. Even so, please soften my heart so I can extend love, kindness, and patience to all people, even to those who I feel don't deserve it.

Have you hardened your heart toward a spouse, family member, or other loved one? Allow Jesus' words in Matthew chapter 19 to inspire you to soften your heart and nurture your relationships. When being confronted by religious leaders regarding divorce, Jesus referred them back to God's Word, explaining that God's desire and will is for husbands and wives to be "united into one" and to stay together (v. 5). But because of the hardness of the people's hearts, Moses permitted divorce.

All relationships have their challenges, and a relationship can thrive only when both members intentionally work at it and do their part. Yet regardless of how another person may or may not invest in the relationship, believers are to do everything possible to instill love, kindness, faithfulness, patience, hope, and endurance in all relationships, most especially their marriages.

COURAGE FOR TODAY

Is there someone in your life who is difficult to love? Read the passage below and vow to be courageously caring and kind today, regardless of the actions and attitudes of others.

Love is patient and kind. Love is not jealous or boastful or proud or rude. It does not demand its own way. It is not irritable, and it keeps no record of being wronged. It does not rejoice about injustice but rejoices whenever the truth wins out. Love never gives up, never loses faith, is always hopeful, and endures through every circumstance.

1 CORINTHIANS 13:4–7

THE COURAGE TO
Seek God's Protection

I was ashamed to ask the king for soldiers and horsemen to accompany us and protect us from enemies along the way. After all, we had told the king, "Our God's hand of protection is on all who worship him, but his fierce anger rages against those who abandon him." So we fasted and earnestly prayed that our God would take care of us, and he heard our prayer.

EZRA 8:22–23

Father, when the steps I take are within your will, you oversee my journey and keep me safe. Help me courageously seek and rely on your guidance and protection daily.

Do you truly trust God to protect you? Consider the prophet's remarks in Ezra chapter 8 when he assembled a large group of Israelites to return with him from Babylon to Jerusalem. As Ezra prepared the caravan for an approximately nine-hundred-mile journey, he refused to ask King Artaxerxes for help because he had great confidence in God's protection.

Instead of seeking outside assistance, Ezra gave orders "for all of us to fast and humble ourselves before our God" (v. 21), to seek God's protection for their pilgrimage. Ezra faithfully believed that if they pursued God's will, worshiped God faithfully, and trusted God unquestionably, that God would save them from enemies and bandits throughout their trip.

COURAGE FOR TODAY

Do you pray for God's care daily, or is his protection your last resort? Meditate on the following two verses from Psalm 91 and ask God for the courage to trust him completely with your circumstances and concerns today.

*He will cover you with his feathers. He will shelter you with his wings.
His faithful promises are your armor and protection.
Do not be afraid of the terrors of the night, nor the arrow that flies in the day.*

PSALM 91:4–5

THE COURAGE TO

Honor God's Temple

*Don't you realize that all of you together are the temple of God
and that the Spirit of God lives in you?*

1 CORINTHIANS 3:16

Father, I need to improve certain areas of my life. Help me recognize my
weaknesses and give me courage to make necessary changes so I can
effectively honor you and the temple of your Holy Spirit, my body.

How attentive are you in caring for your mind and body? Are you careful to stay
away from people, places, and things that jeopardize your spiritual, emotional,
physical, and relational health? Let the apostle Paul's message in 1 Corinthians
chapter 3 challenge you to be more intentional in honoring your body.

In his letter to the Corinthian church, Paul explained to its members that
he and his missionary partners had been working to build them up in their
faith. He described himself by saying, "I have laid the foundation like an expert
builder" (v. 10), and then he builds on that groundwork hoping each Christ
follower will become strong enough to withstand testing and judgment. Paul
then reminded the Corinthians that God's Spirit lives within them, therefore
making them each "the temple of God" (v. 16).

COURAGE FOR TODAY

List the ways you currently honor and protect your spiritual, emotional,
physical, and relational health. Then read the passage below and vow to
value your body by courageously making any necessary changes,
starting today.

*Don't you realize that your body is the temple of the Holy Spirit, who lives in you
and was given to you by God? You do not belong to yourself, for God bought you
with a high price. So you must honor God with your body.*

1 CORINTHIANS 6:19–20

THE COURAGE TO

Fear God

"The fear of the Lord is true wisdom;
to forsake evil is real understanding."

JOB 28:28

Father, to fear you is to respect and obey you. Give me the courage, will, and ability to resist temptation so I can faithfully honor you in my thoughts, speech, and behavior.

Do you fear God's ability to control your surroundings and circumstances? Consider in Job chapter 28 Job's discourse on where we find true wisdom and understanding. Job was a godly and faithful man who was wealthy, successful, and had a large family. Then one day, God allowed Satan to take away everything Job owned, including his health and children. In the following chapters, Job mourned his tragedy while he listened and responded to friends who accused him of sinning against God, believing his misfortunes were the consequences of that sin. Finally, the weary Job asked and answered the following questions: "Do people know where to find wisdom? Where can they find understanding? No one knows where to find it" (vv. 12–13).

After acknowledging that we cannot discover wisdom or understanding in treasured possessions, nor can we find them within a person, Job concluded that true wisdom is "the fear of the Lord," and real understanding is "to forsake evil" (v. 28).

COURAGE FOR TODAY

Do you respectfully fear God, knowing that he is all-knowing, all-powerful, and ever-present? Meditate on the following verses and decide today to walk in courageous faith knowing that God is in complete control.

Oh, the joys of those who take refuge in him! Fear the LORD, you his godly people, for those who fear him will have all they need.

PSALM 34:8–9

THE COURAGE TO
Avoid Enabling

Dear brothers and sisters, we give you this command in the name of our Lord Jesus Christ: Stay away from all believers who live idle lives and don't follow the tradition they received from us.

2 THESSALONIANS 3:6

Father, you command me to help others who are burdened. But you also remind me to let each person carry their own load. Give me wisdom and discernment to know when to be charitable and when not to enable.

Do you sometimes feel compelled or pressured to help a person who isn't really helpless? Is it easy for people to take advantage of you? If so, be motivated by the apostle Paul's instructions in 2 Thessalonians chapter 3. Paul commanded Thessalonian believers to stop enabling members who were living idle lives. For Paul had worked hard to support himself without relying on handouts for his livelihood. So he urged Christ followers to stop supporting laziness and instead to allow the natural consequences for individuals who were unwilling to work: "Those unwilling to work will not get to eat" (v. 10).

Paul then reminded believers that those living idle lives were also the ones causing problems by "meddling in other people's business" (v. 11). So he commanded idle members to settle down and start working. At the same time, Paul urged those who were faithful and hardworking to never tire of doing good.

COURAGE FOR TODAY

Do you struggle to say "no" to individuals who are consistently looking for handouts? Read the verse below and describe how you can courageously love and encourage others and stop enabling them today.

*Lazy people want much but get little,
but those who work hard will prosper.*

PROVERBS 13:4

THE COURAGE TO
Wait on God

He asked the LORD what he should do, but the LORD refused to answer him,
either by dreams or by sacred lots or by the prophets.

1 SAMUEL 28:6

Father, I sometimes rely on other sources for advice rather than waiting for your guidance. Give me great patience and help me courageously trust only in you, no matter how long I must wait.

Are you ever tempted to rely on guidance from anything or anyone other than God? Note how Saul continued his practice of disobeying God in 1 Samuel chapter 28. Saul had asked the Lord what he should do about the enemy army gathering nearby, but rather than waiting for God to respond, Saul then sought the advice of a psychic.

God's prophet Samuel had been Saul's trusted advisor throughout Saul's reign as king of Israel. But when Samuel died, Saul was left to rely on his own relationship with God. Yet God, in response to King Saul's habitual disobedience, chose to remain silent when Saul asked him for help. Rather than humbly confessing his sinful nature and waiting for God's response, Saul asked a medium to call up the spirit of Samuel even though God strictly forbade the practice of consulting mediums.

COURAGE FOR TODAY

Do you ever get impatient when waiting for God to answer your prayers? Read the passage below and consider if there might be a reason for God's silence. Is there a sin you need to turn from and confess before the Lord? Humbly confess to God any wrongdoing or doubt today and commit to courageously awaiting his response no matter how long it takes.

If I had not confessed the sin in my heart, the Lord would not have listened. But God did listen! He paid attention to my prayer. Praise God, who did not ignore my prayer or withdraw his unfailing love from me.

PSALM 66:18–20

THE COURAGE TO
Show Hospitality

Don't forget to show hospitality to strangers, for some who have done this have entertained angels without realizing it!

HEBREWS 13:2

Father, you call me to help those who cannot help themselves. Give me the courage to reach out and care for someone in need of kindness and compassion today.

Have you ever invited a newcomer to join you for a meal or a small group gathering? Consider the writer's final instructions in Hebrews chapter 13. The author of the letter to Hebrews described basic principles that are important in living out the Christian life. Beginning within the family of God, believers are commanded to "keep on loving each other as brothers and sisters" (v. 1). But it requires courage to fulfill the author's next instruction: "to show hospitality to strangers" (v. 2).

At times, this might include housing a stranger overnight or even longer. For who knows—a believer could be entertaining an angel. The Bible records Abraham, Lot, Gideon, and others having entertained God's messengers. Such acts of kindness make an impact for the kingdom of God and sometimes lead to the salvation of a lost soul.

COURAGE FOR TODAY

Do you need more courage to step outside your comfort zone and extend kindness to a stranger? Meditate on Jesus' teaching below and let it inspire you today to lend a hand to someone you don't know.

"I was hungry, and you fed me. I was thirsty, and you gave me a drink. I was a stranger, and you invited me into your home. I was naked, and you gave me clothing. I was sick, and you cared for me. I was in prison, and you visited me."

MATTHEW 25:35–36

THE COURAGE TO
Celebrate God

David sang this song to the LORD on the day the LORD rescued him from all his enemies and from Saul. He sang: "The LORD is my rock, my fortress, and my savior; my God is my rock, in whom I find protection. He is my shield, the power that saves me, and my place of safety. He is my refuge, my savior, the one who saves me from violence."

2 SAMUEL 22:1–3

Father, you are my refuge in times of trouble, my strength when I am weak, and my courage when I am afraid. Help me always seek shelter in your loving arms and embrace courage in your presence.

Where do you turn in times of trouble? Reflect on and be inspired by David's song of praise and thanksgiving in 2 Samuel chapter 22. In the first four verses of his poem, David praised God for delivering him from his enemies. The psalm continues by recalling David's dire situation, and the following verses describe how God "reached down from heaven and rescued" David (v. 17).

The remaining verses of David's song provide a beautiful description of the incomparable attributes of almighty God, the perfection of his ways, and his faithfulness. As we meditate on God's character, we, too, should celebrate his sovereignty, power, and presence in our lives.

COURAGE FOR TODAY

Does God's presence and character inspire you to rely on him at all times? Read the first two verses of Psalm 91 and write a letter thanking God for his faithfulness. What courageous steps of faith will you take today?

Those who live in the shelter of the Most High will find rest in the shadow of the Almighty. This I declare about the LORD: He alone is my refuge, my place of safety; he is my God, and I trust him.

PSALM 91:1–2

THE COURAGE TO
Recognize Your Sin

Everyone has sinned; we all fall short of God's glorious standard. Yet God, in his grace, freely makes us right in his sight. He did this through Christ Jesus when he freed us from the penalty for our sins.

ROMANS 3:23–24

Father, at times I judge others for their sins while overlooking my own wrongdoings. Help me recognize that I, too, will always be a sinner in need of a Savior.

Does your pride tempt you to ignore your sins while focusing on the faults of others? Consider the apostle Paul's teaching in Romans chapter 3. In his letter to the Roman church, Paul discussed the need for believers to accept that "all people...are under the power of sin," even those who believe they are religiously superior (v. 9). He then quoted Psalm 14:1–3, which states that "no one is righteous—not even one" (Romans 3:10).

After describing the various ways in which people sin against God, Paul explained that "no one can ever be made right with God by doing what the law commands. The law simply shows us how sinful we are" (v. 20). Therefore, God made one way for humankind "to be made right with him...by placing our faith in Jesus Christ" (vv. 21–22).

COURAGE FOR TODAY

Do you recognize your continual need for God's forgiveness? Let the verse below open your eyes to your endless need for God's grace. Then confess your sinful nature and courageously commit to extend God's mercy to those around you today.

If we claim we have no sin, we are only fooling ourselves and not living in the truth. But if we confess our sins to him, he is faithful and just to forgive us our sins and to cleanse us from all wickedness.

1 JOHN 1:8–9

THE COURAGE TO

Help and Rely on Others

I observed that most people are motivated to success because they envy their neighbors. But this, too, is meaningless—like chasing the wind…And yet, "Better to have one handful with quietness than two handfuls with hard work and chasing the wind."

ECCLESIASTES 4:4, 6

Father, you created me to be in relationship with you and others. When I am caught in the trap of self-reliance and self-satisfaction, remind me that pleasure is short-lived and can't bring lasting joy.

Are there people in your life who love, encourage, and support you? Do you offer the same to them in return? Let King Solomon's words in Ecclesiastes chapter 4 motivate you to focus on developing healthier and happier relationships with others.

In this chapter of Scripture, Solomon teaches that there will always be people who look out only for themselves and who prey on other people. Focusing on oneself leads to isolation and loneliness, whereas healthy, mutually supportive relationships generate joy, success, endurance, and strength. Regardless of what others may do, it's best for us to concentrate on pursuing comfort and peace in our relationships.

COURAGE FOR TODAY

Make a list of friends and loved ones you can count on. Add the names of those who know they can depend on you. Be challenged by the apostle Paul's words below and describe the courageous steps you will take today to nurture God-honoring relationships.

Make me truly happy by agreeing wholeheartedly with each other, loving one another, and working together with one mind and purpose.

PHILIPPIANS 2:2

THE COURAGE TO
Witness to Unbelievers

Live wisely among those who are not believers,
and make the most of every opportunity.

COLOSSIANS 4:5

Father, you call me to be a vocal witness of your great love and faithfulness. Give me the courage to speak up and act as your representative in the presence of those who do not know you.

Do non-believers within your sphere of influence know you are a Christ follower? Be inspired by the apostle Paul's closing remarks in Colossians chapter 4. Paul wrote to the church in Colossae to encourage believers in their faith and to correct any false teaching that would jeopardize their relationship with God. In his letter, he urged church members in Colossae to live in ways that encourage others to seek salvation too.

Paul used the word *believer* to describe a person who trusts in Jesus, relies on him for guidance, and assembles with other Christ followers. He pressed church members to communicate in ways that display God's grace. In doing so, their conversations would be a blessing to those who were lost. For Paul knew that if believers set their minds on God, including his promises and his peace, they would intuitively conduct themselves in ways that would lead others to the Lord.

COURAGE FOR TODAY

Do you need more courage to speak out about your faith? Meditate on the following verse and describe how you can be a more courageous witness for the Lord today.

You must worship Christ as Lord of your life.
And if someone asks about your hope as a believer,
always be ready to explain it.

1 PETER 3:15

THE COURAGE TO
Respect God's Word

"You have discouraged the righteous with your lies, but I didn't want them to be sad. And you have encouraged the wicked by promising them life, even though they continue in their sins."

EZEKIEL 13:22

Father, your Word is trustworthy and true. Help me uncover worldly lies as I rely on your Scripture to tell me the truth.

Have you ever fallen prey to false teaching? If so, how did you uncover the truth? Consider God's stern warning to the false prophets in Ezekiel chapter 13. God called Ezekiel to be a prophet to the Israelites who were living in exile in Babylon in 593 BC. While Ezekiel chapters 4 through 11 describe God's case against his rebellious people, God's message in chapter 13 is directed specifically to false teachers.

These deceitful leaders, who were living among the Israelites, were inventing their own prophecies and "[deceiving] my people by saying, 'All is peaceful' when there is no peace at all!" (v. 10). So Ezekiel condemned the dishonest prophets who were removing any incentive for God's people to repent, and he pronounced God's judgment against them that would uncover their lies. For God longed for the behavior of his people to change.

COURAGE FOR TODAY

Do you listen to popular promises of definitive prosperity and question whether they are 100 percent true? Read God's warning below and describe how you plan to ground yourself in God's Word today so you can courageously denounce worldly lies and rely on the truth.

A time is coming when people will no longer listen to sound and wholesome teaching. They will follow their own desires and will look for teachers who will tell them whatever their itching ears want to hear.

2 TIMOTHY 4:3

THE COURAGE TO
Live Humbly

Don't be selfish; don't try to impress others. Be humble, thinking of others as better than yourselves. Don't look out only for your own interests, but take an interest in others, too.

PHILIPPIANS 2:3–4

Father, so often I think more of myself than I think of others. Help me to break away from selfishness and find ways to esteem others.

Do you tend to want all things done your way? Do you often think that your needs are more important than others? Be challenged by the apostle Paul's words in Philippians chapter 2. Paul wrote to the Philippian church to remind them to live in unity. While pride and selfishness would tear them apart, being humble, helpful, encouraging, comforting, and compassionate would bring the congregation together.

The church at Philippi was the first church Paul birthed in Europe, and his heart was deeply connected to them. While the ancient Greeks considered humility to be a weakness, Paul assured believers this principle is a virtue. The ultimate example of humility can be found in Jesus Christ, who gave up his divine privileges and left his heavenly home to appear on earth for the glory of God and the salvation of humankind. Therefore, Paul urged believers to "have the same attitude that Christ Jesus had" (v. 5), "thinking of others as better than yourselves" (v. 3).

COURAGE FOR TODAY

Do your personal desires often trump the needs of others? Meditate on the verses below and embrace the courage today to break free from a "me first" mentality.

We should help others do what is right and build them up in the Lord...May God, who gives this patience and encouragement, help you live in complete harmony with each other, as is fitting for followers of Christ Jesus.

ROMANS 15:2, 5

THE COURAGE TO
Rely on God

When Joseph was taken to Egypt by the Ishmaelite traders, he was purchased by Potiphar, an Egyptian officer. Potiphar was captain of the guard for Pharaoh, the king of Egypt.

GENESIS 39:1

Father, you have told me that in this life I will face many trials and sorrows. But in you, I can find peace and hope. Help me to remember that you make all things work together for good, even my hardships and suffering.

Even when bad things happen, good things can result. Consider Genesis chapter 37 where we are introduced to Joseph and we learn about his father's favoritism and his brothers' jealousy. By the end of this chapter, Joseph's brothers had conspired against him, thrown him in a pit, and sold him into slavery. Genesis chapters 39–41 record the account of Joseph's years of suffering.

These chapters reveal that Joseph was seduced, accused of sexual assault, thrown into jail, and betrayed. Then one day, he was asked to interpret Pharaoh's dream. As a young man, Joseph suffered rejection, abuse, false accusations, and imprisonment. Yet through it all, God was with him and gave him favor. Joseph knew that his strength, hope, and courage came from almighty God, and in response, he honored God and gave him all the credit.

COURAGE FOR TODAY

Read the verse below and describe a personal experience in which God used your struggle or pain to ultimately improve your life or the lives of others. How does God's ability to control all outcomes give you more courage for today?

We know that God causes everything to work together for the good of those who love God and are called according to his purpose for them.

ROMANS 8:28

THE COURAGE TO
Have Compassion

"Which of these three would you say was a neighbor to the man who was attacked by bandits?" Jesus asked. The man replied, "The one who showed him mercy." Then Jesus said, "Yes, now go and do the same."

LUKE 10:36–37

Father, help me see the world through your eyes of compassion. Give me the ability and desire to help others who are in need.

Do you respond quickly when you see someone in need? Or do you hope someone else will help? Let Jesus' parable in Luke chapter 10 challenge you to have more compassion. After reciting God's greatest commandments, "Love the LORD your God with all your heart, all your soul, all your strength, and all your mind," and "Love your neighbor as yourself" (v. 27), Jesus taught a parable about a man who demonstrated love and mercy to an unlikely neighbor.

In his story, Jesus explained that a Jewish man was attacked by thieves and left for dead by the side of the road. When a priest and a temple assistant walked by, they looked the other way, not wanting to get involved. Yet when a Samaritan came along, a race despised by the Jews, he stopped, soothed the man's injuries, carried him to an inn, and even took care of his expenses, displaying both love for God and for his neighbor.

COURAGE FOR TODAY

Do you truly have compassion for those who are struggling? Meditate on the verses below and name ways you will courageously care for someone's needs today.

We know what real love is because Jesus gave up his life for us. So we also ought to give up our lives for our brothers and sisters. If someone has enough money to live well and sees a brother or sister in need but shows no compassion—how can God's love be in that person?

1 JOHN 3:16–17

THE COURAGE TO
Choose Rightly

Asa began to rule over Judah in the twentieth year of Jeroboam's reign in Israel...
Asa did what was pleasing in the LORD's sight, as his ancestor David had done.

1 KINGS 15:9, 11

Father, you give me free will to choose right from wrong. Help me courageously choose to do what is right in your sight and remain devoted to you all the days of my life.

Do you make godly decisions even when they are unpopular? Consider the following kings' lives recorded in 1 Kings chapters 14–15. Because of King Solomon's divided heart, God divided Israel into two territories: the Northern Kingdom, Israel, and the Southern Kingdom, Judah. After Solomon's death, his son Rehoboam became king over Judah, and Jeroboam, his former warrior and servant, became king over Israel.

First Kings chapter 14 outlines the reigns of Jeroboam and Rehoboam, who both chose evil over good. But King Asa, Rehoboam's grandson, broke the cycle of disobedience. When he became king, Asa chose rightly, and his heart was fully devoted to God all the days of his life.

COURAGE FOR TODAY

When presented with the option, do you choose obedience to God over the ways of the world? Read the passage below and list any changes you need to make to courageously choose rightly before God today.

With the Lord's authority I say this: Live no longer as the Gentiles do, for they are hopelessly confused...But that isn't what you learned about Christ. Since you have heard about Jesus and have learned the truth that comes from him, throw off your old sinful nature and your former way of life, which is corrupted by lust and deception.

EPHESIANS 4:17, 20–22

THE COURAGE TO
Be Unified

"I pray that they will all be one, just as you and I are one—as you are in me, Father, and I am in you. And may they be in us so that the world will believe you sent me."

JOHN 17:21

Father, I sometimes choose to keep to myself. Help me realize my need for healthy relationships so I can seek wise counsel, be encouraged, receive help, and offer support to friends and loved ones in return.

How much time do you spend with other Christ followers? Be inspired by Jesus' request in John chapter 17. Jesus knew there is strength in numbers, so just before his arrest, conviction, and crucifixion, he asked God to unify believers "that they will all be one." While praying for everyone who would ever believe in him, Jesus asked the Father to unite his followers in the same way the Father and the Son were united.

"Just as you and I are one—as you are in me, Father, and I am in you... may they be in us" (v. 21) so that all believers might also experience perfect unity. This way, the world would know that God had sent Jesus to earth and that the Father loves Christ's followers as much as he loves his Son.

COURAGE FOR TODAY

List the ways you spend time with other believers. Then meditate on King Solomon's counsel below and describe how you will courageously reach out and spend more time with people of faith today.

If one person falls, the other can reach out and help. But someone who falls alone is in real trouble...A person standing alone can be attacked and defeated, but two can stand back-to-back and conquer. Three are even better, for a triple-braided cord is not easily broken.

ECCLESIASTES 4:10, 12

THE COURAGE TO
Boast in the Lord

"Those who wish to boast should boast in this alone: that they truly know me and understand that I am the LORD who demonstrates unfailing love and who brings justice and righteousness to the earth, and that I delight in these things. I, the LORD, have spoken!"

JEREMIAH 9:24

Father, you created all things and are in control of all things. Help me remember that my opportunities, achievements, and prosperity come from you and that you even allow me to experience challenges for a reason.

Are you quick to take credit for your progress? Or do you regularly acknowledge God's involvement in your good fortune? Let the Weeping Prophet's words in Jeremiah chapter 9 challenge you to boast only in the Lord. God called Jeremiah to inform the Israelites about their coming judgment and future restoration.

In this chapter, Jeremiah described their corruption and expressed sorrow over their behavior. He announced Israel's destruction and revealed the destitution and suffering they would endure because of their faithlessness. In verses 22–24, Jeremiah confirmed that the only relief his people would receive would result from understanding God's character, his "unfailing love…justice and righteousness" (v. 24). Therefore, if anyone wanted to boast, they were to boast in the things that God delights in, not their own wisdom or power.

COURAGE FOR TODAY

Do you regularly recognize God's hand at work in your life? Meditate on the verses below and describe how you will courageously boast in the Lord today.

God chose things the world considers foolish in order to shame those who think they are wise. And he chose things that are powerless to shame those who are powerful…Therefore, as the Scriptures say, "If you want to boast, boast only about the LORD."

1 CORINTHIANS 1:27, 31

THE COURAGE TO
Utilize Your Gifts

*A spiritual gift is given to each of us
so we can help each other.*

1 CORINTHIANS 12:7

Father, you have given me unique talents and abilities. Give me the
courage I need to use my gifts to help others and to bring glory
to your name.

Do you recognize your gifts and talents? Or do you struggle to identify ways
the Holy Spirit has equipped you to benefit God and others? Be inspired by the
apostle Paul's encouraging words to believers in 1 Corinthians chapter 12. The
church members in Corinth had been serving themselves and their worthless
idols. So Paul urged them to mature in their faith and help one another.

Paul described the various God-given gifts they could possess, such as the
ability to give wise advice, to heal, to preach, or to prophesy. Yet he was quick to
remind them that no one gift is more important than another. To further explain
his point, Paul described how every part of the human body is necessary for the
whole body to function well. And the same is true for the church and among
believers, that every person and every gift is special and necessary. "All of you
together are Christ's body, and each of you is a part of it" (v. 27).

COURAGE FOR TODAY

Do you truly appreciate how God made you and the unique gifts you
possess? Read the following verse and describe how you will utilize your
talents and abilities to serve God and others today.

*God has given each of you a gift from his great variety of spiritual gifts.
Use them well to serve one another.*

1 PETER 4:10

THE COURAGE TO

Be Broken

Unseal my lips, O Lord, that my mouth may praise you. You do not desire a sacrifice, or I would offer one. You do not want a burnt offering. The sacrifice you desire is a broken spirit. You will not reject a broken and repentant heart, O God.

PSALM 51:15–17

Father, when I sin, you don't ask me to embrace shame and self-condemnation. On the contrary, you seek only authentic contrition and a willingness to change. Give me the courage to confess my sin before you and the genuine desire to change my ways.

Do you hold on to guilt and shame over past sins, or are you stubbornly denying that you've done anything wrong? Let King David's words in Psalm 51 inspire you to courageously own your mistakes, adopt a heart of repentance, and enthusiastically receive God's generous gifts of compassion, forgiveness, and restoration.

David wrote this psalm after Nathan the prophet confronted him about David's sin of adultery with Bathsheba. David knew that God's love and compassion would completely cleanse him from his wrongdoing, but God required one thing in return: "a broken spirit…a broken and repentant heart" (v. 17). King David eagerly embraced the truth and longed to be completely clean so that his joy and rejoicing would return.

COURAGE FOR TODAY

Are you genuinely broken over your wrongdoings? Meditate on the familiar verse below and let God's unconditional love and forgiveness bring you comfort. Confess your sorrow and commit to leave any sin and shame behind today so you can courageously embrace the life God has planned for you.

The LORD is close to the brokenhearted;
he rescues those whose spirits are crushed.

PSALM 34:18

THE COURAGE TO
Listen before Speaking

Understand this, my dear brothers and sisters:
You must all be quick to listen, slow to speak, and slow to get angry.
JAMES 1:19

Father, you command me to stop and think before I speak. Help me be a better listener, carefully considering my words and always being thoughtful of who I am speaking to.

Do you regard yourself as a good listener or a fast talker? Be encouraged by the words of Jesus' disciple in James chapter 1. The Bible offers the best advice for healthy communication. The apostle James laid out three great principles for communication in his letter to Jewish believers. "Be quick to listen, slow to speak, and slow to get angry" (v. 19).

James understood the struggle many people have with being anxious to share their point of view. Too often, people completely disregard the thoughts and opinions of others. James also knew that "human anger does not produce the righteousness God desires" (v. 20). Therefore, he taught believers that they need to listen without interrupting and rid themselves of the filth in their lives so they can fully and humbly accept and obey God's Word and will. For if Christ followers observe God's instructions and do what he commands, God will bless them for doing it.

COURAGE FOR TODAY

Do you need to be a better listener and a more cautious speaker? Read the following verse and list the courageous changes you need to make, beginning today, to be more thoughtful and considerate with your words.

Spouting off before listening to the facts
is both shameful and foolish.
PROVERBS 18:13

THE COURAGE TO
Impact Culture

The LORD was with Jehoshaphat because he followed the example of his father's early years and did not worship the images of Baal…He was deeply committed to the ways of the LORD. He removed the pagan shrines and Asherah poles from Judah.

2 CHRONICLES 17:3, 6

Father, you control all things and have allowed my current circumstances for a reason. Help me realize where and how I can exercise courage and be a godlier influence on others.

How important is it to you to influence others? Consider how King Jehoshaphat used his position of influence to inspire the people of Judah to have a closer relationship with God and his Word. King Jehoshaphat followed King David's example and faithfully honored God's commandments. In the third year of his reign, he sent leaders throughout Judah to teach God's Word to all the people.

Judah grew rich and militarily strong under Jehoshaphat's leadership, and other nations feared them because of their close relationship with God. Everyone has the privilege and opportunity to be a positive role model. Whether in our homes, workplaces, communities, churches, states, or nation, we must courageously strive to positively impact those around us.

COURAGE FOR TODAY

In what ways do you impact today's culture? Meditate on the verse below and consider how you can inspire others to embrace God's goodness. List courageous ways you can become a greater influence today.

You are a chosen people. You are royal priests, a holy nation, God's very own possession. As a result, you can show others the goodness of God, for he called you out of the darkness into his wonderful light.

1 PETER 2:9

THE COURAGE TO
Lay Down Your Life

As they stoned him, Stephen prayed, "Lord Jesus, receive my spirit." He fell to his knees, shouting, "Lord, don't charge them with this sin!" And with that, he died.

ACTS 7:59–60

Father, give me the courage to share your Word and your truth even if it costs me my life.

Are you willing to risk everything—including your life—to share Jesus with others? Be inspired by Stephen's courage in Acts chapter 7. Scripture describes Stephen as "a man full of faith and the Holy Spirit" (6:5), and many religious leaders felt threatened by his boldness. In attempt to rid themselves of Stephen, they persuaded men to lie and had him arrested. Yet that didn't discourage the great man of faith. He continued to share his testimony, even among those who were hostile.

When Stephen accused religious leaders of murdering the Messiah, they became furious and refused to hear it. So they stoned him to death for boldly declaring God's truth. In his final moments here on earth, Stephen looked to the heavens, cried out, "Lord Jesus, receive my spirit" and mercifully begged the Lord to forgive his murderers (vv. 59–60).

COURAGE FOR TODAY

How often do you share your faith with others? Are you willing to speak up around people who are hostile toward God? Read the verse below and make a commitment today to courageously share Jesus every opportunity you get.

Never be ashamed to tell others about our Lord. And don't be ashamed of me, either, even though I'm in prison for him. With the strength God gives you, be ready to suffer with me for the sake of the Good News.

2 TIMOTHY 1:8

THE COURAGE TO
Build on the Cornerstone

"Look! I am placing a foundation stone in Jerusalem, a firm and tested stone.
It is a precious cornerstone that is safe to build on.
Whoever believes need never be shaken."

ISAIAH 28:16

Father, you are my rock and my salvation, and with you, my hope will never be shaken. Give me wisdom and courage to build my life on your trustworthy promises and powerful presence.

Are you reluctant to fully rely on the Lord? Let God's assurances in Isaiah chapter 28 encourage you to build your life on him. Isaiah was a prophet who delivered God's messages of judgment and hope to the people of Israel. This chapter not only focuses on God's warning to the prideful and self-sufficient, but it also celebrates the rewards of those who consider God their pride and joy. Verse 16 offers a powerful prediction of salvation and hope.

In this verse, God announces that he will place a precious and tested cornerstone in Jerusalem, one that is safe to build on. This magnificent stone was established when God offered eternal salvation through his one and only Son, Jesus Christ. When we make God the foundation of our life, we will always be properly prepared to face any challenge or hardship that arises.

COURAGE FOR TODAY

Do you need more courage to weather the storms of life? Meditate on Jesus' words below and courageously decide today to truly make him the foundation upon which you build your life.

"Anyone who listens to my teaching and follows it is wise, like a person who builds a house on solid rock…But anyone who hears my teaching and doesn't obey it is foolish, like a person who builds a house on sand."

MATTHEW 7:24, 26

THE COURAGE TO
Fight Sin

I know that nothing good lives in me, that is, in my sinful nature.
I want to do what is right, but I can't. I want to do what is good, but I don't.
I don't want to do what is wrong, but I do it anyway.

ROMANS 7:18–19

Father, sometimes I struggle to honor you with my thoughts, words, choices, and actions. Help me fight the good fight and consistently resist my sinful cravings.

How hard do you strive to resist making poor choices in your life? Consider the apostle Paul's struggle with sin and let his confession inspire you to fight even harder. Paul was faithful to God, but he still struggled against the desires of his flesh. In his letter to the Roman church, Paul admitted that he often did the opposite of what he truly wanted to do because of the sin living in him. Instead of doing what was right in God's sight, Paul sometimes fell short and did what was wrong.

Realizing that nothing "good" comes from his sinful nature, Paul felt it was important to confess his struggle and acknowledge the one person who frees him from a "life that is dominated by sin and death"—Jesus Christ (vv. 24–25).

COURAGE FOR TODAY

Do you put up a good fight against sin in your life? Read the verse below and let it inspire you today to seek God's guidance, withstand your temptations, and courageously choose the way out.

The temptations in your life are no different from what others experience. And God is faithful. He will not allow the temptation to be more than you can stand. When you are tempted, he will show you a way out so that you can endure.

1 CORINTHIANS 10:13

THE COURAGE TO
Deliver God's Message

"Upon hearing this, Daniel (also known as Belteshazzar) was overcome for a time, frightened by the meaning of the dream. Then the king said to him, 'Belteshazzar, don't be alarmed by the dream and what it means.' Belteshazzar replied, 'I wish the events foreshadowed in this dream would happen to your enemies, my lord, and not to you!'"

DANIEL 4:19

Father, so many people need to hear your words of hope, healing, and warning. Help me be courageous and kind when I share your messages with others.

How often do you share God's Word with others? And when you have the chance, do you do so firmly or with love and compassion? Be challenged by a conversation recorded in Daniel chapter 4. Daniel was taken captive by the king of Babylon in 605 BC. Having been given great favor, wisdom, and knowledge by God, Daniel served the pagan king faithfully and became ruler over an entire Babylonian region under King Nebuchadnezzar.

One day, after the king had a terrifying vision, he called on Daniel because none of Nebuchadnezzar's other advisors could interpret his dream. Upon hearing the king's dream, even Daniel was "frightened by the meaning of the dream" and wished the events were not prophesied for the ruler (v. 19). Yet, out of respect for both God and the king, he gently explained its meaning and urged King Nebuchadnezzar to turn from his wicked ways.

COURAGE FOR TODAY

Do you need more courage to share biblical messages with unbelievers? Let the following verse challenge you to courageously share God's truth in loving ways today.

We will speak the truth in love, growing in every way more and more like Christ, who is the head of his body, the church.

EPHESIANS 4:15

THE COURAGE TO
Work through Pain

"My grace is all you need. My power works best in weakness." So now I am glad to boast about my weaknesses, so that the power of Christ can work through me.

2 CORINTHIANS 12:9

Father, please give me the courage to live above my pain.
Help me to not wallow in it but to rise above it.

Have you suffered physically, emotionally, or relationally with no end in sight? Consider the apostle Paul, one of God's greatest servants, who understood suffering and learned how to endure. In 2 Corinthians chapter 12, Paul spoke of visions and revelations so wonderful that he struggled not to boast about them. He shared his experiences and described how God also gave him "a thorn" (v. 7).

While Paul never specifically identified his ailment, he did reveal that it came from Satan, caused him great pain, and kept his pride in check. Although he repeatedly prayed for relief, God did not heal him. Yet through this experience, Paul heard the Lord say to him, "My grace is all you need. My power works best in weakness" (v. 9). Instead of wallowing in self-pity or giving up on his ministry, Paul relied on God's strength to replace his weakness.

COURAGE FOR TODAY

Are you currently in pain? Do you need God's help to overcome it? Meditate on Jesus' words below and courageously vow to rely on God's peace and power today to see you through.

"Come to me, all of you who are weary and carry heavy burdens, and I will give you rest. Take my yoke upon you. Let me teach you, because I am humble and gentle at heart, and you will find rest for your souls."

MATTHEW 11:28–29

THE COURAGE TO
Extend Compassion

He complained to the LORD about it: "Didn't I say before I left home that you would do this, LORD? That is why I ran away to Tarshish! I knew that you are a merciful and compassionate God, slow to get angry and filled with unfailing love. You are eager to turn back from destroying people."

JONAH 4:2

Father, thank you for always extending compassion to me. Help me let go of negative feelings that hinder my compassion toward others.

Have you ever wished for someone to "get what they deserve?" Perhaps you believe that "what goes around comes around." Let Jonah chapter 4 challenge your attitude. Jonah was thankful for God's compassion when God rescued him, but when God chose to deliver Nineveh from destruction, Jonah's heart was filled with anger, and he wanted to die.

While Jonah hoped for destruction, God desired deliverance. Jonah praised God for forgiving him, but he was disappointed in God's compassion for his enemy. God reminded Jonah of the one hundred twenty thousand souls in Nineveh who morally didn't know their right hand from their left. Jonah could not accept that the God who showed mercy to him would display the same grace for the barbaric people of Nineveh.

COURAGE FOR TODAY

Have you ever been so angry at someone that you wished they would receive punishment rather than mercy? Read the following verse, meditate on God's unconditional love and forgiveness, and ask the Lord to give you the courage today to extend compassion toward those who have hurt you.

The Lord isn't really being slow about his promise, as some people think. No, he is being patient for your sake. He does not want anyone to be destroyed, but wants everyone to repent.

2 PETER 3:9

THE COURAGE TO
Listen to the Truth

We must listen very carefully to the truth we have heard,
or we may drift away from it.

HEBREWS 2:1

Father, your truth gives me insight and allows me to discern right from wrong. Give me the courage and ability to receive your instructions and faithfully obey your commands.

Do you ever find it difficult to obey God's commands? What steps do you regularly take to protect your relationship with God and his Word? Consider God's wise words and warnings in Hebrews chapter 2. The writer of Hebrews addressed all Christ followers and urged them to listen to and heed Jesus' teachings. By using the term "drift away," the author explained how easy it is to fall away from God's truth. While believers don't normally wake up one day and simply choose to turn their backs on God, it can easily happen if Christians don't intentionally and consistently nurture their relationship with him.

Because the Hebrew believers were being persecuted for their beliefs, they faced an added temptation to compromise their commitment to the Lord. But the writer of this letter reminds readers that since Christ suffered and was tested, "he is able to help us when we are being tested" (v. 18). Therefore, the author urged them to cherish God's truth and hold fast to their salvation.

COURAGE FOR TODAY

Do you ever grow tired of reading, hearing, and obeying God's truth? Draw strength and motivation from the verses below and describe how you plan to consistently listen to God's Word and courageously apply it to your life in practical ways today.

Jesus said to the people who believed in him, "You are truly my disciples if you remain faithful to my teachings. And you will know the truth, and the truth will set you free."

JOHN 8:31–32

THE COURAGE TO
Choose Joy

Light shines on the godly, and joy on those whose hearts are right.
May all who are godly rejoice in the LORD and praise his holy name!
PSALM 97:11–12

Father, happiness is only temporary, but true joy can be found only in you. Help me set aside any distractions or discouraging circumstances so I can courageously choose joy every day.

Do you intentionally adopt a joyful perspective each day? In a fast paced, high-pressure society that focuses on instant gratification, immediate responses, and overloaded schedules, it can be difficult to maintain a spirit of joy. Be inspired by Psalm 97, which highlights the majesty of almighty God and reminds all who worship him that joy shines on those "whose hearts are right" (v. 11).

In this psalm, our Creator's character is celebrated. The forces of nature reveal his power, authority, and glory. In response, all the earth should rejoice. Because of God's greatness, all believers are to hate evil and rejoice in the Lord while faithfully praising his holy name.

COURAGE FOR TODAY

Are you willing to adopt an attitude of gratitude even when your circumstances aren't favorable? Reflect on the passage below and let your salvation give you peace and your privileged position as a child of God inspire you to courageously choose joy today.

Since we have been made right in God's sight by faith, we have peace with God because of what Jesus Christ our Lord has done for us. Because of our faith, Christ has brought us into this place of undeserved privilege where we now stand, and we confidently and joyfully look forward to sharing God's glory.
ROMANS 5:1–2

THE COURAGE TO
Receive God's Blessings

All praise to God, the Father of our Lord Jesus Christ, who has blessed us with every spiritual blessing in the heavenly realms because we are united with Christ.

EPHESIANS 1:3

Father, you are loving, forgiving, and overly generous. Help me to cherish the many blessings you give me and inspire me to use them in ways that honor you and benefit others.

Are you comfortable receiving gifts, compliments, and blessings? Meditate on the apostle Paul's words in Ephesians chapter 1 that include his reminder of the many blessings God bestowed upon the church in Ephesus, which included the following:

1. Becoming united with and complete in Christ.
2. Becoming holy and faultless in God's eyes.
3. Being adopted into God's family.
4. Being showered with kindness.
5. Receiving forgiveness, freedom, and life-lifting power.
6. Receiving wisdom, understanding, and insight to grow in knowledge.
7. Participating in God's good plan.
8. Being chosen to receive an inheritance from God.
9. Receiving the Holy Spirit.
10. Having confident hope.

COURAGE FOR TODAY

Do you struggle to recognize or believe you've been blessed? Meditate on the passage below and describe how you can courageously use your blessings to honor God and help others today.

God will generously provide all you need. Then you will always have everything you need and plenty left over to share with others. As the Scriptures say, "They share freely and give generously to the poor. Their good deeds will be remembered forever."

2 CORINTHIANS 9:8–9

THE COURAGE TO
Repent

"I take back everything I said, and I sit in dust and ashes to show my repentance."
JOB 42:6

Father, sometimes I believe that I am in complete control of my circumstances. Reveal my ungodly ways and give me an attitude of humility that leads to genuine repentance.

Are you genuinely remorseful when you misbehave or mistreat others? How willing are you to repent and change your ways? Consider Job's response to God's rebuke and challenge in Job chapter 42. Job was a godly, faithful, and successful man with a large family. Yet, God allowed Satan to test Job by removing everything he possessed, including his health and his children.

Job pleaded with God and questioned the reasons why he suffered so much. At the same time, he listened and responded to friends, who accused him of sinning against God. Finally, God responded to Job's assertive questions and comments, reminding Job not only of God's power and omniscience but also of his mercy and steadfast love. Job realized that he had been talking about things he "knew nothing about, things far too wonderful" for a mere human to know (42:3). Job recognized his insufficiencies and humbled himself before the Lord. Job was genuinely remorseful and confessed his ignorance.

COURAGE FOR TODAY

Do you quickly adopt an attitude of repentance when God convicts you of destructive thinking or wrong behavior? Read the following verse and describe the courageous changes you will begin making today. Then humble yourself, repent of your wrongdoing, and thank God for his unconditional love and grace.

If my people who are called by my name will humble themselves and pray and seek my face and turn from their wicked ways, I will hear from heaven and will forgive their sins and restore their land.
2 CHRONICLES 7:14

THE COURAGE TO
Give Away

Mary took a twelve-ounce jar of expensive perfume made from essence of nard,
and she anointed Jesus' feet with it, wiping his feet with her hair. The house was
filled with the fragrance.

JOHN 12:3

Father, I need the courage to be generous. Help me resist the urge to cling
to all you have given me.

Are you generous, frugal, or stingy? Be motivated by Mary's generosity in John
chapter 12. When the Passover celebration was held in the home of Jesus'
friends, there was great gratitude for Jesus' healing of Lazarus just weeks
before. During the meal, Mary, Lazarus' sister, performed a humble and selfless
act. She poured perfume valued at "a year's wages" (v. 5) onto the feet of Jesus.

Mary had sat at Jesus' feet to learn from him, fallen at his feet in
surrender to him, and then anointed his feet to honor him. Mary displayed
great courage when she let her hair down in public to wipe Jesus' feet. She
dismissed the worry of the cost and public opinion, for her one desire was to
worship her Lord. When Judas criticized Mary for her actions, Jesus quickly
defended her: "Leave her alone. She did this in preparation for my burial. You
will always have the poor among you, but you will not always have me" (v. 7–8).

COURAGE FOR TODAY

Do you need courage to be a generous giver like Mary? Meditate on the
following verse and choose at least one way you will courageously give
something away today.

Give freely and become more wealthy; be stingy and lose everything.
The generous will prosper; those who refresh others will themselves be refreshed.

PROVERBS 11:24–25

THE COURAGE TO

Return to Worship

"Ever since the days of your ancestors, you have scorned my decrees and failed to obey them. Now return to me, and I will return to you," says the Lord of Heaven's Armies. "But you ask, 'How can we return when we have never gone away?'"

MALACHI 3:7

Father, I've been guilty of going through the motions of religion. Help me return to you with a heart of repentance and true worship.

Are your motives for serving God self-seeking or sincere? Let the hearts of the Israelites in Malachi chapter 3 serve as a warning. During their seventy years of captivity, God's people had no physical place to worship the Lord. And after returning from Babylon, they took twenty years to rebuild their temple. Rather than delighting in the Lord, their hearts quickly grew cold, and they dishonored God. Even the priests were disobedient and were leading people astray.

So God commissioned the prophet Malachi to rebuke his people for their unfaithfulness and call them to return to worship. While God admonished them for their wayward behavior, he also offered them mercy and an opportunity to come back to him with pure hearts. "'Return to me, and I will return to you,' says the Lord" (3:7). The people then created a scroll of remembrance that recorded the names of those who feared him. Those whose names were written on the scroll the Lord regarded as his "own special treasure" (v. 17), his obedient children. After Malachi's prophetic words, God remained silent for the next four hundred years.

COURAGE FOR TODAY

Has your love for God become stale and your religious activities meaningless? Be encouraged by the verse below and vow today to courageously love and worship God wholeheartedly.

"You must love the Lord your God with all your heart, all your soul, and all your mind."

MATTHEW 22:37

THE COURAGE TO
Let Go of Fear

God has not given us a spirit of fear and timidity,
but of power, love, and self-discipline.

2 TIMOTHY 1:7

Father, your Holy Spirit resides within me and gives me power, love, and self-discipline. Help me set aside my fears so I can live out my faith, and courageously share my love and devotion for you with others.

Do you ever hesitate to share your faith with others? Consider the apostle Paul's message in 2 Timothy chapter 1 and let his encouraging words challenge you to let go of any fear. Paul began his second letter to Timothy by expressing his affection for him, a man whom Paul considered to be like a son.

Because of his confidence in Timothy's strong and genuine faith, Paul reminded him to "fan into flames the spiritual gift" that God had given him and let fear go (v. 6). He expected Timothy to courageously tell others about Jesus and be prepared to suffer for his faith. For Paul knew that the "spirit of fear" does not come from God. Instead, the Lord places his Holy Spirit within each believer to provide "power, love, and self-discipline" (v. 7).

COURAGE FOR TODAY

Do you ever fear rejection? Take King David's psalms below to heart and set aside any concerns you currently have. Then determine the courageous steps you will begin taking today to pursue God's will and calling on your life.

The LORD is my light and my salvation—so why should I be afraid? The LORD is my fortress, protecting me from danger, so why should I tremble?

PSALM 27:1

THE COURAGE TO
Endure Obstacles

God tested Abraham's faith. "Abraham!" God called. "Yes," he replied. "Here I am."
GENESIS 22:1

Father, this life is full of possibility and adversity. Open the eyes of my heart and mind so that I will consider every obstacle an opportunity to trust you more.

Do you realize that a tested faith is an opportunity to grow closer to God and spiritually stronger? Consider how God tested Abraham's faith in Genesis chapter 22. In previous chapters of Genesis, we read about Abraham's walk of faith and observe his stumbles and victories. Throughout each experience, Abraham's faith in the Lord grew stronger. So much so, that God knew he was ready for the ultimate test.

Sometime after the birth of Abraham's only son, Isaac, God told Abraham to offer Isaac as a sacrifice, and Abraham obeyed God without question. When he and Isaac reached their destination, Abraham prepared his son to be sacrificed, all while having complete faith that God would either provide an alternate sacrifice or bring Isaac back to life (Hebrews 11:17–19). Abraham trusted God implicitly and proved his faith conclusively.

COURAGE FOR TODAY

Do life's challenges cause you to doubt God's faithfulness? Or do they inspire you to trust him more? Read the passage below and describe ways your faith has been tested. How can you develop a more courageous faith in the midst of adversity today?

You say you have faith, for you believe that there is one God. Good for you! Even the demons believe this, and they tremble in terror. How foolish! Can't you see that faith without good deeds is useless? Don't you remember that our ancestor Abraham was shown to be right with God by his actions when he offered his son Isaac on the altar? You see, his faith and his actions worked together. His actions made his faith complete.
JAMES 2:19–22

THE COURAGE TO
Receive God's Peace

Just as they were telling about it, Jesus himself was suddenly standing there among them. "Peace be with you," he said.

LUKE 24:36

Father, it is so easy to get caught up in the demands of this hectic and pressure-filled world. Help me resist the temptation to give in to stress and anxiety so that I can receive and embrace your perfect peace today.

Do you sometimes struggle to embrace peace in your life? Throughout Scripture, God consistently speaks about receiving his peace. Consider Jesus' blessing on his disciples recorded in Luke chapter 24. After Mary, Mary Magdalene, and several other women learned about Jesus' resurrection, they quickly told the other disciples. Peter raced to the tomb, but most of Jesus' followers did not know what to believe.

While two of the disciples were walking along and discussing the events that had taken place, Jesus appeared to them. Not recognizing him, the disciples explained what had happened over the past few days and how their Savior's body was missing from the burial tomb. In response, Jesus rebuked them: "You find it so hard to believe all that the prophets wrote in the Scriptures?" (v. 25). So when Jesus appeared to them again in the presence of a group of disciples, Jesus addressed their distress and said, "Peace be with you" (v. 36). When we genuinely believe God and trust in his promises, we can embrace his peace at all times.

COURAGE FOR TODAY

Are you truly at peace? Do you foster peace in the home, at work, and in other places you go? Decide how you will courageously receive and share Christ's peace today.

Let the peace that comes from Christ rule in your hearts. For as members of one body you are called to live in peace. And always be thankful.

COLOSSIANS 3:15

THE COURAGE TO
Embrace God's Perspective

O LORD, you have examined my heart and know everything about me...
You saw me before I was born. Every day of my life was recorded in your book.
Every moment was laid out before a single day had passed.

PSALM 139:1, 16

Father, I am uniquely and wonderfully created by you. Help me rid my mind of the world's opinion of me so I can exclusively focus on your trustworthy view.

Do you sometimes get sidetracked by what others think? Be encouraged by King David's song in Psalm 139. This psalm begins by celebrating God's omniscience, for the Lord knows every move we make and every thought we have. The next four verses profess God's presence, for there is nowhere we can go or hide that God won't be there too. "Even there your hand will guide me" (v. 10).

God created us delicately, meticulously, marvelously, and with great purpose. The psalmist proclaims, "Thank you for making me so wonderfully complex!" (v. 14). And God's thoughts of us are loving, dependable, and never-ending. While there will always be people who reject, criticize, or insult us, we should ask God to search our hearts, point out our weaknesses, and lead us toward godlier behavior.

COURAGE FOR TODAY

Do you place more faith in the world's view or in God's opinion? Meditate on Jesus' words below and list the courageous ways you will adopt and exhibit God's perspective of you today.

"If the world hates you, remember that it hated me first. The world would love you as one of its own if you belonged to it, but you are no longer part of the world. I chose you to come out of the world, so it hates you."

JOHN 15:18–19

THE COURAGE TO
Remain Forever Faithful

Don't be afraid of what you are about to suffer. The devil will throw some of you into prison to test you. You will suffer for ten days. But if you remain faithful even when facing death, I will give you the crown of life.

REVELATION 2:10

Father, no matter what the future holds, I long to be forever faithful to you. Help me set aside my fear of mistreatment, rejection, or harm and endure any persecution I receive because of my faith.

Is there anything that could cause you to lose faith in God? Let Jesus' instructions in Revelation chapter 2 motivate you to be forever faithful. Jesus was pleased with his followers in Smyrna because they had endured poverty and persecution, yet they had still maintained a rich and loyal faith.

But even more suffering was on their horizon. Jesus instructed John to remind church members to put aside their fears and embrace courage to protect their faith. For some would be thrown into prison and some would even face death as a result of their belief in the Messiah. Therefore they needed to heed Jesus' warning: "If you remain faithful even when facing death, I will give you the crown of life" (v. 10).

COURAGE FOR TODAY

Is your confidence in God strong enough to keep your faith from being undermined? Memorize the verse below and vow today to courageously maintain your hope in the Lord as you trust in him to always keep his promises.

Let us hold tightly without wavering to the hope we affirm, for God can be trusted to keep his promise.

HEBREWS 10:23

THE COURAGE TO
Walk God's Way

Moses told the people to celebrate the Passover in the wilderness of Sinai as twilight fell on the fourteenth day of the month. And they celebrated the festival there, just as the Lord had commanded Moses.

NUMBERS 9:4–5

Father, you know the best direction for my life. Help me to understand where you want me to go and give me courage to walk confidently in the direction of your will.

Are you willing to accept that God knows best, and will you heed his guidance? Consider the account of Israel's wanderings and how God faithfully led them from slavery toward prosperity in Numbers chapter 9. As God's people prepared to depart their encampment at Mount Sinai, God instructed them to celebrate the Passover, commemorating their exodus from slavery in Egypt.

God used a cloud by day and fire at night to guide his people. Whether God beckoned them to remain in one place for a period of time or to move their camp often, the Israelites trusted that God knew best, so they complied. While the cloud and fire indicated God's presence to that generation, God's presence today is evident by the Holy Spirit that lives within every believer.

COURAGE FOR TODAY

Do countless distractions and self-imposed demands keep you from seeking God's guidance? Read the following verse and ask God to give you wisdom and insight into what he wants you to accomplish. List specific steps you will take today to courageously walk his way.

"He is the Holy Spirit, who leads into all truth. The world cannot receive him, because it isn't looking for him and doesn't recognize him. But you know him, because he lives with you now and later will be in you."

JOHN 14:17

THE COURAGE TO
Be Transformed

*All of us who have had that veil removed can see and reflect the glory of the Lord.
And the Lord—who is the Spirit—makes us more and more like him as we are
changed into his glorious image.*

2 CORINTHIANS 3:18

Father, your Spirit lives within me and continually prompts me to become more like you. Help me surrender to your will and be transformed into the person you created and desire for me to be.

Do you accept that God wants you to become more like Jesus every day? Let the apostle Paul's message in 2 Corinthians chapter 3 inspire you to ask God to give you the courage to make any necessary changes today. Paul's words in this chapter reflect his humility and reliance on God.

He explained that the old covenant practice of animal offerings to cover sins had been replaced by a far superior sacrifice—that of Jesus Christ. Those who held on to their old beliefs were veiled to God's truth, "like Moses, who put a veil over his face" (v. 13), but those who embraced their new life in Christ have been set free by God's Spirit. And when the Spirit sets a believer free, they begin the transformation process of becoming "more and more like [Jesus] as we are changed into his glorious image" (v. 18).

COURAGE FOR TODAY

Have you embraced your never-ending transformation as a believer in Jesus? Meditate on King David's words below and ask God to give you the desire to make courageous and necessary changes to your attitudes and behaviors today.

*Create in me a clean heart, O God. Renew a loyal spirit within me…
Restore to me the joy of your salvation, and make me willing to obey you.*

PSALM 51:10, 12

THE COURAGE TO
Celebrate God's Presence

The trumpeters and singers performed together in unison to praise and give thanks to the LORD. Accompanied by trumpets, cymbals, and other instruments, they raised their voices and praised the LORD with these words: "He is good! His faithful love endures forever!" At that moment a thick cloud filled the Temple of the LORD.

2 CHRONICLES 5:13

Father, since I received your Holy Spirit at salvation, you are with me at all times and in all places. Help me to not only be aware of your presence but also to always trust in and depend on you for guidance, strength, and courage.

How often do you celebrate God's presence? Be inspired by Israel's preparation, worship, and celebration recorded in 2 Chronicles chapter 5. When the temple's construction was complete and the dedicated items were installed, King Solomon instructed Israel's leaders to bring the ark of the covenant into the temple's inner sanctuary.

Every detail was important, and nothing was overlooked in order for the people to properly honor God and prepare for his presence to be among them. Then all of Israel celebrated, sacrificed, and praised God as "the glorious presence of the LORD filled the Temple of God" (v. 14). Today, as believers, we are God's temple, and his Holy Spirit resides within us.

COURAGE FOR TODAY

Do you regularly acknowledge, rely on, and celebrate God's presence in your life? Describe how you believe God's Holy Spirit can give you more courage for your life today.

My old self has been crucified with Christ. It is no longer I who live, but Christ lives in me. So I live in this earthly body by trusting in the Son of God, who loved me and gave himself for me.

GALATIANS 2:20

THE COURAGE TO
Expect Rejection

Some were persuaded by the things he said,
but others did not believe.

ACTS 28:24

Father, you call me to represent your love and salvation in front of everyone, regardless of their response. Help me anticipate and overcome any rejections so I can continue to share your truth everywhere I go.

Do you ever hesitate to speak up out of fear of rejection? Consider the apostle Paul's experience in Acts chapter 28. After being imprisoned and transported from Caesarea to Rome, Paul appeared before local Jewish leaders to explain why he was placed under house arrest. When he confessed his faith in Jesus, the leaders expressed their interest in hearing more.

When the day came for Paul to speak, he testified from morning until night about Jesus being the Messiah. He explained how Jesus had fulfilled the law of Moses and had satisfied every prophecy spoken by their ancestors. While some were persuaded to believe in Christ, others rejected Paul's beliefs. So Paul accepted that some people's hearts were hardened, yet he never stopped "boldly proclaiming the Kingdom of God and teaching about the Lord Jesus Christ" (v. 31).

COURAGE FOR TODAY

Are you willing to set aside hesitation and respectfully speak up about your love for your Savior? Consider the encouraging words below and vow to courageously share your faith with someone you meet today.

"Anyone who accepts your message is also accepting me. And anyone who rejects you is rejecting me. And anyone who rejects me is rejecting God, who sent me."

LUKE 10:16

THE COURAGE TO

Fulfill Your Calling

"I knew you before I formed you in your mother's womb. Before you were born I set you apart and appointed you as my prophet to the nations."

JEREMIAH 1:5

Father, thank you for creating me with my own set of gifts and talents. Give me the courage to use my abilities to glorify you, to benefit others, and to fulfill your intended purpose in my life.

Do you believe you were made on purpose and for a purpose? Let the words God spoke to the prophet in Jeremiah chapter 1 give you courage to fulfill your God-given calling. At the time of his assignment, Jeremiah was a young man who felt inadequate to be God's spokesperson. Behind his excuse crouched an element of fear. "I can't speak for you! I'm too young!" (v. 6).

In response to Jeremiah's hesitation, God comforted the inexperienced prophet by telling him, "I have put my words in your mouth!" (v. 9). The Lord knew his message of judgment would be met with resistance, so God reassured Jeremiah and empowered him to speak boldly before kings, priests, and the people of Judah. Through words and visions, God strengthened and prepared Jeremiah, reassuring him that he would be with him every step of the way.

COURAGE FOR TODAY

Do you feel unprepared for the assignment God has for you? If so, you're not alone. Be inspired by the words of encouragement below that King David spoke to his son Solomon, and describe how you will embrace your God-given courage today.

"Be strong and courageous, and do the work. Don't be afraid or discouraged, for the LORD God, my God, is with you. He will not fail you or forsake you. He will see to it that all the work related to the Temple of the LORD is finished correctly."

1 CHRONICLES 28:20

THE COURAGE TO
Tell the Truth

*One of the household slaves of the high priest, a relative of the man whose ear
Peter had cut off, asked, "Didn't I see you out there in the olive grove with Jesus?"
Again Peter denied it. And immediately a rooster crowed.*

JOHN 18: 26–27

Father, give me the courage to speak the truth regardless of the
consequences that may follow.

Have you ever lied or stretched the truth to keep yourself from trouble? If so, how
did you feel afterward? Learn from one of Jesus' closest disciples, who denied
knowing him even though he loved Jesus deeply and followed him closely.

Jesus repeatedly warned his disciples that he would be leaving them,
but they were unable to truly grasp the gravity of the situation. After Jesus was
arrested, his followers were terrified. While Peter loved Jesus and believed he
was the Son of God, Peter also feared for his own life. Three times, bystanders
questioned Peter about being one of Christ's disciples, and three times he
lacked the courage to be truthful. Jesus had warned Peter that before the
rooster crowed that day, Peter would deny knowing his Savior, and that's
exactly what happened. But fortunately for Peter, the story didn't end there.
When Jesus returned after his death, he allowed Peter to redeem himself.

COURAGE FOR TODAY

Do you need more courage to be honest at all costs? Meditate on the
verses below and courageously commit to telling the truth today.

*Now is the time to get rid of anger, rage, malicious behavior, slander, and dirty
language. Don't lie to each other, for you have stripped off your old sinful nature
and all its wicked deeds.*

COLOSSIANS 3:8–9

THE COURAGE TO
Praise God's Word

Ezra stood on the platform in full view of all the people. When they saw him open the book, they all rose to their feet. Then Ezra praised the LORD, the great God, and all the people chanted, "Amen! Amen!" as they lifted their hands. Then they bowed down and worshiped the LORD with their faces to the ground.

NEHEMIAH 8:5–6

Father, your words are transformational when I apply them to my life. Help me to always cherish and respect the Bible as I commit to reading it every day.

How often do you read and study Scripture and put it into practice? Consider Nehemiah chapter 8, which reveals the respect and devotion God's people had for the Word of God. In this chapter, we learn that the people of Judah gathered in Jerusalem to listen to God's Word.

When Ezra opened the book, the people stood, lifted their hands, then bowed down and worshiped God. After hearing the Scriptures, they celebrated, realizing that this day was "a sacred day before the LORD" (v. 9). The next day, out of a desire to learn more, they gathered again to hear Ezra read the Scriptures. Upon hearing God's law, the people were moved to take action.

COURAGE FOR TODAY

Are you genuinely moved by God's words? Read the passage below and describe how you will courageously celebrate the Bible and make it part of your life today.

The instructions of the LORD are perfect, reviving the soul. The decrees of the LORD are trustworthy, making wise the simple. The commandments of the LORD are right, bringing joy to the heart. The commands of the LORD are clear, giving insight for living. Reverence for the LORD is pure, lasting forever. The laws of the LORD are true; each one is fair.

PSALM 19:7–9

THE COURAGE TO
Humble Yourself

"Those who exalt themselves will be humbled,
and those who humble themselves will be exalted."

MATTHEW 23:12

Father, when I am tempted to exalt myself above others, remind me that I, too, am human and capable of mistakes, struggles, and failure.

Do you ever elevate your own goodness, importance, or accomplishments? While confidence is helpful, arrogance is always harmful. Consider Jesus' rebuke in Matthew chapter 23. Religious teachers and leaders had placed themselves on pedestals while judging everyone else according to their ability to follow their heavy laws.

Jesus pointed to the behavior of the Pharisees and teachers, explaining how they didn't practice what they preached, did everything for show, and cherished their authority, recognition, and privileges above all else. So Jesus cautioned his audience against this and announced that "those who exalt themselves will be humbled, and those who humble themselves will be exalted" (v. 12). He then described their legalistic practices and the misery that awaited them, calling them hypocrites who pretended to be perfect.

COURAGE FOR TODAY

Do you practice what you preach? Let the verse below inspire you to take an honest inventory of your attitudes and behaviors and commit today to courageously humbling yourself in any area of your life that is needed.

Because of the privilege and authority God has given me, I give each of you this warning: Don't think you are better than you really are. Be honest in your evaluation of yourselves, measuring yourselves by the faith God has given us.

ROMANS 12:3

THE COURAGE TO
Choose Discipline

My child, if sinners entice you, turn your back on them…
My child, don't go along with them! Stay far away from their paths.

PROVERBS 1:10, 15

Father, you have given me your Holy Spirit and your Word as a guide for godly living. Give me an open mind that longs for your guidance and willingly applies it to my everyday life.

Are you quick to turn your back on temptation? Or do you sometimes play with fire, expecting not to get burned? Take to heart the words of King Solomon in Proverbs chapter 1. Solomon wrote many proverbs to give instruction in wise living. While a wise person receives godly counsel and applies it to their life, "fools despise wisdom and discipline" and choose instead to go their own way (v. 7).

In this Proverb, Solomon describes two opposing directions in life, and each person is given the opportunity to choose for themselves whether they will lead lives of discipline or foolishness. While the foolish path leads to violence, greed, immorality, and severe consequences, the disciplined path leads to justice, honor, success, and true peace.

COURAGE FOR TODAY

Do you live a disciplined life? What life changes do you sense God is calling you to make? Read Paul's message below and let it inspire you today to choose discipline courageously and consistently.

All athletes are disciplined in their training. They do it to win a prize that will fade away, but we do it for an eternal prize. So I run with purpose in every step. I am not just shadowboxing. I discipline my body like an athlete, training it to do what it should. Otherwise, I fear that after preaching to others I myself might be disqualified.

1 CORINTHIANS 9:25–27

THE COURAGE TO
Let God Provide

Jesus said, "You feed them." "With what?" they asked. "We'd have to work for months to earn enough money to buy food for all these people!"

MARK 6:37

Father, you promise to supply all I need, including everything that is essential to accomplish your calling. Help me align my wants with your will and trust that you will provide exactly what I need.

Are you able to remain confident even when you believe you are lacking what you need to move forward or carry out God's will? Consider Jesus' illustration recorded in Mark chapter 6. No matter how profound his teaching was or how many miracles he performed, religious leaders in Jesus' day refused to accept that he was their long-awaited Messiah, God in the flesh. Unfortunately, his disciples sometimes struggled with doubts as well.

When Jesus saw a large crowd that had followed him, he commanded his disciples to feed them. But in response to Jesus' request, they complained about how much it would cost to feed a crowd that large. When Jesus asked them how much food they had, they replied, "We have five loaves of bread and two fish" (v. 38). Using their meager resources, Jesus blessed the food and provided all that was needed to feed five thousand men and their families.

COURAGE FOR TODAY

Do you truly believe God will provide your needs? Memorize the verse below and describe how you will courageously trust God today to give you everything you need to pursue and accomplish his will for you.

This same God who takes care of me will supply all your needs from his glorious riches, which have been given to us in Christ Jesus.

PHILIPPIANS 4:19

THE COURAGE TO
Embrace Christ's Sacrifice

He was pierced for our rebellion, crushed for our sins.
He was beaten so we could be whole.
He was whipped so we could be healed.

ISAIAH 53:5

Father, Jesus gave his life so I could be eternally set free from
the penalty of my sins. Help me live in ways that truly honor his selfless
and incredible sacrifice.

How often do you reflect upon the agonizing sacrifice Christ endured for our
freedom? Meditate on the concluding verses of the fourth prophetic Servant
Song in Isaiah chapter 53. Let these fulfilled predictions of our Savior genuinely
sink in. The Messianic prophecies recorded in this chapter are quoted
numerous times by New Testament authors when referring to Christ's life,
ministry, and crucifixion.

Though Jesus performed many miracles, people still refused to believe
in him. Jesus suffered unjustly, was pierced for our sins, and "he was led like a
lamb to the slaughter. And…he did not open his mouth" (v. 7). Though Jesus
had done no wrong, they mocked and mistreated him like he was a rebel, and
they killed and buried him like he was a criminal.

COURAGE FOR TODAY

Are you humbled by Christ's sacrifice? Let the following familiar verse
help you to fully grasp God's love and inspire you to embrace a more
courageous faith today.

"This is how God loved the world: He gave his one and only Son,
so that everyone who believes in him will not perish but have eternal life."

JOHN 3:16

THE COURAGE TO
Be Strong

Be on guard. Stand firm in the faith.
Be courageous. Be strong.

1 CORINTHIANS 16:13

Father, my hope and faith are challenged at times. Give me courage and strength so I can stand firm in my faith and persevere through any hardship or adversity.

Are you able to courageously defend your faith when difficulties come your way or when someone challenges your beliefs? Take to heart Paul's message in 1 Corinthians chapter 16 and let it inspire you to be strong when your faith is challenged.

As Paul concluded his first letter to the Corinthian church, he encouraged believers to generously support others who were helping spread and defend the gospel, and he mentioned his desire to visit the Corinthians soon. But in the meantime, Paul urged believers to welcome his ministry partners and persevere in their faith. Because of his concern over false teaching, Paul advised the Corinthians to "be on guard. Stand firm in the faith. Be courageous. Be strong" (v. 13). He then also reminded them to "do everything with love" (v. 14).

COURAGE FOR TODAY

Is it easy for you to remain strong in your faith when life gets hard or your beliefs are challenged? Recite the following portions of Moses' praise song to the Lord and describe how you will rely on God's strength today to help you courageously persevere.

"The LORD is my strength and my song; he has given me victory.
This is my God, and I will praise him—my father's God, and I will exalt him!
With your unfailing love you lead the people you have redeemed.
In your might, you guide them to your sacred home."

EXODUS 15:2, 13

THE COURAGE TO
Acknowledge God's Character

*The Lord is good, a strong refuge when trouble comes. He is close to those who trust
in him. But he will sweep away his enemies in an overwhelming flood.
He will pursue his foes into the darkness of night.*

NAHUM 1:7–8

Father, no matter what I endure, I will remember that, although you are
slow to get angry, vengeance is yours, not mine. Help me affirm your
character and rely on your promises in every situation I encounter.

Do you accept that God is both loving and just? That anyone who opposes
him and attacks his people also welcomes his wrath? Consider the description
of God's character in Nahum chapter 1. About one hundred years had passed
since the city of Nineveh had repented after the prophet Jonah had warned
them of God's judgment. Yet once again, the Assyrians of Nineveh had become
merciless enemies of God's people.

In Nahum's opening message, he described God as "a jealous God,
filled with vengeance and rage" against his enemies (v. 2). Yet the prophet
also affirmed that God is "slow to get angry…a strong refuge when trouble
comes…[and] close to those who trust in him" (vv. 3, 7). Although the Assyrians
had many allies, God vowed to destroy them and make them disappear in
response to their scheming and evil plots against him and his people. Yet at the
same time, God promised peace to the Israelites.

COURAGE FOR TODAY

Do you consider God's whole character when evaluating your situations
and decisions? Meditate on the verse below and allow the attributes of
almighty God to give you courage and confidence today.

*How great is our Lord! His power is absolute!
His understanding is beyond comprehension!
The Lord supports the humble, but he brings the wicked down into the dust.*

PSALM 147:5–6

THE COURAGE TO
Be Sincerely Remorseful

*Zacchaeus stood before the Lord and said, "I will give half my wealth to the poor, Lord,
and if I have cheated people on their taxes, I will give them back four times as much!"*

LUKE 19:8

Father, make me aware of situations and times when I have treated others
badly. Give me a remorseful spirit along with the desire and ability to
make amends for the hurt I've caused.

Can you name the times when you've intentionally or unintentionally
mistreated others? Let Zacchaeus' story in Luke chapter 19 inspire you to
confess your wrongdoing and make up for any hurt you've caused. When Jesus
entered Jericho, he came across a man who had climbed a sycamore tree to
see him.

Zacchaeus was a wealthy tax collector who frequently cheated people
on their taxes. So as Jesus walked by the tree where the man perched, he called
Zacchaeus by name. "Quick, come down! I must be a guest in your home today,"
Jesus said to the tax collector (v. 5). While others criticized Jesus for being the
guest of a notorious sinner, Zacchaeus was grateful and sincerely remorseful.
So he vowed before the Lord to give half of his wealth to the poor and to repay
those he had stolen from—four times what he had taken.

COURAGE FOR TODAY

Are you remorseful over mistreating other people? Allow the verse below
to cause you to courageously change your ways today and discover
opportunities to make up for the hurt you've caused.

*I am glad I sent it, not because it hurt you, but because the pain caused you to
repent and change your ways. It was the kind of sorrow God wants his people to
have, so you were not harmed by us in any way.*

2 CORINTHIANS 7:9

THE COURAGE TO
Speak Up

Queen Esther replied, "If I have found favor with the king, and if it pleases the king to grant my request, I ask that my life and the lives of my people will be spared."

ESTHER 7:3

Father, sometimes I hesitate to speak up. Give me your wisdom to know what to say and when to say it, and give me the courage to lovingly speak the truth no matter who is listening.

Do you defend God, your faith, and others, regardless of opposition? Consider Queen Esther's courage, recorded in Esther chapter 7. Esther found herself in a precarious situation when Haman, a court official, convinced Esther's husband, King Ahasuerus, to issue an order to have all Jews destroyed. Prior to confronting the king about the fate of her people, Esther, a Jewish woman herself, prepared herself to "speak up" by personally fasting and praying and asking the Jewish community to do the same.

After seeking God's favor and guidance, Esther went before the king. Esther chapter 7 records her respectful plea for the lives of her people. Because of Esther's faith and courage, King Ahasuerus turned against Haman, and the Jewish population was saved.

COURAGE FOR TODAY

How often do you speak up for God, your faith, and others? Meditate on the verse below and describe the courageous steps you will take today to speak up.

I am not ashamed of this Good News about Christ.
It is the power of God at work, saving everyone who believes—
the Jew first and also the Gentile.

ROMANS 1:16

THE COURAGE TO
Embrace Your Gifts

In his grace, God has given us different gifts for doing certain things well. So if God has given you the ability to prophesy, speak out with as much faith as God has given you. If your gift is serving others, serve them well. If you are a teacher, teach well.

ROMANS 12:6–7

Father, you have given me many talents and abilities. Help me recognize and embrace my gifts so I can use them to honor and serve you every day.

How often do you use your skills and resources to serve God and others? Let the apostle Paul's teaching in Romans chapter 12 prompt you to identify your God-given talents and use them to honor the Lord and help others.

After urging believers to let their bodies "be a living and holy sacrifice" to God (v. 1), Paul discussed the many talents and abilities believers possess. From prophesying to teaching, giving, loving, serving, and leading, everyone has something they can contribute to the kingdom. In the same way our earthly bodies have many parts, each with individual functions, God has given each person specific abilities and skills that can complement and contribute to the work of all believers.

COURAGE FOR TODAY

Are you currently using your gifts and talents in ministry and to serve others? Read the passage below and explain how you will make further use of your God-given abilities to courageously pursue the Lord's will and calling today.

There are different kinds of spiritual gifts, but the same Spirit is the source of them all. There are different kinds of service, but we serve the same Lord. God works in different ways, but it is the same God who does the work in all of us. A spiritual gift is given to each of us so we can help each other.

1 CORINTHIANS 12:4–7

THE COURAGE TO
Worry Not

Don't worry about the wicked or envy those who do wrong. For like grass, they soon fade away. Like spring flowers, they soon wither. Trust in the LORD and do good. Then you will live safely in the land and prosper.

PSALM 37:1–3

Father, I worry way too often. Help me courageously replace all my concerns with peace and confidence in you.

How often do you worry about people, places, and things? Meditate on Psalm 37 and let God's words inspire you to trust him with your problems. It can be discouraging to live in a world where power, greed, and wealth seem to prosper, while those who are gentle, generous, and godly often struggle.

But in Psalm 37, God encourages believers to exchange worry and envy for faith and "delight in the LORD" (v. 4). For when we commit all we do to God, have faith in his help, and wait patiently for him to act, he promises we will be justified, and eventually, "he will make your innocence radiate like the dawn" (v. 6). Therefore, let us be confident that God will guide, protect, and bless us when we lay down our worry and anger and embrace courageous patience and faith.

COURAGE FOR TODAY

Will you give your worries to God and trust him with your circumstances? Read the familiar verses below and commit to courageously laying your concerns at the feet of Jesus today, where his presence and promises will bring you peace.

Don't worry about anything; instead, pray about everything. Tell God what you need, and thank him for all he has done. Then you will experience God's peace, which exceeds anything we can understand. His peace will guard your hearts and minds as you live in Christ Jesus.

PHILIPPIANS 4:6–7

THE COURAGE TO
Lead Carefully

Keep a close watch on how you live and on your teaching. Stay true to what is right for the sake of your own salvation and the salvation of those who hear you.

1 TIMOTHY 4:16

Father, you place me in positions of influence within my family, community, and among friends. Give me wisdom and courage to lead others carefully and faithfully as I strive to be true to your calling and your Word.

Do you consistently guard how you live and watch what you say so that your words and actions build others up and encourage them to live godly lives? Consider the apostle Paul's warning and encouragement in 1 Timothy chapter 4 and let it inspire you to be more careful in how you lead others.

Paul explained to Timothy that there would come a time when people would abandon their faith and follow "hypocrites and liars" (v. 2). He then encouraged Timothy to explain the truth but not to waste his time arguing over people's lies. Instead, Paul told Timothy to "be an example to all believers in what you say, in the way you live, in your love, your faith, and your purity" (v. 12). For if he stayed true to what was right, kept a close eye on how he lived, and faithfully taught God's truth, he would protect his own salvation and the salvation of those who heard him.

COURAGE FOR TODAY

Explain the ways you inspire others to be generous, loving, and kind while also motivating them to grow in their relationship with the Lord. Then memorize the verse below and describe how you will courageously and intentionally lead others toward godlier living today.

Let us think of ways to motivate one another to acts of love and good works.

HEBREWS 10:24

THE COURAGE TO
Ask for Understanding

God gave these four young men an unusual aptitude for understanding every aspect of literature and wisdom. And God gave Daniel the special ability to interpret the meanings of visions and dreams.

DANIEL 1:17

Father, you are the giver of true wisdom and understanding. Give me a longing to come before you daily to seek your wisdom and guidance.

Do you regularly rely on God for wisdom and knowledge? Be inspired by the predicament of four young men in Daniel chapter 1. In 605 BC, King Nebuchadnezzar overthrew Israel's capital city, captured an elite group of Israelites, and took them back to Babylon. Daniel and his three friends, Hananiah (Shadrach), Mishael (Meshach), and Azariah (Abednego), were young men when they were taken into captivity and chosen by Nebuchadnezzar for royal service.

While the trauma of his abduction could have left him bitter and unwilling to submit, Daniel instead treated the king's chief of staff with great respect while remaining firm in their dedication to God's laws. Because of this, "God had given the chief of staff both respect and affection for Daniel" (v. 9). And he gave the four young men great knowledge and intelligence along with giving Daniel the ability to understand visions and dreams.

COURAGE FOR TODAY

How often do you seek understanding from God? Read the following passage and begin courageously placing your faith in God's wisdom and guidance above everything and everyone else's today.

If you need wisdom, ask our generous God, and he will give it to you. He will not rebuke you for asking. But when you ask him, be sure that your faith is in God alone. Do not waver, for a person with divided loyalty is as unsettled as a wave of the sea that is blown and tossed by the wind.

JAMES 1:5–6

THE COURAGE TO

Forgive and Restore

It is time to forgive and comfort him. Otherwise he may be overcome by
discouragement. So I urge you now to reaffirm your love for him.

2 CORINTHIANS 2:7–8

Father, I sometimes struggle to forgive those who've offended me.
Give me your compassion and equip me to extend grace and mercy to
others like you do.

Do you struggle to forgive those who have hurt you? Do you feel that restoring your relationship with them is out of the question? Consider Paul's words in his second letter to the Corinthians, in which he urged believers to forgive and welcome back a sinful man.

Paul understood that all people need both forgiveness and love. While he had likely encouraged church members to discipline the sinful man, apparently the man had repented and now needed restoration. If believers had continued to ostracize him, the broken man may have become overwhelmingly discouraged. Therefore, restoration was needed so the man wouldn't lose heart. If the church had not reconciled with its sinful member, Satan might have again gotten an upper hand in his life.

COURAGE FOR TODAY

God commands us to forgive all people, and he urges us to restore our relationships with those who are genuinely repentant. Meditate on the verse below and ask God for the courage today to forgive those who've hurt you and to take practical steps toward restoration with those who are repentant.

Most important of all, continue to show deep love for each other,
for love covers a multitude of sins.

1 PETER 4:8

THE COURAGE TO
Confess Your Sins

David confessed to Nathan, "I have sinned against the LORD."
2 SAMUEL 12:13

Father, thank you for loving me unconditionally and for forgiving me as I humbly confess my sin. Help me to accept the consequences of my disobedience and inspire me to continually worship you even when I'm hurting.

When you sin, are you immediately remorseful, or are you more upset once you've been found out? Recall how King David responded after he heartlessly took another man's wife in 2 Samuel chapters 11 and 12. David lusted after Bathsheba and was willing to take her even though she was married to Uriah. When Bathsheba discovered she was pregnant while her husband was off in battle, David then plotted to cover up his sin and had Uriah murdered.

While David ended up taking the widowed Bathsheba as his wife, God didn't let David get away with his secret sin. God sent the prophet Nathan to confront King David, saying, "Why…have you despised the word of the LORD and done this horrible deed?" (v. 9). God forgave David's sin, but he also allowed David to experience consequences for his actions, which included the death of his and Bathsheba's son. Yet, while David mourned his son's death, he was also broken and remorseful, choosing to worship God in the midst of his great loss.

COURAGE FOR TODAY

How do you respond when you sin? Is there a sin you need to confess before God? Read the passage below and courageously confess your sins today, trusting God to forgive and restore you.

When I refused to confess my sin, my body wasted away, and I groaned all day long…Finally, I confessed all my sins to you and stopped trying to hide my guilt. I said to myself, "I will confess my rebellion to the LORD." And you forgave me! All my guilt is gone.
PSALM 32:3, 5

THE COURAGE TO
Spread God's Love

"I am giving you a new commandment: Love each other.
Just as I have loved you, you should love each other.
Your love for one another will prove to the world that you are my disciples."

JOHN 13:34–35

Father, you love all people unconditionally. Help me follow your example and love other believers despite any differences or conflicts.

Do you love others well even when you disagree with their views? Let Jesus' instructions in John chapter 13 encourage you to demonstrate your love for other believers. After giving his disciples an example of humble leadership by washing their feet, Jesus predicted Judas' betrayal and Peter's denial. Then he gave them a new commandment.

Having earlier clarified God's two greatest commandments, "You must love the LORD your God with all your heart, all your soul, and all your mind" and "Love your neighbor as yourself" (Matthew 22:37, 39), Jesus then commanded his disciples to "Love each other" just as he had loved them (John 13:34). For when the world sees believers' love for one another, it will recognize them as Christ's disciples.

COURAGE FOR TODAY

Are you currently at odds with another believer? Are you willing to love them despite your differences? Meditate on the verse below and let it inspire you to courageously love and pray for anyone with whom you are in conflict today.

If someone says, "I love God," but hates a fellow believer, that person is a liar;
for if we don't love people we can see, how can we love God, whom we cannot see?

1 JOHN 4:20

THE COURAGE TO

Restrain Your Desires

The LORD said to Elijah, "Go down to meet King Ahab of Israel, who rules in Samaria.
He will be at Naboth's vineyard in Jezreel, claiming it for himself."

1 KINGS 21:17–18

Father, I am sometimes tempted to believe the grass is greener on the
other side. Help me realize that the desires of my flesh are merely illusions
that seek to keep me from your will.

Have you or do you long for something that belongs to someone else?
Consider King Ahab's desire for another man's vineyard in 1 Kings chapter
21. This passage of Scripture reveals a conversation between Ahab and his
neighbor, Naboth, in which Ahab offered to purchase Naboth's vineyard.
　　When Naboth explained to Ahab that God had forbidden him to give up
his inheritance, Ahab became angry and depressed. But Queen Jezebel assured
her husband that she would get him what he wanted. "Don't worry about it. I'll
get you Naboth's vineyard!" (v. 7). She made good on her promise by resorting
to deception and murder. In response, God promised that Ahab would reap the
consequences of all he had put into motion. Yet, when Ahab showed genuine
remorse, God mercifully stayed his hand, promising instead to end Ahab's dynasty.

COURAGE FOR TODAY

Envy is like a disease. Left untreated, it will wreak havoc on your life. Has
envy stolen your peace? Read the verses below and write a commitment
to courageously set aside your worldly cravings today to pursue God's will
for your life.

Let the Holy Spirit guide your lives. Then you won't be doing what your sinful nature
craves. The sinful nature wants to do evil, which is just the opposite of what the
Spirit wants. And the Spirit gives us desires that are the opposite of what the sinful
nature desires. These two forces are constantly fighting each other, so you are not
free to carry out your good intentions.

GALATIANS 5:16–17

THE COURAGE TO
Grow Your Faith

"You don't have enough faith," Jesus told them. "I tell you the truth, if you had faith even as small as a mustard seed, you could say to this mountain, 'Move from here to there,' and it would move. Nothing would be impossible."

MATTHEW 17:20

Father, I sometimes struggle with distrust and discouragement. Give me a passion to consistently grow my faith so I can conquer my fears and defeat my doubts.

How strong is your faith? Can it carry you through difficult times? Does it give you strength to overcome your fears? Let Jesus' challenge in Matthew chapter 17 motivate you to consistently grow your faith. Even though his disciples had walked with Jesus, sat under his teaching, and experienced his miracles, their faith still struggled at times.

After Jesus' divinity was confirmed by his transfiguration, he came upon a man who begged Jesus to help his son. The man had asked Jesus' disciples for help, but even though Jesus had empowered them to perform miracles, they could not heal the man's son. The disciples wanted to know why they were unable to help the boy, and Jesus replied, "You don't have enough faith" (v. 20). For if one's faith is strong enough, "Nothing would be impossible" (v. 20).

COURAGE FOR TODAY

In what ways do you nurture your faith? Study the verses below and describe the steps you will take, beginning today, to grow stronger, more secure, and courageous in your faith.

You already know these things, dear friends. So be on guard; then you will not be carried away by the errors of these wicked people and lose your own secure footing. Rather, you must grow in the grace and knowledge of our Lord and Savior Jesus Christ. All glory to him, both now and forever! Amen.

2 PETER 3:17–18

THE COURAGE TO
Embrace God's Power

David replied to the Philistine, "You come to me with sword, spear, and javelin,
but I come to you in the name of the LORD of Heaven's Armies—
the God of the armies of Israel, whom you have defied."

1 SAMUEL 17:45

Father, too often I rely on my own strength and means to sustain me in challenging times. Remind me that you alone can protect me from my enemies and equip me to truly succeed.

Do you rely on your own strength and possessions to protect you? Consider the story of David and Goliath in 1 Samuel chapter 17. While this is a familiar Bible story we tell our children, it shows fundamental principles we should all put into practice throughout every stage of life.

Early in the chapter, we discover that Israel was at war with the Philistines and that the Philistines' largest and most powerful champion, Goliath, had challenged any Israelite warrior to fight him. But all the men in Israel's army were terrified of the nine-foot giant. As David questioned his homeland's soldiers, he asserted that Goliath had no business taunting God's army. Though David was young, his confidence in God was impenetrable. David was convinced that God would protect him and would give him victory if he fought the Philistine giant. Before handily taking Goliath's life, David calmly told him, "You come to me with sword, spear, and javelin, but I come to you in the name of the LORD…today the LORD will conquer you" (vv. 45–46).

COURAGE FOR TODAY

Are you confident in God's ability to empower you for victory?
Read the verse below and let God's words give you strength for your current situation.

"The LORD your God is going with you! He will fight for you against your enemies,
and he will give you victory!"

DEUTERONOMY 20:4

THE COURAGE TO
Overcome Intimidation

*"I declare today that I have been faithful. If anyone suffers eternal death,
it's not my fault, for I didn't shrink from declaring all that God wants you to know."*
ACTS 20:26–27

Father, some people attempt to discourage my faith. Help me reject their tactics and overcome their efforts to dampen my love and dedication to you.

Do you respond to intimidation with courage and confidence? Let Paul's persistence in Acts chapter 20 motivate you to resist bullying and peer pressure. When Paul's preaching and teaching threatened the wealth and welfare of idol makers in Ephesus, several artisans rioted, fearing their businesses would suffer and their false goddess would lose her influence. But Paul never backed down from the truth.

As Paul traveled near the province of Asia, he asked the church elders in Ephesus to meet with him. When they gathered before him, Paul reminded them that, from the first day he arrived in Asia, he had consistently, courageously, and faithfully served God. And, although he had endured suffering and rejection, he "never shrank back" or abandoned his calling to speak the truth (v. 20). Paul resisted all intimidation and persistently encouraged everyone to repent and receive Jesus as their Savior.

COURAGE FOR TODAY

Is anyone discouraging or distracting you from your dedication to God and his Word? Meditate on the verses below and let Paul's reassurance give you courage to overcome intimidation so you can grow closer and more courageous in your walk with God today.

Don't be intimidated in any way by your enemies. This will be a sign to them that they are going to be destroyed, but that you are going to be saved, even by God himself. For you have been given not only the privilege of trusting in Christ but also the privilege of suffering for him.
PHILIPPIANS 1:28–29

THE COURAGE TO
Count on Jesus

A child is born to us, a son is given to us. The government will rest on his shoulders. And he will be called: Wonderful Counselor, Mighty God, Everlasting Father, Prince of Peace.

ISAIAH 9:6

Father, I can easily get discouraged when I listen to the news. Help me remain hopeful in my relationship with you and dependent on your promises for my future and eternity.

Do you sometimes get discouraged by the corruption in our culture? Do you ever question whether God really cares? Consider the Israelite's hardship and God's promise of hope recorded in Isaiah chapter 9. Isaiah was a godly prophet who lived during a difficult and dark time in his homeland. But through Isaiah, God not only sent messages of judgment for Israel, but the Lord also wanted to remind his people that hope was on the horizon.

The prophecies in this book of Scripture describe how, one day, God's light and prosperity would abound again in the land of Israel. For "a child" would be born, and "the government [would] rest on his shoulders" (v. 6). God used four names to describe the coming Savior: "Wonderful Counselor," meaning an extraordinary advisor; "Mighty God," meaning a powerful and divine being; "Everlasting Father," meaning an eternal overseer; and "Prince of Peace," meaning a leader who secures peace and tranquility for those who receive him.

COURAGE FOR TODAY

Where do you find hope? Read the passage below and vow today to courageously count on Jesus.

We were given this hope when we were saved. (If we already have something, we don't need to hope for it. But if we look forward to something we don't yet have, we must wait patiently and confidently.)

ROMANS 8:24–25

THE COURAGE TO
Embrace Aging

Teach the older men to exercise self-control, to be worthy of respect, and to live wisely. They must have sound faith and be filled with love and patience.

TITUS 2:2

Father, you teach me that there is a time and season for everything under heaven. Give me the courage to grow older gracefully and be a faithful witness for you to the end of my life.

Have you encountered a grumpy older person? Perhaps you have experience with aging parents, friends, or loved ones who became preoccupied with their problems as they aged. Be inspired by the apostle Paul's wise words in Titus chapter 2. Paul wrote to his disciple Titus with instructions for the older men and women in the church. Their behavior needed to reflect godliness in the presence of younger believers.

Men were to live wisely, exhibiting self-control, sound faith, love, and patience. And the women were to honor God by watching their words and behaviors, teaching "the younger women to love their husbands and their children...to work in their homes...and to...not bring shame on the word of God" (vv. 4–5). Though still a young man and teacher, Titus needed to set an example for other believers. Living with integrity and good works would keep his reputation and relationships above reproach.

COURAGE FOR TODAY

Do you need encouragement to embrace your current season of life and to be a godly example for younger believers? Meditate on the following verse and determine the courageous steps you will begin taking today to leave a lasting and honorable legacy.

Now that I am old and gray, do not abandon me, O God. Let me proclaim your power to this new generation, your mighty miracles to all who come after me.

PSALM 71:18

THE COURAGE TO
Apply God's Word

Shaphan also told the king, "Hilkiah the priest has given me a scroll."
So Shaphan read it to the king. When the king heard what was written in the Law,
he tore his clothes in despair.

2 CHRONICLES 34:18–19

Father, I acknowledge that the Bible is your living, breathing Word. Help me understand how to apply your life lessons to my current circumstances in practical, courageous, and transformational ways.

Do you regularly apply God's Word to your life? Consider 2 Chronicles chapter 34, where we learn that King Josiah sought God at a young age, and he humbled himself and took action when the scrolls of the book of the law of Moses were read to him.

During the early years of Josiah's reign, he followed in the faithful footsteps of King David and sought God rather than pursuing selfish ambitions. At age twenty-six, King Josiah had the temple of God repaired. When Hilkiah the priest discovered the ancient scrolls, Josiah heard God's words for the first time and immediately humbled himself and "tore his clothes in despair" (v. 19). Then King Josiah sought God's will. Upon hearing God's response, Josiah took immediate action and commanded the people of Judah to also faithfully worship, honor, and obey the Lord.

COURAGE FOR TODAY

How often do you apply the Bible to your life? Write down the verses below and circle the ways Scripture can impact your life. Make a commitment to courageously implement God's guidance, commands, and warnings found in his Word today.

All Scripture is inspired by God and is useful to teach us what is true and to make us realize what is wrong in our lives. It corrects us when we are wrong and teaches us to do what is right. God uses it to prepare and equip his people to do every good work.

2 TIMOTHY 3:16–17

THE COURAGE TO
Reject Pride

"I tell you, this sinner, not the Pharisee, returned home justified before God. For those who exalt themselves will be humbled, and those who humble themselves will be exalted."

LUKE 18:14

Father, you command me to be humble, gentle, and kind. Help me see myself and others through your compassionate eyes and remind me to set my pride aside when it raises its ugly head.

Do you pride yourself on following the rules or in achieving worldly success? Let Jesus' parable in Luke chapter 18 cause you to reconsider your attitude. After teaching about a persistent widow and the importance of prayer, Jesus compared the dispositions of a Pharisee and a tax collector.

Both men went into the temple to pray. Yet while the Pharisee thanked God that he was more faithful and religious than other people, the tax collector humbled himself and prayed, "O God, be merciful to me, for I am a sinner" (v. 13). After telling this story, Jesus clarified that the sinner was more justified than the prideful Pharisee because those who are humble, respectful, and repentant will be exalted by God while those who are full of pride and arrogance will be humbled by the Lord.

COURAGE FOR TODAY

Are you consistently humble, gentle, and kind? Let the verses below challenge you to be more modest, considerate, and compassionate toward others. Explain ways you will courageously exercise humility, peace, and empathy today.

Always be humble and gentle. Be patient with each other, making allowance for each other's faults because of your love. Make every effort to keep yourselves united in the Spirit, binding yourselves together with peace.

EPHESIANS 4:2–3

THE COURAGE TO
Partner with Others

When Moses' father-in-law saw all that Moses was doing for the people, he asked,
"What are you really accomplishing here? Why are you trying to do all this alone
while everyone stands around you from morning till evening?"

EXODUS 18:14

Father, a pitfall to success is trying to go it alone. Give me the wisdom
to realize when I am over-obligated and give me the courage to not only
seek wise counsel but to also delegate appropriate tasks to trustworthy
and dependable people.

Are you overwhelmed, exhausted, worried, or stressed out? Do you often take
on responsibilities without asking for help or advice? In important life situations,
God calls us to seek wise counsel and consider delegating some tasks to others.
Consider the interaction between Jethro and Moses in Exodus chapter 18.

Jethro, Moses' father-in-law, came to faith when he heard how God had
rescued Moses and the Israelites. When Jethro arrived in the area where the
Israelites were encamped, he observed Moses' enormous responsibility and
leadership style. He immediately realized that Moses was overwhelmed by his
workload. So Jethro advised Moses to "select from all the people some capable,
honest men who fear God and hate bribes. Appoint them as leaders" (v. 21).
Moses listened to his father-in-law's wise counsel and courageously appointed
capable leaders to help him oversee the needs of the people.

COURAGE FOR TODAY

Do you feel as if you are the only person who can properly complete
a particular task? Are you reluctant to ask for help or advice? Read the
verse below and ask God to reveal to you the name of a godly advisor.
Courageously reach out for wise counsel today and make a commitment
to follow it.

Get all the advice and instruction you can, so you will be wise the rest of your life.
PROVERBS 19:20

THE COURAGE TO
Remain Dedicated

A third time he asked him, "Simon son of John, do you love me?" Peter was hurt that Jesus asked the question a third time. He said, "Lord, you know everything. You know that I love you." Jesus said, "Then feed my sheep."

JOHN 21:17

Father, when I am unsuccessful or make mistakes, I sometimes get frustrated and think about quitting. Help me remember that failure is an opportunity for growth and that I should never give up.

Is someone or something creating an obstacle in your life? Are you looking at your situation as an opportunity to learn something new? Or are you tempted to give up? Be inspired by Jesus and Peter's conversation in John chapter 21. When Jesus had been arrested and led to the high priest's home, Peter, as predicted, denied knowing his friend and Savior three times in front of a crowd.

Yet after his resurrection, Jesus appeared before his disciples at the Sea of Galilee. When Peter realized who it was, he jumped from the boat and headed for the shore. After sharing breakfast with his disciples, Jesus asked Peter, three times, "Do you love me?" and each time Peter responded, "You know I love you" (vv. 15–17). Although Peter was initially hurt when Jesus questioned him, he persisted in passionate dedication to reaching, teaching, and ministering to believers for the remainder of his days.

COURAGE FOR TODAY

Do you ever feel like quitting? Meditate on the verse below and make a commitment today to embrace your God-given courage to persevere through any obstacle that tempts you to give up.

*"Be strong and courageous,
for your work will be rewarded."*

2 CHRONICLES 15:7

THE COURAGE TO
Revere God

The LORD answered Job from the whirlwind: "Who is this that questions my wisdom with such ignorant words? Brace yourself like a man, because I have some questions for you, and you must answer them."

JOB 38:1–3

Father, you are all-knowing, all-powerful, ever-present, and completely in control. Help me revere you no matter what circumstances or situations I experience.

Do you faithfully worship, adore, and revere almighty God? Consider God's response to Job, recorded in Job chapter 38. Job was a God-fearing and faithful man who had a large family, success, and great wealth. However, one day, God allowed Satan to test Job's faithfulness. Satan took away Job's possessions, his ten children, and his health.

While Job mourned his calamity, he also pleaded with God to explain the purpose of his suffering and conversed with friends, who accused him of sinning. In Job chapter 38, we begin reading God's response to Job's painful questions. Here, God reminds Job of his limitations and contrasts Job's human weakness to God's incomparable power, might, and complete control. God wanted Job to accept that no matter what happens in this life, whether good or bad, Job should always believe in, trust, and revere almighty God.

COURAGE FOR TODAY

Amid life's struggles, do you maintain a consistent attitude of reverence and respect for almighty God? Read the familiar verses below out loud and make a commitment today to courageously honor and worship the Lord despite any hardship or challenges you are currently facing.

Since we are receiving a Kingdom that is unshakable, let us be thankful and please God by worshiping him with holy fear and awe. For our God is a devouring fire.

HEBREWS 12:28–29

THE COURAGE TO
Walk by Faith

We are always confident, even though we know that as long as we live in these bodies we are not at home with the Lord. For we live by believing and not by seeing.

2 CORINTHIANS 5:6–7

Father, while the world urges me to trust in people, pleasure, and possessions, you offer me hope, spiritual healing, and eternal life. Give me an unshakable faith so I can walk confidently and consistently in your perfect will.

Do you walk by faith and not by sight? Let the apostle Paul's message in 2 Corinthians chapter 5 motivate you to live according to God's promises and not by the world's standards.

Paul knew what it was like to grow weary of life on earth. His extensive experience with rejection, mistreatment, and incarceration caused him to long for eternal life in God's presence. For he knew "that as long as we live in these bodies we are not at home with the Lord" (v. 6). But he never let his hardships deter him from serving God and living by faith. So in order to persevere, Paul relied on his faith in Jesus and drew confidence from God's promise of eternity.

COURAGE FOR TODAY

Are you focused on the here and now? Or does your faith in God and eternal life impact the way you live today? Meditate on the verse below and vow to take your eyes off your troubles so you can courageously walk by faith today.

We don't look at the troubles we can see now; rather, we fix our gaze on things that cannot be seen. For the things we see now will soon be gone, but the things we cannot see will last forever.

2 CORINTHIANS 4:18

THE COURAGE TO
Be Satisfied

Sing out your thanks to the Lord; sing praises to our God with a harp. He covers the heavens with clouds, provides rain for the earth, and makes the grass grow in mountain pastures.

PSALM 147:7–8

Father, I am grateful for all you have given me. Help me overcome my worldly lusts and desires so I can be satisfied with all I have.

Do you lust for more possessions or long for different circumstances? Be challenged by the psalmist's song in Psalm 147. In this prayer, we learn that God builds up those who follow him, and he heals and supports those who need him.

God's wisdom and power are visible as he attends to every detail of our world. God blesses, strengthens, and satisfies the hunger of all who rely on him "with the finest wheat" (v. 14), and his Word gives wisdom and guidance to everyone who engages and applies it to their life. God gives us everything we need to live healthy, happy, and successful lives, and all he asks for in return is our faith, love, humility, and trust.

COURAGE FOR TODAY

Are you satisfied with all you currently have? Do you trust God to provide all you truly need? Read the apostle Paul's inspiring words below and vow to be courageously content and to trust God's guidance for any necessary changes today.

Not that I was ever in need, for I have learned how to be content with whatever I have. I know how to live on almost nothing or with everything. I have learned the secret of living in every situation, whether it is with a full stomach or empty, with plenty or little. For I can do everything through Christ, who gives me strength.

PHILIPPIANS 4:11–13

THE COURAGE TO
Stand against Satan

Stay alert! Watch out for your great enemy, the devil.
He prowls around like a roaring lion, looking for someone to devour.

1 PETER 5:8

Father, you are far greater than the devil. Help me stand firm against
Satan's many deceptions and temptations.

Do you ever feel helpless in your circumstances or powerless when fighting
temptation? Consider the apostle's advice in 1 Peter chapter 5. The apostle
Peter knew what it was like to fall prey to fear and enticement. Peter had
followed Jesus, had seen his miracles, and knew he was the promised Messiah.
Yet when he thought his life was at stake, Peter denied his relationship with
Christ three times. But after Jesus' resurrection, Peter became bold and
courageous in his faith and warned believers to "stay alert" and watch out for
Satan's tactics (v. 8).

Like enemy combatants setting land mines in strategic places, the devil
knows where and when to plant temptation and deception that can devour a
believer's faith and testimony. Because followers were under persecution, Peter
sought to encourage them. "Stand firm against [the devil], and be strong in
your faith. Remember that your family of believers…is going through the same
kind of suffering you are" (v. 9). Prayer would be their greatest defense, for
God's power trumps Satan's every time.

COURAGE FOR TODAY

Do you need more courage to resist Satan's tactics? Memorize the
following familiar verse and vow to ask God to help you courageously turn
away from any temptation or sin in your life today.

Put on all of God's armor so that you will be able to stand firm
against all strategies of the devil.

EPHESIANS 6:11

THE COURAGE TO
Speak Out

*If I say I'll never mention the L*ORD *or speak in his name, his word burns in my heart like a fire. It's like a fire in my bones! I am worn out trying to hold it in! I can't do it!*

JEREMIAH 20:9

Father, in this world that is desperate for hope and guidance, you are the only answer. Give me the courage to speak your name in any situation and in the presence of any person.

Are you sometimes hesitant to speak God's name in the presence of a particular person or group? Are you ever concerned you will be labeled or rejected? Be inspired by the great prophet's perseverance in Jeremiah chapter 20. Jeremiah spoke boldly even though he became unpopular and his hearers threatened his life. God's message of justice invoked hatred rather than inspiring the people of Israel to repent and return to worshiping their Creator.

Hopelessness overcame Jeremiah, and for a moment, he tried to remain silent. "I'll never mention the LORD or speak in his name" (v. 9). But God's presence was greater than the prophet's self-pity, and Jeremiah declared he could no longer stay quiet. For what he knew to be true about God and his Word burned like fire in Jeremiah's bones.

COURAGE FOR TODAY

Do you need more courage to share God's truth in the face of rejection? Meditate on the verse below and name at least one way you will courageously speak out about God today.

I am not ashamed of this Good News about Christ. It is the power of God at work, saving everyone who believes—the Jew first and also the Gentile.

ROMANS 1:16

THE COURAGE TO
Renew Your Life

"Who are you, lord?" Saul asked. And the voice replied, "I am Jesus, the one you are persecuting! Now get up and go into the city, and you will be told what you must do."

ACTS 9:5–6

Father, you call me to embrace my new life in Christ. Help me begin again, putting you at the center of everything I do.

Have you ever longed for a second chance? Are you ready for a fresh start today? Consider Saul's transformation recorded in Acts chapter 9. Saul was determined to eliminate all Christians. Steeped in self-righteousness and hatred, he threatened Jesus' disciples and was eager to kill them. But God had a different plan for Saul's life.

On his way to Damascus, a heavenly light blinded him, and he fell to the ground in fear. Jesus called him by name. "Why are you persecuting me?…I am Jesus, the one you are persecuting!" (vv. 4–5). When Jesus told him to get up and wait for further instructions about his future, Saul arose a blind man, completely dependent upon others. Saul was led where the Lord directed, and he sat without food for three days. Humbled, broken, and completely transformed, Saul became Paul, one of the most courageous Christ followers ever documented. The heartless persecutor became the great proclaimer.

COURAGE FOR TODAY

Changing your life takes courage and self-discipline. Memorize the verse below and decide today to make necessary and courageous changes in your circumstances, relationships, and behavior.

Throw off your old sinful nature and your former way of life, which is corrupted by lust and deception. Instead, let the Spirit renew your thoughts and attitudes. Put on your new nature, created to be like God—truly righteous and holy.

EPHESIANS 4:22–24

THE COURAGE TO
Preserve Your Reputation

Choose a good reputation over great riches;
being held in high esteem is better than silver or gold.

PROVERBS 22:1

Father, you give me the privilege and responsibility of being a positive influence on others. Remind me of the importance of my reputation and give me the determination and willpower to preserve it.

When making important decisions, do you stop to think about how your choices might impact your reputation? Be challenged by the wise teachings of King Solomon in Proverbs chapter 22. Solomon opens this chapter by stating the importance of having a good name. He then compares the benefits and blessings of godly behavior with the downfall and destruction of foolishness, wickedness, slander, and corruption.

While the opinions of others should never weigh us down or supersede God's view of us, we must always consider the importance of our influence on others and carefully consider our steps. Our actions not only affect us, but they may also influence others in their Christian walk. Solomon concludes his teaching by urging listeners to pay attention to his advice and to apply it in practical ways.

COURAGE FOR TODAY

Do you regularly consider the ways you influence others? Are you willing to turn away from compromising behavior that might lead someone toward immorality or wrongdoing? Meditate on the verse below and consider your character. Then take courageous steps to achieve the life changes God is encouraging you to make today.

You yourself must be an example to them by doing good works of every kind.
Let everything you do reflect the integrity and seriousness of your teaching.

TITUS 2:7

THE COURAGE TO
Live in Harmony

I appeal to you, dear brothers and sisters,
by the authority of our Lord Jesus Christ,
to live in harmony with each other.

1 CORINTHIANS 1:10

Father, you call me to love, lift up, and pray for others. Give me the ability
to politely disagree without being argumentative.

Do you find it difficult to communicate with believers who think differently
than you? Are you quick to quarrel, or are you willing to have civil
conversations? Be inspired by the apostle Paul's letter to the church at Corinth,
recorded in the book of 1 Corinthians. Sin had crept into the church, and
divisions had taken place. Paul's heart was broken over the disputes, so he
courageously and compassionately addressed the problem.

   The people had taken their eyes off God and had begun looking to one
another with an air of superiority. They quarreled over leaders and disagreed
about who deserved their loyalty. But Paul quickly clarified that the wisdom,
strength, and power of God belong to only one man, Jesus Christ. The followers
of mere men are easily misguided. Instead, they needed to focus solely on their
Savior and become believers who furthered the cause of Christ and promoted
harmony within the church.

COURAGE FOR TODAY

Living in unity with others who think differently can be a challenge. Are
you willing to approach your differences with courage and compassion?
Read the following verse and ask God to give you words of wisdom and
courage to speak lovingly to those with whom you are in conflict today.

Live in harmony with each other. Don't be too proud to enjoy the company
of ordinary people. And don't think you know it all!

ROMANS 12:16

THE COURAGE TO
Believe God's Word

"I will go before you, Cyrus, and level the mountains. I will smash down gates of bronze and cut through bars of iron. And I will give you treasures hidden in the darkness—secret riches. I will do this so you may know that I am the LORD, the God of Israel, the one who calls you by name."

ISAIAH 45:2–3

Father, your Word is trustworthy and true. Give me a longing to be in my Bible daily, learning your ways and seeking your will.

Do you sometimes doubt that Scripture accurately predicts the future? Consider the prophecy recorded in Isaiah chapter 45. Cyrus was called by name to restore the people of Israel more than two hundred years before he became the king of Persia. God promised to prepare and appoint Cyrus to free his people (vv. 1–8), and he did exactly that.

In 539 BC, this pagan king of Persia easily conquered Babylon, and in the first year of Cyrus' reign, God fulfilled both Isaiah's and Jeremiah's prophecies (see Jeremiah 25:12–14) and freed the Israelites from captivity. When God stirred the heart of Cyrus, the king issued a proclamation allowing the people of Israel, who had been exiled in Babylon for seventy-five years, to return to their homeland and rebuild their holy temple.

COURAGE FOR TODAY

Do you rely on God's Word as a guide for daily living? Meditate on the verse below and describe how believing in Scripture can give you more courage for life.

The word of God is alive and powerful. It is sharper than the sharpest two-edged sword, cutting between soul and spirit, between joint and marrow. It exposes our innermost thoughts and desires.

HEBREWS 4:12

THE COURAGE TO
Follow Christ

As Jesus walked by, John looked at him and declared,
"Look! There is the Lamb of God!"
When John's two disciples heard this, they followed Jesus.

JOHN 1:36–37

Father, this world sometimes perceives Christians negatively. Give me the courage to follow you regardless of how it affects the way others view me.

Have you ever given up something good for an opportunity to have something greater? Be inspired by the courage of Jesus' first followers in John chapter 1. When John the Baptist identified Jesus as "the Lamb of God" (v. 36), two of John the Baptist's disciples left him to follow Jesus. They trusted that Jesus was "the very person Moses and the prophets wrote about" (v. 45) and the One all men had been anticipating.

Andrew, a Christ follower, then left to find his brother Peter. When Peter met the Messiah, Jesus invited Peter to follow him. Others also joined until Jesus had acquired many faithful disciples. Men and women left their families, jobs, and even their reputations to follow their Savior. They dedicated their lives to him, became his disciples, and served until it cost them everything, including, for some, their lives.

COURAGE FOR TODAY

Has following Jesus ever cost you anything? At times, it can take great courage to identify as a Christ follower. Draw comfort from the verse below and determine today that you will courageously follow Jesus, no matter what it costs.

Jesus spoke to the people once more and said, "I am the light of the world. If you follow me, you won't have to walk in darkness, because you will have the light that leads to life."

JOHN 8:12

THE COURAGE TO
Stay Encouraged

"Does anyone remember this house—this Temple—in its former splendor?
How, in comparison, does it look to you now? It must seem like nothing at all!"

HAGGAI 2:3

Father, I often fall into the comparison trap, measuring myself and my accomplishments against those of others. Allow me to consistently be encouraged by you and not to be discouraged by any negativity around me.

One of Satan's greatest tools to lead us toward defeat is comparison. Feelings of not measuring up to our former success or to someone else's achievements often tempt us to give up. Consider Haggai chapter 2. The prophet Haggai had previously proclaimed God's message to abandon selfishness and idolatry and to rebuild God's temple, and the people had obeyed. But before long a new wave of discouragement had taken over.

The older generation remembered the original temple's magnificence, so the new structure appeared inferior to them on every level, "like nothing at all" (v. 3). In response to their pessimism, God told Haggai to deliver words of encouragement. The Lord commanded his people, "Be strong…for I am with you…My Spirit remains among you, just as I promised…So do not be afraid" (vv. 4–5). The prophet then revealed God's plans of greater peace, prosperity, victory, and a national blessing on his people, if only they obey God.

COURAGE FOR TODAY

Are you guilty of looking around for encouragement instead of looking up? Take hold of the following verse and describe how God's words give you courage today.

"I am leaving you with a gift—peace of mind and heart.
And the peace I give is a gift the world cannot give.
So don't be troubled or afraid."

JOHN 14:27

THE COURAGE TO
Make Disciples

*"Go and make disciples of all the nations, baptizing them in the name of the
Father and the Son and the Holy Spirit. Teach these new disciples to obey all the
commands I have given you. And be sure of this: I am with you always, even to the
end of the age."*

MATTHEW 28:19–20

Father, you call me to lead others to you and teach them your Word. Give
me wisdom and understanding to know who I am to disciple.

Are you being discipled, and are you discipling others? Let Jesus' words in
Matthew chapter 28 challenge you to help more people grow in their relationship
with God. The morning after Jesus was crucified and buried, Mary and Mary
Magdalene went to his grave and were startled when his stone was rolled away
and an angel announced, "He isn't here! He is risen from the dead" (v. 6).

After the angel sent the women to tell the disciples the good news,
Jesus appeared before them and said, "Don't be afraid!" (v. 10). He then asked
the women to inform his disciples to meet him in Galilee. When his followers
saw him, they worshiped their risen Savior. Then Jesus instructed them to "go
and make disciples of all the nations" (v. 19), for he would be with them, even
to the end of time.

COURAGE FOR TODAY

How often are you involved in discipleship? Meditate on Paul's instructions
below and describe how you will courageously increase the number of
people you minister to today, who will, in turn, pass on to others their
knowledge and passion for God.

*You have heard me teach things that have been confirmed by many reliable
witnesses. Now teach these truths to other trustworthy people who will be able to
pass them on to others.*

2 TIMOTHY 2:2

THE COURAGE TO
Remember God

Fear God and obey his commands, for this is everyone's duty. God will judge us for everything we do, including every secret thing, whether good or bad.

ECCLESIASTES 12:13–14

Father, I often fall prey to distractions, worries, and wants. Give me the desire to seek you daily and a passion to honor and obey you faithfully.

Are you aware of God's presence every day, or do you only think of him when you're in need? Consider King Solomon's instruction in Ecclesiastes chapter 12. Solomon was a wise and thoughtful king, who listened, acquired knowledge, and experienced life, then passionately "taught the people everything he knew" (v. 9). After years of devotion to God, Solomon was drawn away from the Lord by his relationships with unbelievers. As an older man, this wise and wealthy king took an honest assessment of his life, and this chapter records his conclusion.

After experiencing life's many ups and downs and countless opportunities and challenges, Solomon determined that our most important pursuit should be to remember and honor God in everything we do. Therefore, let us strive each day to respect and obey the Lord, because in the end, "God will judge us for everything we do" (v. 14).

COURAGE FOR TODAY

What is your most important pursuit in life? Read the verses below and decide today to courageously set aside anxiety, impatience, and selfishness, to focus faithfully on respect, gratitude, and obedience to the Lord.

Always be full of joy in the Lord. I say it again—rejoice!…Don't worry about anything; instead, pray about everything. Tell God what you need, and thank him for all he has done.

PHILIPPIANS 4:4, 6

THE COURAGE TO
Embrace God's Victory

The sin of this one man, Adam, caused death to rule over many. But even greater is God's wonderful grace and his gift of righteousness, for all who receive it will live in triumph over sin and death through this one man, Jesus Christ.

ROMANS 5:17

Father, my problems often seek to distract me and steal my joy. Help me maintain an attitude of gratitude so I can fully embrace a victorious life here on earth.

Do you fully embrace God's victory over sin and death? Let the apostle Paul's testimony in Romans chapter 5 inspire you to live life to the fullest. Paul lived a joy-filled life and never missed an opportunity to witness to an unbeliever, even when others ridiculed, opposed, threatened, and imprisoned him. In his letter to the Roman church, Paul encouraged believers to embrace confidence, peace, and joy in their salvation and relationship with God.

Paul explained that trials strengthen endurance, "and endurance develops strength of character, and character strengthens our confident hope of salvation" (v. 4). Therefore, since believers have been "made right in God's sight by the blood of Christ" (v. 9) and "since our friendship with God was restored" (v. 10), Christ followers should embrace every aspect of life and live as victors over sin and death. While happiness is short-lived, lasting joy comes from the hope we have in God's unconditional love, forgiveness, and faithful promises.

COURAGE FOR TODAY

What does living life to the fullest look like to you? Meditate on the verse below and describe how you will courageously embrace a victorious life and let God's presence and promises bring you joy and courage today.

You will show me the way of life, granting me the joy of your presence and the pleasures of living with you forever.

PSALM 16:11

THE COURAGE TO
Respect God above All

Abigail wasted no time. She quickly gathered 200 loaves of bread, two wineskins full of wine, five sheep that had been slaughtered, nearly a bushel of roasted grain, 100 clusters of raisins, and 200 fig cakes. She packed them on donkeys and said to her servants, "Go on ahead."

1 SAMUEL 25:18–19

Father, sometimes I am unsure how to respond or what step to take next. Give me wisdom as I seek your guidance and help me courageously step out in faith as I pursue your will and ways.

Do you ever find yourself in a precarious position, wondering whether to align yourself with a loved one, leader, or employer over God? Consider 1 Samuel chapter 25 and discover how one woman relied on wisdom from God to determine her response to her husband's foolish behavior. Abigail was the wife of Nabal, a ruthless and unkind man.

When David sought provisions in return for the generosity he had shown to Nabal's shepherds, Nabal selfishly refused. In response, David prepared his men to take violent action. But when a servant informed Abigail of Nabal's foolish refusal to share his provisions, Abigail relied on discernment from God to determine her response. She secretly approached David and his troops, seeking forgiveness and supplying their needs.

COURAGE FOR TODAY

Are you ever torn between honoring God or honoring a loved one, leader, or employer? Read the passage below and note the importance of pursuing God's will above all else. What courageous step will you take today to make God's will your priority?

Trust in the LORD with all your heart; do not depend on your own understanding. Seek his will in all you do, and he will show you which path to take.

PROVERBS 3:5–6

THE COURAGE TO
Comfort Others

He comforts us in all our troubles so that we can comfort others. When they are troubled, we will be able to give them the same comfort God has given us.

2 CORINTHIANS 1:4

Father, you call us to lift one another up. Give me the courage to reach out and encourage those around me who need comfort today.

Do you sometimes find it difficult to comfort someone who is hurting? Be encouraged by the apostle Paul's words recorded in 2 Corinthians chapter 1. Throughout his many trials, Paul discovered the greatest source of reassurance—God himself. Because Paul had received encouragement from God and other believers, he urged believers to continually comfort one another. "He comforts us in all our troubles so that we can comfort others" (v. 4).

The Greek term Paul used in his letter to the Corinthians, *paraklesis,* conveyed the idea of strengthening one another, not simply offering sympathetic words. Paul not only knew the benefit of being supported by others, but he also knew that suffering troubles and persecution opens us to God's comfort and leads to our salvation (see 2 Thessalonians 1:5). While believers in the Corinthian church were suffering persecution and hardships, Paul understood that by comforting one another they could endure to the end.

COURAGE FOR TODAY

How often do you encourage others with kind words, prayers, and good deeds? Or just by being present? Meditate on the "one another" verse below and name at least one person you can comfort today.

You have been called to live in freedom, my brothers and sisters.
But don't use your freedom to satisfy your sinful nature.
Instead, use your freedom to serve one another in love.

GALATIANS 5:13

THE COURAGE TO
Refuse Idolatry

"There are some Jews—Shadrach, Meshach, and Abednego—whom you have put in charge of the province of Babylon. They pay no attention to you, Your Majesty. They refuse to serve your gods and do not worship the gold statue you have set up."

DANIEL 3:12

Father, you are worthy of all loyalty, honor, and praise. Help me resist the temptation to worship anything or anyone other than you.

Do worldly possessions and pleasures tempt you to turn your back on God? Let three men's courageous faith, recorded in Daniel chapter 3, inspire you to refuse idolatry and remain loyal to the Lord. Shadrach, Meshach, and Abednego were taken captive when King Nebuchadnezzar of Babylon conquered Jerusalem in 605 BC. God blessed these three young men with great wisdom and knowledge, so when the Babylonian king ordered all people to bow before a golden statue and worship it as a god, Shadrach, Meshach, and Abednego refused.

In response to their disloyalty to the king, Nebuchadnezzar ordered the strongest men in his army to throw them into a fiery furnace. In great faith, the three confessed their devotion to the Lord and refused to worship false gods. For they professed that "the God whom we serve is able to save us. He will rescue us from your power," one way or another (v. 17).

COURAGE FOR TODAY

Do you cherish your possessions, profession, or relationships more than God? The Bible defines an idol as any person or thing you worship in place of the Lord. Read the following verse and vow today to courageously refuse idolatry.

Dear children, keep away from anything that might take God's place in your hearts.

1 JOHN 5:21

THE COURAGE TO
Overcome Favoritism

My dear brothers and sisters, how can you claim to have faith in our glorious Lord
Jesus Christ if you favor some people over others?

JAMES 2:1

Father, you love unconditionally and show no favoritism. Help me be like
you by showing no partiality and loving all people well.

Do you show favoritism to certain people while disregarding others? Is
your generosity inclusive or exclusive? Consider the words of warning and
encouragement in James chapter 2. In his letter, James rebuked believers for
showing favoritism. He said, "If you give special attention and a good seat to
the rich person, but you say to the poor one, 'You can stand over there, or else
sit on the floor'—well, doesn't this discrimination show that your judgments
are guided by evil motives?" (vv. 3–4).

James taught that a faithful life is characterized by good deeds, and he
explained that "faith without good deeds is useless" (v. 20). Using Abraham as
an example, James made it clear that faith and good works always go together
and make one's faith complete. "We are shown to be right with God by what we
do, not by faith alone" (v. 24).

COURAGE FOR TODAY

Do you need to overcome favoritism and grow more active in your faith?
Meditate on the verses below and describe how you will courageously set
aside any discrimination and actively let others see your love for
the Lord today.

Do not withhold good from those who deserve it when it's in your power to help
them. If you can help your neighbor now, don't say, "Come back tomorrow,
and then I'll help you."

PROVERBS 3:27–28

THE COURAGE TO
Model God's Love

The LORD said to me, "Go and love your wife again, even though she commits adultery with another lover. This will illustrate that the LORD still loves Israel, even though the people have turned to other gods and love to worship them."

HOSEA 3:1

Father, you are the author of true love and the source of unconditional acceptance. Give me the courage to care for those who seem unlovable.

Have you been in a relationship that didn't end in "happily ever after"? Unrequited love is painful. Consider Hosea chapter 3 in which God's prophet suffered greatly when he obeyed God's command to rescue and marry a prostitute named Gomer. After the marriage ceremony and three children later, Hosea's wife returned to prostitution. Again, God commanded Hosea to go after Gomer and bring her home.

God wanted Hosea to courageously model forgiveness and redemption with his wife. God said, "This will illustrate that the LORD still loves Israel, even though the people have turned to other gods and love to worship them" (v. 1). Hosea courageously obeyed God's calling and paid the necessary wages to buy back his unfaithful wife. In doing so, he became a living lesson of the lengths to which God will go to rescue those he loves.

COURAGE FOR TODAY

How often do you model God's unconditional love? Consider how God went to great lengths to save each of us even when we didn't deserve it. Just as Hosea modeled God's love to the people of Israel, meditate on the verse below and courageously vow today to love people in your life who seem unlovable.

This is real love—not that we loved God, but that he loved us and sent his Son as a sacrifice to take away our sins.

1 JOHN 4:10

THE COURAGE TO

Accept Correction

All Scripture is inspired by God and is useful to teach us what is true and to make us realize what is wrong in our lives. It corrects us when we are wrong and teaches us to do what is right.

2 TIMOTHY 3:16

Father, your Word is a light for my path and a lamp for my feet. Give me the courage to admit when I am wrong and help me correct any behaviors that dishonor your name.

Do you find it difficult to admit when you're wrong? Are you apt to justify sin when it creeps into your life? Let the apostle Paul's words in 2 Timothy chapter 3 challenge you to take an inventory of your life and perspective.

In his second letter, Paul reminded Timothy that God's Word differentiates right from wrong. And he warned him about lifestyles that would dominate the latter days: such as the love of self and money; the tendency to be arrogant, prideful, and disobedient; the willingness to disrespect and disobey God, parents, and leaders; and the propensity to be unloving, unforgiving, slanderous, cruel, and out of control. Paul urged Timothy, "You must remain faithful to the things you have been taught…the holy Scriptures from childhood" (vv. 14–15).

COURAGE FOR TODAY

Do you need more courage to address and correct bad behaviors in your life? Read King Solomon's bold and insightful words below and vow to accept godly correction and courageously make changes in your behavior, attitude, or surroundings today.

If you reject discipline, you only harm yourself; but if you listen to correction, you grow in understanding.

PROVERBS 15:32

THE COURAGE TO
Focus on God

I will shout for joy and sing your praises, for you have ransomed me. I will tell about your righteous deeds all day long, for everyone who tried to hurt me has been shamed and humiliated

PSALM 71:23–24

Father, your promises reassure me that, in the end, I will triumph over my adversaries. Remind me to take my eyes and ears off the world and keep them consistently focused on you.

Do others criticize your faith or judge you for not living up to their standards? Consider how the author of Psalm 71 focused on God's opinion over that of others. The psalmist put his hope and faith in God alone. Though he said his enemies were "whispering against me…[and] plotting together to kill me" (v. 10), he chose to wholeheartedly believe in God, who protects and defends those who love him.

In response to God's presence and supreme power, the psalmist vowed to praise God and tell others about him. He knew that God would not only defend him (see Psalm 71:1) but would also "humiliate and shame those who want to harm me" (v.13).

COURAGE FOR TODAY

Do hurtful words wound and discourage you? Meditate on the verse below and let God's perspective supersede all others. Focus on God today, let him be your source of courage and strength, and boldly share him with others.

"In that coming day no weapon turned against you will succeed. You will silence every voice raised up to accuse you. These benefits are enjoyed by the servants of the LORD; their vindication will come from me. I, the LORD, have spoken!"

ISAIAH 54:17

THE COURAGE TO
Refrain from Immorality

Run from sexual sin! No other sin so clearly affects the body as this one does.
For sexual immorality is a sin against your own body.

1 CORINTHIANS 6:18

Father, I pray to remain pure before you. Give me the wisdom and courage
to flee from temptation and immorality.

Does living in a sex-saturated society negatively affect you or someone you
love? Reflect on the apostle Paul's words in Corinthians chapter 6. The Corinth
church was located in a city known for its moral depravity. Religious prostitutes
roamed the city, and sexual sin had made its way into the church. God's people
had become accustomed to immorality and simply looked the other way.

But Paul courageously spoke out. In love, he reminded all believers that
"your bodies are actually parts of Christ" (v. 15). Sexual impurity, therefore,
defiled their relationship with God. So Paul urged believers to "run from sexual
sin!" (v. 18). He begged them to remember that their bodies were purchased by
God and are the temple for the Lord's Holy Spirit. God's followers are thereby
called to faithfully glorify the Lord with their bodies.

COURAGE FOR TODAY

Has living in a sexually saturated society caused you to take your eyes
off Christ? If so, confess your sin and receive God's grace and forgiveness
today. Then meditate on the verse below and ask God to help you
courageously refrain from immorality going forward.

God's will is for you to be holy, so stay away from all sexual sin. Then each of you
will control his own body and live in holiness and honor—not in lustful passion like
the pagans who do not know God and his ways.

1 THESSALONIANS 4:3–5

THE COURAGE TO
Bear Burdens

Amos replied, "I'm not a professional prophet, and I was never trained to be one. I'm just a shepherd, and I take care of sycamore-fig trees. But the LORD called me away from my flock and told me, 'Go and prophesy to my people in Israel.'"

AMOS 7:14–15

Father, sometimes your assignments are difficult to endure. Help me carry out your requests without complaining and give me wisdom and courage to finish well without giving up.

Has God ever given you a task that seemed overwhelming? Consider the book of Amos where we learn about the life and ministry of a former shepherd and gardener. Amos, whose name means "burden bearer," had no training as a prophet. Yet God gave him the daunting task of delivering messages of judgment to Israel and its surrounding neighbors.

The people's constant rejection of God and his commandments, lack of worship, mistreatment of the poor, and lack of justice prompted God to act. Although God's calling was a burden on Amos, he willingly accepted his assignment to speak God's truth, even though he knew that the people would not welcome or embrace him or God's message. Despite the constant rejection, Amos remained faithful to God's will.

COURAGE FOR TODAY

When faced with an overwhelming responsibility or a difficult challenge, do you complain and look for ways out? Or are you willing to trust God to help you persevere? Meditate on God's promise below and vow to embrace your God-given courage today to do God's will, no matter the burden.

Those who trust in the LORD will find new strength. They will soar high on wings like eagles. They will run and not grow weary. They will walk and not faint.

ISAIAH 40:31

THE COURAGE TO
Counter Evil with Good

"To you who are willing to listen, I say, love your enemies!
Do good to those who hate you. Bless those who curse you.
Pray for those who hurt you."

LUKE 6:27–28

Father, the last thing my flesh wants is to be kind to my enemies. Help me set aside my hurt and bitterness and resist the urge to be hateful so I can instead counter anyone's ugliness with genuine kindness.

Do you sometimes find it difficult to be nice to certain people? Let Jesus' words in Luke chapter 6 encourage you to maintain a gentle disposition even around people who don't act the same. After responding to religious leaders, healing a man's hand in the synagogue, and choosing his twelve disciples, Jesus stood before a large crowd and began to teach. He spoke of God's compassion and warned those who put their faith in their wealth.

Then Jesus addressed all who would listen, telling them, "Love your enemies! Do good to those who hate you. Bless those who curse you. Pray for those who hurt you" (vv. 27–28). For if we only love people who love us back, there's no credit in that. Therefore, let us be compassionate, kind, and generous to everyone, regardless of their behavior.

COURAGE FOR TODAY

How difficult is it for you to be kind to someone who has mistreated you? Read Jesus' teaching below and explain how you can courageously be considerate and kindhearted toward your adversaries today.

"Love your enemies! Pray for those who persecute you! In that way, you will be acting as true children of your Father in heaven. For he gives his sunlight to both the evil and the good, and he sends rain on the just and the unjust alike."

MATTHEW 5:44–45

THE COURAGE TO
Confront Lies

"Don't say such things," the people respond. "Don't prophesy like that. Such disasters will never come our way!" Should you talk that way, O family of Israel? Will the Lord's Spirit have patience with such behavior? If you would do what is right, you would find my words comforting.

Micah 2:6–7

Father, help me distinguish the truth from a lie and give me the courage to speak up for what is right, even when I stand alone.

Would you rather hear the truth or settle for lies? Nothing good comes from distorting the truth even when we don't get caught. For God knows our every word and understands our every intention. Consider the prophet Micah's era, when the people of Israel scoffed at God's impending judgment.

They desired a god who overlooked sin, disregarded rebellion, and allowed idol worship. They took what they wanted "by fraud and violence" (v. 2). They proudly served manmade gods even though it insulted and grieved the Lord, and they refused to believe Micah's warnings. Yet despite this rebellion, Micah persistently stood up for God's truth and courageously confronted those who only wanted their ears tickled.

COURAGE FOR TODAY

What is your source of truth? Are you swayed by the politically correct opinions of our society? Be challenged by the familiar verse below and courageously commit today to make the study, memorization, and respect of God's Word a priority in your life.

All Scripture is inspired by God and is useful to teach us what is true and to make us realize what is wrong in our lives. It corrects us when we are wrong and teaches us to do what is right.

2 Timothy 3:16

THE COURAGE TO
Walk in Christ's Light

Jesus replied, "My light will shine for you just a little longer.
Walk in the light while you can, so the darkness will not overtake you.
Those who walk in the darkness cannot see where they are going."

JOHN 12:35

Father, you give us all a choice—to walk in Christ's light or to walk in the world's darkness. Give me an endless desire and courage to faithfully choose your lighted path.

Are you walking in God's light? Let Jesus' message in John chapter 12 motivate you to center your life on Christ and walk in his light. Shortly before he was arrested, sentenced, and crucified, Jesus traveled back to Jerusalem. When he entered the city, a large crowd welcomed and worshiped him, but the apostles didn't understand the significance of this event.

As he began preparing his followers for his departure, Jesus explained that he would die by being lifted up and that he would "draw everyone to [himself]" (v. 32). Yet the crowd became confused, asking how could Jesus be the Messiah if he was going to die? In response, Jesus told them, "My light will shine for you just a little longer" (v. 35). So he urged his followers to walk in his light and put their trust in his light while they still could. That way, they would become "children of the light" (v. 36).

COURAGE FOR TODAY

List the ways you are currently walking in Christ's light. Then meditate on the verse below and describe other courageous steps you will take today to let God's light shine in and through you.

If we are living in the light, as God is in the light,
then we have fellowship with each other,
and the blood of Jesus, his Son, cleanses us from all sin.

1 JOHN 1:7

THE COURAGE TO
Trust God's Strength

The man said to me, "Daniel, you are very precious to God, so listen carefully to what I have to say to you. Stand up, for I have been sent to you." When he said this to me, I stood up, still trembling.

DANIEL 10:11

Father, at times, I do not have the strength to handle the challenges before me. God, give me the ability to face my problems by relying on wisdom, courage, and confidence from you.

In times of hardship or grief, do you sometimes find it difficult to stand? If so, where do you turn for courage and strength? Consider Daniel chapter 10 and notice how Daniel's physical and emotional condition exhibited suffering, misery, and weakness. Daniel had been fasting and mourning for three weeks after learning the dismal future that awaited his people. When an angel of the Lord appeared before him, Daniel was speechless, pale, and lacked the ability to stand.

In response to Daniel's humility and prayers, God sent the angel to give Daniel peace, understanding, and strength. Twice the angel said, "Don't be afraid" (vv. 12, 19) and twice he empowered Daniel with bodily strength so he could stand in the midst of one of his weakest and most discouraging times.

COURAGE FOR TODAY

When you need strength and courage, where do you turn? Memorize this encouraging verse below and commit today to rely on God's promise to give you courage during your weakest and most discouraging moments.

"Don't be afraid, for I am with you. Don't be discouraged, for I am your God. I will strengthen you and help you. I will hold you up with my victorious right hand."

ISAIAH 41:10

THE COURAGE TO
Seek God's Will

He went on a little farther and bowed with his face to the ground, praying,
"My Father! If it is possible, let this cup of suffering be taken away from me.
Yet I want your will to be done, not mine."

MATTHEW 26:39

Father, I spend most of my time chasing after my own dreams and desires.
Help me set my selfishness aside so I can make your will a priority
in my life.

Are you willing to set aside your wants and wishes to pursue God's will for
your life? Let Jesus' humble and God-honoring prayer inspire you to seek God's
desires over your own today.

Just after he celebrated his last Passover meal with his disciples, Jesus
went to the garden of Gethsemane to pray. As the time drew near for his arrest,
crucifixion, and death, Jesus became deeply distressed and was filled with
grief. When he bowed before the Lord, he first pleaded with God to "let this cup
of suffering be taken away from me" (v. 39). But right after these words, Jesus
confessed that his greatest desire was for God's will to be done over his. After
checking on his disciples, Jesus prayed twice more, repeating his same request
saying to the Father, "Your will be done" (v. 42).

COURAGE FOR TODAY

When you pray, do you pray for God's will to be done? Recite the verses
below taken from the prayer Jesus taught his disciples, and courageously
seek and surrender to God's will for your life today.

"Pray like this: Our Father in heaven, may your name be kept holy.
May your Kingdom come soon.
May your will be done on earth, as it is in heaven."

MATTHEW 6:9–10

THE COURAGE TO
Uncover Sin

When I refused to confess my sin, my body wasted away, and I groaned all day long. Day and night your hand of discipline was heavy on me. My strength evaporated like water in the summer heat. Finally, I confessed all my sins to you and stopped trying to hide my guilt. I said to myself, "I will confess my rebellion to the LORD." And you forgave me! All my guilt is gone.

PSALM 32:3–5

Father, you know my heart and see my sin. Give me the courage to stop hiding my unfaithfulness and help me fully embrace your forgiveness and restoration.

When you fall into sin, are you immediately remorseful and willing to confess? Or do you attempt to minimize or hide your wrongdoing? Consider King David's compelling words recorded in Psalm 32. In this psalm, we discover how Israel's beloved king compared the torment he experienced when he tried to hide his sin and the relief he felt once he had confessed it.

While the beginning of the psalm express David's delight over God's faithful forgiveness and restoration, it also reveals the suffering he endured when he refused to acknowledge his wrongdoing. "My body wasted away, and I groaned all day long" (v. 3). Finally, David describes the moment when he uncovered his guilt and received God's pardon. The remaining verses record God's merciful invitation for those who trust and obey him to celebrate God's guidance and loving-kindness.

COURAGE FOR TODAY

Is there a sin you need to uncover and confess? Meditate on the verse below, courageously turn away from ungodly attitudes and behaviors, and joyfully receive God's mercy, forgiveness, and restoration today.

People who conceal their sins will not prosper, but if they confess and turn from them, they will receive mercy.

PROVERBS 28:13

THE COURAGE TO
Have Faith

It is impossible to please God without faith. Anyone who wants to come to him must believe that God exists and that he rewards those who sincerely seek him.

HEBREWS 11:6

Father, you remind me that faith is the reality of what I hope for and the evidence of what I cannot see. Help me keep believing, living, and trusting in you by faith.

Does discouragement or unanswered prayers cause you to lose faith in God? Be inspired by the lives of the faithful women and men documented in Hebrews chapter 11. By faith, Abel brought the first pleasing sacrifice to God; Enoch's walk pleased God; Noah built the ark; Abraham, Isaac, and Jacob journeyed to unknown lands; Sarah conceived in her old age; Abraham offered his son as a sacrifice; Moses' parents hid him as a baby; Moses brought the Israelites through the Red Sea; the Israelites marched around Jericho until the walls fell down; Rahab, the prostitute, protected God's spies; and many others suffered because of their trust in God.

These courageous women and men "earned a good reputation because of their faith" (v. 39). Their courage to seek God by faith pleased the Lord and led to eternal rewards.

COURAGE FOR TODAY

Do you need more courage to truly live by faith and to trust God with your challenges? Read the verse below and vow today to courageously have faith, no matter what difficulty you encounter.

"You don't have enough faith," Jesus told them. "I tell you the truth, if you had faith even as small as a mustard seed, you could say to this mountain, 'Move from here to there,' and it would move. Nothing would be impossible."

MATTHEW 17:20

THE COURAGE TO
Be a Godly Influence

*"Don't worry about a thing, my daughter. I will do what is necessary,
for everyone in town knows you are a virtuous woman."*

RUTH 3:11

Father, you call me to be an example, to be a light of hope and encouragement amidst the darkness of this world. Help me to be more intentional and courageous as I strive to be a godly example to others.

A good reputation can easily be spoiled, and a poor reputation can be intentionally restored; it all depends on our choices. How often do you stop to consider how others are affected or influenced by your actions and behavior? Consider Ruth chapter 3 and take note of Ruth and Boaz's reputations among the community.

In the first two chapters of this book of Scripture, we learn that Ruth was loyal, caring, and hard-working, and we discover that Boaz was not only a relative of Naomi's but was also a considerate and generous man and a passionate believer in God. Naomi encouraged Ruth to present herself to Boaz, and Ruth agreed. Boaz responded in a way that coincided with his reputation: he blessed, complimented, and encouraged Ruth while assuring her that her reputation as a wholesome and moral woman was secure.

COURAGE FOR TODAY

How important is it to you to be a godly influence on others? Read the passage below and list ways you can more courageously shine God's light among others today.

*"You are the light of the world—like a city on a hilltop that cannot be hidden.
No one lights a lamp and then puts it under a basket.
Instead, a lamp is placed on a stand, where it gives light to everyone in the house."*

MATTHEW 5:14–15

THE COURAGE TO
Be Diligent

Watch out that you do not lose what we have worked so hard to achieve.
Be diligent so that you receive your full reward.

2 JOHN 1:8

Father, you warn me about false teachings that can tempt me to falter in my faith. Protect me from the many deceptions this world offers and help me stay closely connected to you and your perfect truth.

Are you ever tempted to believe something that contradicts the Word of God? Let the apostle's warning in 2 John caution you to consistently study your Bible so you can easily recognize the difference between God's truth and worldly lies. John wrote this letter to warn his readers of the dangers of entertaining false teaching.

In his introduction, John complimented their faith and dedication to God's truth and reminded them of the importance of loving God and loving others. He then expressed his concern "because many deceivers have gone out into the world" who "deny…Jesus Christ" (v. 7). He wanted to ensure they didn't lose confidence in their faith. For anyone who strays from the truth is in danger of damaging their relationship with the Lord.

COURAGE FOR TODAY

Do you consistently examine what you are learning by comparing it to the Word of God? Read Jeremiah's prophetic words below and explain how you will strive to identify false beliefs and courageously replace them with God's truth today.

"Jeremiah, say to the people, 'This is what the LORD says: 'When people fall down, don't they get up again? When they discover they're on the wrong road, don't they turn back?'"

JEREMIAH 8:4

THE COURAGE TO
Return to God

At the king's command, runners were sent throughout Israel and Judah. They carried letters that said: "O people of Israel, return to the LORD, the God of Abraham, Isaac, and Israel, so that he will return to the few of us who have survived the conquest of the Assyrian kings."

2 CHRONICLES 30:6

Father, at times, I draw closer to you, and at other times, I drift away. Help me return to you in faithfulness and devotion when I backslide.

How strong is your relationship with God? Are you courageously devoted or distant and uncommitted. Consider King Hezekiah's proclamation recorded in 2 Chronicles chapter 30. Hezekiah became king when he was twenty-five years old, and he dedicated his life and leadership to faithfully serving God. He encouraged the people of Judah to return to God in both heart and action and even decreed that they should return to the temple and worship.

In response to King Hezekiah's decree, people throughout Israel and Judah faithfully returned to God and gathered to celebrate and worship the Lord with great joy. Afterward, the people of Judah went through their towns and "smashed all the sacred pillars…and removed the pagan shrines and altars" (31:1). Then they gave generously to the priests to help protect their community's future relationship with the Lord.

COURAGE FOR TODAY

How would you describe your relationship with God? Do you need to return to him with greater faith and dedication? Meditate on the following verse and list ways you will courageously serve God and faithfully influence others today.

This is how the LORD responds: "If you return to me, I will restore you so you can continue to serve me. If you speak good words rather than worthless ones, you will be my spokesman. You must influence them; do not let them influence you!"

JEREMIAH 15:19

THE COURAGE TO
Stop Throwing Stones

They kept demanding an answer, so he stood up again and said,
"All right, but let the one who has never sinned throw the first stone!"
JOHN 8:7

Father, when I am tempted to judge, criticize, or gossip about others who have fallen into sin, remind me that I, too, am a sinner in need of a Savior.

Are you quick to judge others without recognizing your own sin? Consider the account of the sinful woman in John chapter 8. As Jesus was teaching in the temple, a group of religious teachers and leaders brought to him a woman caught in adultery.

They placed her in front of the crowd and confronted Jesus, asking if she should be stoned to death as it stated in Moses' law. He answered them saying, "Let the one who has never sinned throw the first stone" (v. 7). When the religious elites heard Jesus' response, they slipped away one by one until no one was left to accuse her. Then Jesus told the woman that no one remained to condemn her, so "Go and sin no more" (v. 11).

COURAGE FOR TODAY

It's been said, "Never judge another person until you've walked a mile in their shoes." How often do you consider a person's particular situation or life story before judging what they've done? Take Jesus' words to heart and vow to consider other people's experiences and courageously refrain from passing judgment today.

"Do not judge others, and you will not be judged. For you will be treated as you treat others. The standard you use in judging is the standard by which you will be judged."
MATTHEW 7:1–2

THE COURAGE TO
Embrace Perfect Peace

You will keep in perfect peace all who trust in you, all whose thoughts are fixed on you! Trust in the LORD always, for the LORD GOD is the eternal Rock.

ISAIAH 26:3–4

Father, you are trustworthy and true. Help me embrace your perfect peace as I trust you with all my heart and strive to honor your name.

Do you find peace in your relationship with God? Take heed of the Song of Praise in Isaiah chapter 26. The great prophet Isaiah wrote a song to be sung by the faithful, whom the Messiah would one day redeem. This song intermingles God's reliable attributes with the prophet's personal pleas over Israel's status and salvation.

Those who fix their eyes on the Lord and trust in his promises will experience God's peace. And while those who are proud will be humbled and those who are wicked will be judged, those who seek the Lord, trust in him, and honor his holy name will experience salvation, walk without stumbling, be at peace, and enjoy prosperity in this life. Therefore, Isaiah urged God's followers to trust in the Lord always, obey him faithfully, pray to him compassionately, worship him consistently, and wait for him patiently.

COURAGE FOR TODAY

List the people, places, and things in your life that steal your peace. Now meditate on the Scripture verse below and describe how you will make courageous changes today to gratefully embrace God's perfect peace.

May the Lord of peace himself give you his peace at all times and in every situation. The Lord be with you all.

2 THESSALONIANS 3:16

THE COURAGE TO
Extend Kindness

She and her household were baptized, and she asked us to be her guests. "If you agree that I am a true believer in the Lord," she said, "come and stay at my home." And she urged us until we agreed.

ACTS 16:15

Father, you call me to exhibit your love by cheerfully caring for others. Help me to extend kindness to strangers and lead me to open my heart and home to those in need.

Does the thought of inviting people into your home cause you stress? Are you routinely kind to strangers, or do you more often look the other way? Consider a woman named Lydia who was the first convert to Christianity in Europe. Lydia sold expensive fabrics used in making garments for people of wealth and royalty.

One day while Lydia and others were worshiping and praying by a river in Philippi, the apostle Paul arrived and began teaching. The Lord opened Lydia's heart to Paul's words, and she and her household were immediately saved and baptized. Without hesitation, Lydia insisted that Paul and his companion "come and stay at my home" (v. 15). Paul and his partner, Silas, spent time in prison for sharing their faith, and upon their release they returned to Lydia's home to meet with and encourage believers.

COURAGE FOR TODAY

Showing hospitality, even to people you know well, can be uncomfortable and inconvenient. How willing are you to step outside your comfort zone to care for others? Meditate on the verse below and describe how you plan to courageously and unselfishly extend kindness to someone today.

Don't forget to show hospitality to strangers, for some who have done this have entertained angels without realizing it!

HEBREWS 13:2

THE COURAGE TO
Honor God's Glory

Suddenly, the glory of the God of Israel appeared from the east.
The sound of his coming was like the roar of rushing waters,
and the whole landscape shone with his glory.

EZEKIEL 43:2

Father, thank you for your presence in my life. Give me an overwhelming desire to faithfully honor and proclaim your glory in everything I do.

Do you faithfully honor God's glory? Be motivated by the prophet's response in Ezekiel chapter 43. God commissioned Ezekiel to deliver messages of judgment and hope to the Israelites who were exiled in Babylon. In the early chapters of this great book, God told Ezekiel to warn his people that they and their surrounding nations would face punishment for their rebellion. But later, God gave Ezekiel messages of hope for the nation of Israel. And in the last chapters of this book, God provided detailed descriptions of Israel's future prosperity.

Around 573 BC, God gave Ezekiel a vision of Israel's restoration. After showing Ezekiel the new temple, new worship, and new land, God showed him the glory of the Lord. In response, Ezekiel fell face down on the ground. God promised that, in that day, he would "live here forever among the people of Israel" (v. 7). He commanded Ezekiel to tell the people of Israel everything he had seen so that they would once again faithfully honor God and his glory.

COURAGE FOR TODAY

How important is it to you to honor God's glory? Memorize the following verse and vow today to give evidence of God's greatness in everything you do.

Whether you eat or drink, or whatever you do,
do it all for the glory of God.

1 CORINTHIANS 10:31

THE COURAGE TO
Accept God's Word

"Since you didn't believe what I said, you will be silent and unable to speak until the child is born. For my words will certainly be fulfilled at the proper time."

LUKE 1:20

Father, your words are spirit and life. They are powerful, instructional, and life changing. Give me a passion to study Scripture and wisdom to heed your transformative lessons.

Do you take God at his Word? Or do you pick and choose what you want to accept? Consider the results of Zechariah's disbelief in Luke chapter 1. In preparation for the coming Messiah, God sent his angel Gabriel to announce the coming birth of John the Baptist.

The father-to-be and priest, Zechariah, and his wife, Elizabeth, were advanced in age and had been unable to conceive a child. Therefore, when God's angel announced that they would be having a son, Zechariah questioned the accuracy of the prediction. "How can I be sure this will happen?" he doubted (v. 18). In response, Gabriel chastised the priest and rendered him speechless until the baby's birth. Although Zechariah was a leader and teacher of God's Word, he was still vulnerable to human weaknesses and doubt. So God allowed him to experience the consequences of his lack of faith to serve as an example for all who would see and learn about his predicament.

COURAGE FOR TODAY

Do you regularly rely on the Bible for wisdom and guidance? Meditate on the following verse, consider the importance of Scripture in your life, and explain how you will courageously apply God's Word in practical and powerful ways today.

"The Spirit alone gives eternal life. Human effort accomplishes nothing. And the very words I have spoken to you are spirit and life."

JOHN 6:63

THE COURAGE TO
Be Faithful

The LORD had clearly instructed the people of Israel,
"You must not marry them, because they will turn your hearts to their gods."
Yet Solomon insisted on loving them anyway.

1 KINGS 11:2

Father, temptations abound in this life. Give me wisdom and courage to resist Satan's schemes so my heart won't be divided in my devotion to you.

Are you torn between following God and chasing after pleasure? Consider 1 Kings chapter 11. This book of Scripture describes the rise and reign of King Solomon and how his faith was compromised when he gave in to temptation and married foreign women.

In the beginning of his rule, he was humble, faithful, and reliant on God. In response, God granted him incomparable wisdom and blessed him with great riches and fame. God warned Solomon of the consequences should he or the people of Israel turn away and serve other gods. But by the time he was an old man and despite God's warning, Solomon had done just that—he turned away.

COURAGE FOR TODAY

Describe your level of commitment to God. How willing are you to forgo the pleasures of this life that compromise your devotion to God? Read the passage below and describe the courageous changes you will make today to protect your heart from becoming divided.

If you need wisdom, ask our generous God, and he will give it to you. He will not rebuke you for asking. But when you ask him, be sure that your faith is in God alone. Do not waver, for a person with divided loyalty is as unsettled as a wave of the sea that is blown and tossed by the wind.

JAMES 1:5–6

THE COURAGE TO
Resist Satan

"The thief's purpose is to steal and kill and destroy.
My purpose is to give them a rich and satisfying life."

JOHN 10:10

Father, my greatest desire is to embrace the abundant life you offer me. Help me resist Satan's schemes and temptations so I can dedicate each day to serving you and accomplishing your will.

Do you sometimes find it difficult to resist Satan's temptation? Let Jesus' message in John chapter 10 inspire you to hold fast to the abundant life God offers you. While confronting several religious leaders, Jesus described the differences between a good shepherd and a bad one. He highlighted the fact that he is a "good shepherd" (v. 11) providing "good pastures" (v. 9) to those who choose to follow him.

Jesus then described the differences between his aspirations for his followers and Satan's intentions for those who follow him. While Jesus promises believers a rich and satisfying life, one where they know him well and listen to his voice, Satan desires to "steal and kill and destroy" (v. 10) everyone and everything in his path. To further clarify his role and dedication to believers, Jesus then told listeners that a "good shepherd sacrifices his life for the sheep" (v. 11), which is exactly what he did to save all who choose to believe in him.

COURAGE FOR TODAY

How prepared are you to withstand the devil's enticements? Read the verse below and describe how you will humble yourself before the Lord and courageously rely on Jesus to help you say no to Satan today.

Humble yourselves before God.
Resist the devil, and he will flee from you.

JAMES 4:7

THE COURAGE TO
Count on God

*The king asked, "Well, how can I help you?" With a prayer to the God of heaven,
I replied, "If it please the king, and if you are pleased with me, your servant,
send me to Judah to rebuild the city where my ancestors are buried."*

NEHEMIAH 2:4–5

Father, you promise to be with me wherever I go. You are my source of courage and confidence. Help me to always count on you as I prepare for delicate conversations and situations.

Do you consistently count on God? Consider Nehemiah's reliance on God during his encounter with the King in Nehemiah chapter 2. Nehemiah was a cupbearer for King Artaxerxes in approximately 445 BC. Nehemiah was heartbroken over the condition of his homeland, which had been "torn down, and the gates…destroyed by fire" (1:3). He longed to return to his native land to help rebuild its walls.

As an attendant, Nehemiah knew the danger of exposing his emotions before the king. Yet with confidence in God and a quick prayer, when the king asked why he was so sad, Nehemiah explained his sorrow and presented his request: "Send me to Judah to rebuild the city where my ancestors are buried" (2:5). When the governors of the regions mocked Nehemiah for his intentions, he courageously and confidently declared that God's favor was upon him and that God would grant their success.

COURAGE FOR TODAY

To whom do you turn when making significant decisions or preparing for important conversations? Read the following verses and describe courageous changes you will make today to rely more on God for help and guidance.

This is what the LORD says: "Cursed are those who put their trust in mere humans, who rely on human strength and turn their hearts away from the LORD…But blessed are those who trust in the LORD and have made the LORD their hope and confidence."

JEREMIAH 17:5, 7

THE COURAGE TO
Honor God's Grace

Well then, should we keep on sinning so that God can show us more and more of
his wonderful grace? Of course not! Since we have died to sin, how can we continue
to live in it?

ROMANS 6:1–2

Father, when I blatantly sin, I dishonor your grace. Help me resist
temptations so I can faithfully demonstrate my appreciation and respect for
your great sacrifice and forgiveness.

Are you struggling with temptation or sin? Let the apostle Paul's words
encourage you to fight harder to resist your weaknesses and sinful desires. In
his letter to the Roman church, Paul urged believers to realize that their "old
sinful selves" had died with Christ (v. 6) and that they had been granted a new
life through Jesus, setting them free from the power of sin.

Therefore, believers must no longer let sinful desires control their lives.
Instead, they should embrace the freedom found in God's grace and commit
themselves completely to the Lord. That way, their lives would reflect their
relationship with God and bring him glory. Believers either allow themselves to
be slaves to sin or slaves to righteousness—the choice is theirs. For "the wages
of sin is death, but the free gift of God is eternal life through Christ Jesus our
Lord" (v. 23).

COURAGE FOR TODAY

Although we can never earn God's grace, we can show our appreciation
and respect for Christ's great love and sacrifice. Read the following verse
and describe ways you honor—or dishonor—the Lord. How will you
courageously honor God's grace today?

Since it is through God's kindness, then it is not by their good works.
For in that case, God's grace would not be what it really is—
free and undeserved.

ROMANS 11:6

THE COURAGE TO
Persist

I told you, Theophilus, about everything Jesus began to do and teach until the day he was taken up to heaven after giving his chosen apostles further instructions through the Holy Spirit.

ACTS 1:1–2

Father, please give me the courage to keep sharing your truth even when I don't see immediate results.

Have you ever mustered up the courage to share your faith and no one listened? Perhaps you've encouraged family or friends to draw closer to God but saw no results. Giving up can be easy, but persistence is a genuine act of courage. Consider the author of the book of Acts, who many believe was the apostle Luke. The writer earnestly desired for Theophilus to know that Jesus was the Messiah.

Luke had written to Theophilus before, giving him a detailed account of the life of Christ. Whether to a non-believer or a new believer who needed further teaching, Luke persistently shared his faith. Although the Scripture does not record a response from Theophilus, Luke provided facts and details in his second letter to him that left no room for skepticism.

COURAGE FOR TODAY

Witnessing to those who live as skeptics or unbelievers can be difficult and discouraging. Read the verses below and vow to never give up but instead to patiently, lovingly, and persistently share your faith with others today.

Sing to the Lord; praise his name. Each day proclaim the good news that he saves. Publish his glorious deeds among the nations. Tell everyone about the amazing things he does.

PSALM 96:2–3

THE COURAGE TO
Prepare for Christ's Return

*"Then everyone will see the Son of Man coming on a cloud
with power and great glory."*

LUKE 21:27

Father, you tell me to always be ready for your return. Give me wisdom
and guidance to know how I can faithfully be prepared for
Jesus' second coming.

Are you prepared for Christ's return? Let Jesus' words comfort and challenge
you to be ready at all times. After telling his disciples about the poor widow's
extravagant and selfless offering, Jesus spoke to them about the future. He first
warned his followers to be on guard against false prophets who would pretend
to be him.

Then he described worldly events that must take place before his second
coming, such as wars, earthquakes, famines, plagues, strange signs from the
sun, moon, and stars, and great persecution against believers. But Jesus urged
his followers not to worry because he will come again. And in the meantime,
he provides believers with the strength and skills they need to persevere.

COURAGE FOR TODAY

Describe how you are currently preparing for Jesus to come back. Read the
apostle John's prophecy below and explain the courageous steps you will
take, beginning today, to be ready at all times for your Savior to return.

*He is the faithful witness to these things, the first to rise from the dead, and the ruler
of all the kings of the world. All glory to him who loves us and has freed us from
our sins by shedding his blood for us…Look! He comes with the clouds of heaven.
And everyone will see him—even those who pierced him. And all the nations of the
world will mourn for him. Yes! Amen!*

REVELATION 1:5, 7

THE COURAGE TO
Obey God's Call

The LORD gave this message to Jonah son of Amittai:
"Get up and go to the great city of Nineveh.
Announce my judgment against it because I have seen how wicked its people are."
JONAH 1:1–2

Father, your instructions are often challenging, and you sometimes point me in directions where I don't desire to go. Give me the will and courage to set aside my personal plans so I can faithfully fulfill yours.

Has God ever called you to move in a direction that went against your desires? If so, did you obey him, or did you dig in your heels and say no? Consider Jonah chapter 1, where we meet the disobedient prophet, who was intimately acquainted with the Lord but fled thousands of miles in the opposite direction to avoid God's calling.

Nineveh was the capital of Assyria, a bitter enemy of Israel. It was known for its cruelty and ruthlessness, including toward Jonah's people. And while God desired to give the people of Nineveh an opportunity to repent, Jonah wanted no part in their restoration. Twice Scripture states that Jonah ran from the presence of the Lord. So when he boarded a ship to flee, God caused a great storm that resulted in Jonah being thrown overboard.

COURAGE FOR TODAY

Have you ever said no to God? A rebellious spirit can send us into dark places that only leave us with regrets. Read the passage below and describe how God's greatness inspires you to courageously pursue his plans for your life today.

"My thoughts are nothing like your thoughts," says the LORD. "And my ways are far beyond anything you could imagine. For just as the heavens are higher than the earth, so my ways are higher than your ways and my thoughts higher than your thoughts."
ISAIAH 55:8–9

THE COURAGE TO
Embrace Life

"Be happy about it! Be very glad! For a great reward awaits you in heaven.
And remember, the ancient prophets were persecuted in the same way."
MATTHEW 5:12

Father, you tell me that it is okay for me to mourn, hunger, thirst, and
realize my great need for you. Help me always remember to turn to you
first when I need comfort and care.

When bad things happen, are you more apt to get discouraged, or do you
see a bright spot in the middle of your storm? Be inspired by Jesus' words in
Matthew chapter 5. Shortly after he began his ministry, Jesus went up on a
mountain in Galilee and began to teach about the attitudes God's people
should possess. Today, these eight characteristics are known as the Beatitudes.

Throughout this chapter, which covers only a portion of his speech,
Jesus reminds his listeners that God's people are to be overcomers, to bring
livelihood, light, and goodness to the world. The only thing more devastating
than the trauma we may experience in this life is the way we choose to handle
it. Therefore, we must embrace joy in the midst of our pain and life in the
middle of our hardship.

COURAGE FOR TODAY

Do you ever find it difficult to keep a positive outlook? Meditate on the
verses below and describe how you will courageously embrace your life in
Christ today.

"Yes, I am the gate. Those who come in through me will be saved. They will come
and go freely and will find good pastures. The thief's purpose is to steal and kill and
destroy. My purpose is to give them a rich and satisfying life."
JOHN 10:9–10

THE COURAGE TO
Put God First

All the elders of Israel met at Ramah to discuss the matter with Samuel.
"Look," they told him, "you are now old, and your sons are not like you.
Give us a king to judge us like all the other nations have."

1 SAMUEL 8:4–5

Father, you know all things; past, present, and future, and therefore, you always know what is best. Give me the desire and the courage to pursue your will over my selfish wants and wishes.

Are you willing to disregard God's will to have your way? Consider Israel's uncompromising desire for a king recorded in 1 Samuel chapter 8. The ark of the covenant was a wooden box overlayed in gold that represented the very presence of God. In 1 Samuel chapters 4–5, we discover that the Israelites treated the ark like a good luck charm, and as a result, it fell into enemy hands.

When the ark was finally returned to the Israelites, they vowed to honor God faithfully. But it wasn't long before the people of Israel once again exhibited their lack of faith in God when they demanded that Samuel appoint a king to rule over them. When Samuel took their request before the Lord, God let them have their way and anointed a king, but he also revealed the consequences that would result from having a man to reign over them rather than the Lord.

COURAGE FOR TODAY

Is there something you want bad enough to disregard God's will and warnings? Read the passage below and ask God for wisdom regarding your desires. Describe any warning you receive from the Lord and commit to courageously pursue his will over your wants today.

Temptation comes from our own desires,
which entice us and drag us away.

JAMES 1:14

THE COURAGE TO
Be Careful

Don't be fooled by those who say such things,
for "bad company corrupts good character."
1 CORINTHIANS 15:33

Father, for better or for worse, the people I spend time with influence me. Help me set healthy boundaries with toxic friends, loved ones, and others who attempt to hinder my faith and my dedication to you.

Are you careful when it comes to what and whom you expose yourself to? Consider the apostle Paul's warning in 1 Corinthians chapter 15. In his letter to the church in Corinth, Paul explained Christ's sacrifice and resurrection in detail. He then warned Corinthian believers to be careful not to listen to or follow immoral people.

Paul knew they needed encouragement to stop sinning because it made them look as if they didn't know God at all. For God "gives us victory over sin and death through our Lord Jesus Christ" (v. 57); therefore, believers are to be strong and immovable as they strive to honor and be obedient to the Lord.

COURAGE FOR TODAY

Whom do you currently follow and seek advice from? Meditate on the familiar psalm below and vow today to courageously set boundaries with people who negatively influence you and to pursue healthy relationships with those who inspire you to draw closer to God and his Word.

Oh, the joys of those who do not follow the advice of the wicked, or stand around with sinners, or join in with mockers. But they delight in the law of the LORD, meditating on it day and night. They are like trees planted along the riverbank, bearing fruit each season. Their leaves never wither, and they prosper in all they do.
PSALM 1:1–3

THE COURAGE TO
Pursue God's Will

We have not stopped praying for you since we first heard about you.
We ask God to give you complete knowledge of his will
and to give you spiritual wisdom and understanding.

COLOSSIANS 1:9

Father, give me the courage to seek your will and be obedient to it.
I also pray this prayer for my family and friends who are in need of
your daily direction.

How dedicated are you to pursuing God's will? Consider how the apostle
Paul prayed for God's will in Colossians chapter 1. Paul wrote to the church
at Colossae because some members had adopted false teaching. He prayed
that believers would genuinely know and accomplish God's will in their lives.
Without God's knowledge and guidance, their lives would be marked by error,
instability, and sorrow.

So Paul prayed the Colossians would be strengthened by God, be
thankful for all he had done, and live to honor and please him. For Paul
knew that if believers would stand firm in their faith, they could overcome
the difficult people and circumstances they were currently facing. So Paul
encouraged and challenged them further by sharing how he gladly suffered
and depended on God's power to persevere and to do God's will.

COURAGE FOR TODAY

One of the greatest prayers we can pray, for ourselves and others, is to
know and do God's will. Meditate on the verse below and describe how
you will courageously pursue God's will today.

Don't copy the behavior and customs of this world, but let God transform you into
a new person by changing the way you think. Then you will learn to know God's
will for you, which is good and pleasing and perfect.

ROMANS 12:2

THE COURAGE TO
Prepare for Adversity

"I'm not asking you to take them out of the world, but to keep them safe from the evil one. They do not belong to this world any more than I do. Make them holy by your truth; teach them your word, which is truth."

JOHN 17:15–17

Father, I want to embrace the abundant life you have planned for me. Help me to prepare for and persevere through the various obstacles I encounter.

Are you prepared for adversity? Consider John chapter 17 that records Jesus' longest prayer. Earlier, Jesus reminded his apostles—including us—that, "Here on earth you will have many trials and sorrows" (16:33). Yet in this same verse, he also teaches that, despite this reality, we can find peace in him.

Jesus asks that God's will be done. He prays for his disciples and for all believers, even those who will come to the faith in the future. Jesus asks God to protect us from Satan by preparing us in three ways. First, by strengthening us in God's Word. Second, by encouraging us to fellowship with other believers. And third, by challenging us to fellowship with God.

COURAGE FOR TODAY

Describe your relationship with God and name believers you fellowship with. Read the following verses and list the changes you will make so you are better prepared to courageously persevere today.

Stay alert! Watch out for your great enemy, the devil. He prowls around like a roaring lion, looking for someone to devour. Stand firm against him, and be strong in your faith. Remember that your family of believers all over the world is going through the same kind of suffering you are.

1 PETER 5:8–9

THE COURAGE TO
Treasure God's Word

I have hidden your word in my heart,
that I might not sin against you.

PSALM 119:11

Father, you have given us your Word as a guide for life. Give me the desire and ability to apply your teachings so I can live in ways that honor you and accomplish your will.

Is studying the Bible a priority in your life? How often each week do you read and apply God's Word? Meditate on Psalm 119 that celebrates the Bible's many benefits. Blessed are those who seek God with all their heart and walk according to his ways. Cleansed are those who treasure, meditate on, and do not forget God's Word.

While consequences await those who wander from God's commandments, those who choose faithfulness to the Lord's instructions receive revival, encouragement, comfort, hope, and understanding. Therefore, the psalmist urges his audience to seek, keep, trust in, delight in, meditate on, and never forget the words of the Lord.

COURAGE FOR TODAY

What is your current Bible study routine? As you learn from God's Word, do you look for ways to apply it to your daily life? Read the passage below and vow today to consistently apply Scripture in both practical and courageous ways.

"Study this Book of Instruction continually. Meditate on it day and night so you will be sure to obey everything written in it. Only then will you prosper and succeed in all you do. This is my command—be strong and courageous! Do not be afraid or discouraged. For the LORD your God is with you wherever you go."

JOSHUA 1:8–9

THE COURAGE TO
Live with Integrity

Be careful to live properly among your unbelieving neighbors. Then even if they
accuse you of doing wrong, they will see your honorable behavior, and they will
give honor to God when he judges the world.

1 PETER 2:12

Father, in a culture that prefers power, possessions, and pleasures over faith
in you and good deeds, it can be hard to live a faithful life. Give me the
desire, ability, and courage to make integrity a priority in my life each day.

Do you strive to live with integrity? Consider the apostle's message in 1 Peter
chapter 2 and let it motivate you to be set apart from the ways and behaviors
of this world. Peter longed for believers to persevere in their faith while living
in a sinful society. So he consistently urged followers of Christ to "get rid of all
evil behavior" (v. 1).

As representatives of the Lord and witnesses of God's saving grace,
believers were to stay away from behaviors like "deceit, hypocrisy, jealousy,
and all unkind speech" (v. 1). As a part of the body of Christ and as the Lord's
possession, believers are called to leave this world's darkness behind so they
can live in God's perfect light. For life on earth is only temporary. Therefore,
Christ followers must be cautious and live honest and godly lives so unbelievers
will witness their integrity and credit the Lord for all the good they do.

COURAGE FOR TODAY

How important is it to you to live an upright and honest life? Meditate on
King Solomon's wisdom below and explain how you plan to courageously
live with integrity today.

People with integrity walk safely,
but those who follow crooked paths will be exposed.

PROVERBS 10:9

THE COURAGE TO
Keep Your Faith

I will rejoice in the LORD! I will be joyful in the God of my salvation!
The Sovereign LORD is my strength! He makes me as surefooted as a deer,
able to tread upon the heights.

HABAKKUK 3:18–19

Father, you know the beginning, the end, and everything in between, and your ways and timing are always perfect. Strengthen my faith so I will confidently and constantly trust in you.

Does your faith remain firm regardless of your circumstances? Consider the perspective of God's prophet in Habakkuk chapter 3. Habakkuk was a man who courageously approached God with his questions. Twice, he presented his concerns about the evil he was witnessing, and twice God replied and encouraged him to be patient, that judgment was forthcoming.

In his conclusion, Habakkuk's questions turned into a song of praise that would be sung by the Israelites in worship. While he celebrated God's presence and proclaimed his majesty, Habakkuk also acknowledged God's wrath. In the final four verses of this chapter, Habakkuk describes his faith. Although he was afraid of the coming judgment, the prophet vowed to wait patiently and be joyful in God, whom he faithfully trusted for strength and salvation.

COURAGE FOR TODAY

Do you keep your faith when adversity comes? Let Paul's assurance below inspire you to demonstrate courageous faith today.

We can rejoice, too, when we run into problems and trials, for we know that they help us develop endurance. And endurance develops strength of character, and character strengthens our confident hope of salvation. And this hope will not lead to disappointment. For we know how dearly God loves us, because he has given us the Holy Spirit to fill our hearts with his love.

ROMANS 5:3–5

THE COURAGE TO
Ask for Help

The two sisters sent a message to Jesus telling him,
"Lord, your dear friend is very sick."

JOHN 11:3

Father, I am sometimes afraid to ask you for help. Give me the courage, faith, and desire to come to you for all my needs.

Has sin, unbelief, or doubt ever kept you from going to God? Do you accept that God wants you to come to him no matter what you've done? Consider the story of Jesus' friends, Mary and Martha, recorded in John chapter 11. Their brother Lazarus, whom Jesus loved, had become deathly ill. In desperation, the two sisters courageously sent a message to Jesus, saying, "Lord, your dear friend is very sick" (v. 3). They believed their miracle-working friend would rush to their aid and heal their brother. But Jesus waited for Lazarus to die.

Sickness and death do not disprove God's love. Delayed answers aren't signs that God is denying, neglecting, or punishing us. Instead, Jesus allowed Lazarus to die "for the glory of God so that the Son of God will receive glory" from the miracle (v. 4). Jesus returned to Bethany and brought Lazarus back to life. And as a result of his miracle, many more believed in him.

COURAGE FOR TODAY

Do you need more courage to ask God for help? Read the verse below and go courageously before the Lord today with your needs and requests.

Let us come boldly to the throne of our gracious God. There we will receive his mercy, and we will find grace to help us when we need it most.

HEBREWS 4:16

THE COURAGE TO
Obey God

"As for you, if you faithfully follow me as David your father did, obeying all my commands, decrees, and regulations, then I will establish the throne of your dynasty. For I made this covenant with your father, David, when I said, 'One of your descendants will always rule over Israel.'"

2 CHRONICLES 7:17–18

Father, I want to receive and make the most of your every blessing. Remind me daily that my obedience to you and your will directly affects my ability to pursue the many opportunities and advantages you offer me.

How eager are you to receive God's blessings? Are you willing to obey God's commands even when it's difficult? Consider God's promise and warning recorded in 2 Chronicles chapter 7. At the conclusion of King Solomon's prayer in the previous chapter, God's glory filled Israel's newly constructed temple. Later that evening, God came to Solomon and reaffirmed his covenant.

God promised to bless his people in response to their obedience. But he also warned that "if you or your descendants abandon me and disobey" calamity would come (vv. 19–20). These promises still stand today. While God's grace and forgiveness through Jesus offer to cleanse us from our sins and release us from eternal judgment, many of God's blessings are still set in motion in response to our obedience.

COURAGE FOR TODAY

Do you pursue obedience to God no matter how challenging or painful it is? Meditate on the verse below and list ways you will courageously obey God's commands today.

"Give, and you will receive. Your gift will return to you in full—pressed down, shaken together to make room for more, running over, and poured into your lap. The amount you give will determine the amount you get back."

LUKE 6:38

THE COURAGE TO
Recognize Deception

During that time the devil came and said to him, "If you are the Son of God, tell these stones to become loaves of bread." But Jesus told him, "No! The Scriptures say, 'People do not live by bread alone, but by every word that comes from the mouth of God.'"

MATTHEW 4:3–4

Father, you warn me about Satan's desire to take me down. Help me recognize his deception and resist his temptations by relying on your Holy Spirit and your Word.

How often do you entertain your inner voice that tempts you to engage in bad behaviors or negative attitudes? Let Matthew chapter 4 inspire you to replace worldly lies with God's truth. After Jesus was baptized by John the Baptist, God sent Jesus into the wilderness to prepare him for ministry. Jesus fasted for forty days and nights, and when he was weak and hungry, Satan tempted him with food, pride, and power. In response to each temptation, Jesus responded by reciting Scripture.

Today, Satan uses the same tactics on both believers and unbelievers. So to recognize the devil's deception and resist his temptation, we must know God's Word and stand firmly on its truth.

COURAGE FOR TODAY

How difficult is it for you to overcome Satan's temptations? Read the following verses and describe your commitment to recognize and courageously combat the devil's deception by replacing his lies with truth of God's Word today.

I fear that somehow your pure and undivided devotion to Christ will be corrupted, just as Eve was deceived by the cunning ways of the serpent…But I am not surprised! Even Satan disguises himself as an angel of light.

2 CORINTHIANS 11:3, 14

THE COURAGE TO

Heed God's Word

When the king heard what was written in the Book of the Law,
he tore his clothes in despair.

2 KINGS 22:11

Father, your Word has power and can transform my life. But I must put your teachings into practice for my life to change. Help me heed your words and warnings and consistently choose faithfulness over sin.

Is there a profound difference in your life today as a result of your relationship with God? Consider the life of King Josiah recorded in 2 Kings chapters 22 and 23. Josiah was the fifteenth king to rule over the Southern Kingdom, Judah, after it was separated from Israel in 931 BC. At eight years old, Josiah became king, and he had a choice: follow in the footsteps of his evil father and grandfather or heed God's Word.

When Josiah heard God's law, he responded in humility. Not only did King Josiah humble himself, but he also took action. Josiah "pledged to obey the LORD…with all his heart and soul…and all the people pledged themselves to the covenant" (23:3). Following this, Josiah cleansed Judah of all pagan worship and honored the Lord with all is heart, soul, and strength.

COURAGE FOR TODAY

Are you willing to heed God's Word? What specific command has he placed on your heart? Meditate on the following verses and describe courageous ways you will put these verses into action today.

The man answered, "'You must love the LORD your God with all your heart, all your soul, all your strength, and all your mind.' And, 'Love your neighbor as yourself.'"
"Right!" Jesus told him. "Do this and you will live!"

LUKE 10:27–28

THE COURAGE TO
Tell Others

*After seeing him, the shepherds told everyone what had happened
and what the angel had said to them about this child.*

LUKE 2:17

Father, my life is filled with hope and healing because you are my Lord
and Savior. Give me countless opportunities to share my testimony with
others and inspire me to tell them about your incredible love
and faithfulness.

How often do you tell others about God? Remember the shepherds'
enthusiasm in Luke chapter 2 when Mary and Joseph were in Nazareth. Mary
gave birth to God's Son, the Messiah. Because there was nowhere else to stay,
they took shelter in a stable among the livestock. Suddenly an angel of the
Lord appeared before several shepherds who were tending to their flocks in a
nearby field.

Realizing they were terrified, God's messenger told them not to be afraid
and shared with them the great news of their Savior's birth. After witnessing a
host of angels rejoicing, the shepherds hurried with excitement to Bethlehem
to search for the child of God. When they found him lying in a manger, they
told everyone about Jesus and praised God for all they had seen and heard.
We, too, can demonstrate the same enthusiasm when sharing the glory of God
with others.

COURAGE FOR TODAY

Meditate on Paul's confession below and explain your comfort level in sharing
your testimony and God's good news with family members, friends, and
acquaintances. How will you courageously share Christ with others today?

*I am eager to come to you in Rome, too, to preach the Good News. For I am not
ashamed of this Good News about Christ. It is the power of God at work, saving
everyone who believes—the Jew first and also the Gentile.*

ROMANS 1:15–16

THE COURAGE TO
Resist Temptation

God was very displeased with the census, and he punished Israel for it.
Then David said to God, "I have sinned greatly by taking this census.
Please forgive my guilt for doing this foolish thing."

1 CHRONICLES 21:7–8

Father, no matter how spiritually mature I strive to become, I will always be vulnerable to Satan's deception. Help me recognize Satan's schemes and overcome the temptation to sin against you.

Are you on guard daily against the tactics and temptations from Satan? Consider King David's predicament in 1 Chronicles chapter 21. God called David "a man after my own heart" (Acts 13:22), but he was not without fault. From the time he was a boy, David displayed great faith in and reliance on God.

Throughout his life he faced temptation, suffered the consequences of his sins, and experienced God's unconditional love, mercy, and amazing grace. Yet, even after all this, David was still susceptible to Satan's persuasion. In the first verse of 1 Chronicles chapter 21, we learn that Satan influenced him to take a census to assess Israel's military strength, an act of pride that was sinful in God's eyes. On earth, we will always struggle with temptation, yet with God's help, we truly have the power to resist it.

COURAGE FOR TODAY

How successful are you in resisting Satan's schemes? Read the verse below and describe how God's warning and willingness to provide a way of escape helps you courageously resist temptation today.

The temptations in your life are no different from what others experience.
And God is faithful. He will not allow the temptation to be more than you can stand.
When you are tempted, he will show you a way out so that you can endure.

1 CORINTHIANS 10:13

THE COURAGE TO
Examine Yourself

*"Anyone with ears to hear must listen to the Spirit
and understand what he is saying to the churches."*
REVELATION 2:29

Father, it is far too easy for me to focus on my busy life and neglect my
relationship with you. Prompt me to regularly evaluate my faith in you
so I can avoid the pitfalls I read about within your letters to
the seven churches.

How often do you consider your spiritual health? Are you growing closer
to God, or are you drifting farther away? Consider Revelation chapters 2–3,
which describe spiritual conditions that many believers struggle with. Christ's
messages to the churches in these chapters should inspire us to constantly
examine our faithfulness to God.

Ask yourself, *Is my love for God as strong as it once was, or am I loveless
like Ephesus? Do I fear rejection, persecution, or suffering, or am I courageous like
Smyrna? Am I solely devoted to God or indecisive like Pergamum? Do I tolerate sin
like Thyatira? Have I become lifeless like Sardis? Am I committed to keeping God's
Word and honoring his name like Philadelphia? Or am I lukewarm like Laodicea?*

COURAGE FOR TODAY

How often do you evaluate your faith in God? Does your relationship with
him compare to any of the churches' conditions mentioned in Revelation
chapters 2 and 3? Read the following verses and list the courageous steps
you will take today to repair any weak areas in your devotion to the Lord.

*We have not stopped praying for you since we first heard about you.
We ask God to give you complete knowledge of his will and to give you
spiritual wisdom and understanding.*
COLOSSIANS 1:9

THE COURAGE TO
Obey God

*I heard the Lord asking, "Whom should I send as a messenger to this people?
Who will go for us?" I said, "Here I am. Send me."*

ISAIAH 6:8

Father, help me get out of my comfort zone and inspire me to go where
you lead without any reservation. Give me the courage to always look
to you for wisdom, guidance, and validation and not to long
for worldly success.

Would you take a job knowing all your efforts would be fruitless? That no
matter how hard you tried, nothing would prevail? Be inspired by the great
prophet's response in Isaiah chapter 6. The first five chapters of the book of
Isaiah describe Israel's immoral condition and God's plans for judgment. During
that time, a prosperous, yet disobedient king had died. The people mourned
their leader and overlooked the fact that their worldly prosperity had left them
spiritually lifeless.

When Isaiah encountered the Lord in all his holiness, he confessed
his sinfulness and that of his people. "I am a sinful man…and I live among a
people with filthy lips" (v. 5). Yet when God asked for a volunteer to confront
the people about their sin, Isaiah eagerly said, "Here I am. Send me" (v. 8). Even
though God warned him that the people would reject him, Isaiah still willingly
and eagerly obeyed God.

COURAGE FOR TODAY

When your tasks are overwhelming and nothing goes as planned, do you
give up or stay the course? Let the following verse encourage you to
eagerly say "yes" to God today and courageously persevere.

*"This is my command—be strong and courageous! Do not be afraid or
discouraged. For the LORD your God is with you wherever you go."*

JOSHUA 1:9

THE COURAGE TO
Keep a Clear Conscience

Cling to your faith in Christ, and keep your conscience clear.
For some people have deliberately violated their consciences;
as a result, their faith has been shipwrecked.

1 TIMOTHY 1:19

Father, as your spirit moves within me, help me think and act in ways that
honor you and keep my conscience clear.

How important is it to you to maintain a close relationship with God? Consider
the apostle Paul's instructions in 1 Timothy chapter 1. It was important to Paul
to live before God with a pure heart, genuine faith, and a clear conscience. Paul
met Timothy on his second missionary journey and arranged for Timothy to
accompany him as he went from church to church teaching.

When Paul left Ephesus, he asked Timothy to stay and shepherd the
believers in that area. In order for Timothy to effectively pastor the Ephesians,
he needed to cling to Christ. "For some people have deliberately violated their
consciences," Paul warned, and "as a result, their faith has been shipwrecked"
(v. 19). Two men in particular had blatantly disrespected their relationship with
God. So Paul threw them out of the church.

COURAGE FOR TODAY

How strong is your desire to please God in everything you do? Read Job's
inspirational words below and describe the courageous changes you will
make, beginning today, to live before God with a pure heart, genuine faith,
and a clear conscience.

As long as I live, while I have breath from God, my lips will speak no evil,
and my tongue will speak no lies…I will maintain my innocence without wavering.
My conscience is clear for as long as I live.

JOB 27:3–4, 6

THE COURAGE TO
Stand Firm

Elijah stood in front of them and said, "How much longer will you waver, hobbling between two opinions? If the LORD is God, follow him! But if Baal is God, then follow him!" But the people were completely silent.

1 KINGS 18:21

Father, sometimes I am surrounded by people who reject my devotion to you. Help me to courageously stand firm in my faith and give me the right words to say that will plant seeds of belief in the lives of those I encounter.

When your faith is challenged, do you stand firm, or do you waver? Consider Elijah's dangerous contest with the pagan prophets of Ahab and Jezebel in 1 Kings chapter 18. Previously in Scripture, we discover how God prepared Elijah to stand firm in his faith. God called Elijah to personally deliver a message to King Ahab, and the prophet obeyed.

Elijah challenged the king's false prophets to a contest. When the 850 false prophets arrived, Elijah challenged the people of Israel, "If the Lord is God, follow him! But if Baal is God, then follow him!" (v. 21). He then tested Jezebel's false prophets in order to prove the existence of the one true God. When the people witnessed God's power, they fell to the ground and humbly acknowledged, "Yes, the LORD is God!" (v. 39).

COURAGE FOR TODAY

When someone opposes or challenges your faith in God, do you stand firm? Memorize the verse below and make a commitment to courageously and respectfully stand up for God and for your faith in him today no matter what.

Put on all of God's armor so that you will be able to stand firm against all strategies of the devil.

EPHESIANS 6:11

Acknowledgments

I would like to thank my heavenly Father for his presence and his Word, which give me courage every day to pursue the abundant life he offers me.

I am sincerely grateful to Dawn Mooring, author, amazing Bible teacher, and dear friend, who contributed countless hours, wonderful teachings, and inspiring content to this project.

I am especially thankful for my sweet family, who gave me grace, space, support, and prayer while I dedicated hours and months to writing and to praying that these devotions would encourage countless people to embrace their God-given courage for life.

About the Author

"The greatest enemy of our courage is fear,
and the greatest way to conquer our fear is through our faith."

ANN WHITE

FOUNDER OF ANN WHITE MINISTRIES, LLC, AND COURAGE FOR LIFE, INC.

Ann White is an author, speaker, and Bible teacher whose global ministry, Courage for Life, has a special focus on those who desire to grow in their relationship with God.

In 2019, Courage for Life developed and released the first female-voiced audio Bible app. The app is free to download on Apple and Android devices.

Ann's book *Courage for Life* provides step-by-step direction and guidance with intentional, doable actions that will alter your life no matter what difficult situation you're experiencing.

Ann has also published two unique New Living Translation Study Bibles with Tyndale House Publishers: *Courage for Life Study Bible for Men* and *Courage for Life Study Bible for Women*. These Bibles are designed to provide readers with applicable, easy-to-understand, inspiring content to grow in their relationship with God.

To learn more about Ann White and Courage for Life, visit AnnWhite.com and CourageForLife.org. You can also find her on Facebook and Instagram @GodGivesCourage.